*Medieval Music*

# Medieval Music

John Caldwell

Indiana University Press
Bloomington

MANUFACTURED IN THE UNITED STATES OF AMERICA

**Library of Congress Cataloging in Publication Data**

Caldwell, John, 1938-
  Medieval music.

  Bibliography: p.
  Includes indexes.
  1. Music—History and criticism—Medieval, 400-1500.  I.  Title.
  ML172.C28      780'.902      77-94060
  ISBN 0-253-33731-3

3 4 5 6 7 8 83 82 81

To my parents

# Acknowledgements

The author and publishers are indebted to the original publishers for permission to reprint the following musical examples:

Examples 42, 80–2, 92, 93 and 94: The American Institute of Musicology

Examples 63–4, 65, 66, 67, 68, 69, 72, 73 and 74: Editions de L'Oiseau-Lyre

Examples 70–1: The Medieval Academy of America

Examples 83, 84 and 86: Stainer and Bell Ltd, Publishers to the Royal Musical Association

# Contents

# List of Tables

# *Preface*

In writing this book I have had in mind the needs of undergraduates and others who require a straightforward account of medieval music, above all in its technical aspects. There is in these pages little biography and almost no sociology, topics on which others are better equipped to write; on the other hand considerable attention is paid to notation, so often the key to musical style. I have regarded the Middle Ages as a phenomenon of the Christian West, with the consequent omission of Byzantine chant (except in passing in connection with the subject of modes), not to mention the music of Islam and 'medieval' oriental music generally. This has excluded the possibility of comparisons between these musical cultures and that of the West; but apart from my own lack of expertise it has to be confessed that this is an area in which subjective opinion counts for much and in which very little can be demonstrated with confidence.

Latin chant, on the other hand, is dealt with rather fully, since apart from its intrinsic interest it represents a basic substratum of musical experience throughout the entire period. I have taken the end of the musical Middle Ages to coincide with the emergence of harmony as a structural factor, and the end of the reliance on *cantus firmi* and *formes fixes*, at around 1500. The treatment of the fifteenth century, however, is in no way intended to be comprehensive.

An invaluable recent guide to the available literature is Hughes, *Medieval Music* (Toronto and Buffalo, 1974). Two works of a general nature may be particularly recommended to those who are new to medieval studies. For the earlier part of the period there is R. H. C. Davis, *A History of Medieval Europe from Constantine to St Louis* (London, 1957), and for the later—though it is a very different kind of book—Huizinga's *The Waning of the Middle Ages* (Penguin Books, 1955 etc.).

9

Gramophone records of medieval music are now very numerous; but it must be remembered that all performances rely much more heavily on conjecture than is the case with later music, and the apparent authority of a recording can be an illusion. Readers who wish to know what is available should consult J. Coover and R. Colvig, *Medieval and Renaissance Music on Long-Playing Records* (Information Coordinators, Inc., Detroit, 1964), and its *Supplement, 1962–71* (1973) (Detroit Studies in Music Bibliography, nos. 6, 26).

It is my pleasant task to thank those who have been of assistance in the preparation of this book. The late Sir Jack Westrup read the typescript and made a number of helpful suggestions; above all he exerted a guiding hand over my translations from the Latin. Mr C. A. Robson of Merton College, Oxford, has performed a similar service in connection with the other languages; indeed the translations from the Provençal are entirely his work. Nevertheless, I must take final responsibility for the texts as they stand. I owe much to the guidance and enthusiasm of Mr M. B. Parkes, of my own college, in matters of palaeography, while Dr F. W. Sternfeld has been a constant source of encouragement. And lastly with gratitude I mention my wife, who has done most of the typing and vicariously shouldered many of the burdens of authorship.

JOHN CALDWELL
KEBLE COLLEGE, OXFORD
JUNE 1976

Note: the system of reference by symbol or short title is explained in the general *Bibliography* beginning on p. 260. References to official liturgical books are not always to the most recent editions; nor does mention of the 'modern' Roman rite take into account liturgical changes following the Second Vatican Council (1962–5).

# 1 *The chant of the Latin liturgies to c. 950*

## *Late antiquity and early Christianity*

The culture of the ancient Greeks and Romans enjoyed a long and glorious sunset—in some respects, indeed, the light never quite faded. In the East, the closing of the Athenian Academy in A.D. 529 after nine centuries of existence marked a formal conclusion to philosophical study; but it was not too difficult to assimilate some of the doctrines of the neo-Platonists to Christian theology, and in many ways the old spirit lived on. The classics continued to be copied and read, and these copies are often our earliest sources of ancient Greek texts, including those of musical theory. In the West, where there was no artificial restraint placed upon the study and imitation of classical models, the gradual separation from the East in politics and religion from the fifth to the eleventh centuries led to the falling into oblivion of the Greek language; but the Latin side of classical culture lingered on, kept alive in periods of relative ignorance by men such as Bede or Fulbert of Chartres, and rising to comparative heights in the Carolingian era and in the twelfth century, until there occurred that final revival under Petrarch which from a literary point of view it is reasonable to call the Renaissance. From the time of the edict of Milan (313), the Christian and pagan cultures could interact freely upon one another, producing such figures as St Ambrose and St Augustine, Boethius and Cassiodorus, Fortunatus and Eugenius of Toledo (d. 658), whom Raby described as 'one of the last products of the old schools'. This was also the era of the Vulgate Bible and the *Rule* of St Benedict (d. 543), exemplifying in written form that trend towards a simpler Latinity which when combined with regional differences in pronunciation ultimately gave rise to the Romance languages.

This culture was primarily one of letters. To what extent a musical interaction occurred must remain an open question. Our ignorance of Graeco-Roman music is almost complete. The transcription of the surviving fragments of Greek music, from the second century B.C. to the fourth century A.D., is not always certain, since the late theorists who preserve the notation (principally Alypius in the fourth century) reveal an ignorance of its theoretical basis at earlier times; and of Roman music not one fragment has come down to us. What is clear, however, is that it was an art in decline, like the drama with which it was so closely linked. The music of the Roman Empire at its highest was devoted to the glorification of a gifted performer; at its lowest, it served as a crude accompaniment to gladiatorial contests. Its academic study was confined to philosophical speculation, harmonic theory (a branch of mathematics unrelated to practical music or to harmony in our sense), rhythm and metrics. The Church Fathers were suspicious of its all-pervading influence, though they reserved their most forceful imprecations for musical instruments—David may have played the harp, but St Jerome counselled a total abstention. Even its academic study was regarded as frivolous: St Augustine failed to complete his *De Musica* (as we have it a treatise on rhythm and metre). However, St Augustine himself partially attributed his conversion to the charms of church music; and at a later date Boethius (d. 524) and Cassiodorus (d. *c.* 580), both Christians, transmitted the harmonic theory of the Greeks to the Latin West. It will be necessary to return to some aspects of this theory when considering the psalm-tones and their associated modes.

It was the infant art of the Church itself, however, which was destined to become the parent of modern Western music. Its basis lay in the practice of the Jewish synagogue at the time of Our Lord, and consisted of the cantillation of lessons and prayers and the singing of psalms, both unaccompanied. Cantillation was a kind of heightened reading with special attention to punctuation and intonation. In the West at least, this method ultimately became standardized as a recitation or ecphonesis on a single note with very simple musical formulae for punctuation. Contrasted with this is the 'lyrical' principle, found both in short, syllabic melodies with simple, well-balanced phrases and in highly elaborate melismatic melodies based on standard formulae (cf. Example 22 below), as well as in an intermediate style nowadays called neumatic.

By comparing the melodies of the West with those of isolated communities of Jews in the East it has been possible to show that a good many melodic elements which have survived into Latin chant are of ancient oriental origin (Idelsohn, *Thesaurus*). This is especially true of the psalm-tones, which may represent a modification on ecphonetic lines of originally 'lyrical' melodies. It is interesting that as late as the fourth century St Augustine contrasted 'the lovely chants to which the psalms of David are habitually sung' with a method attributed to Athanasius, bishop of Alexandria, 'who used to oblige the lectors to recite the psalms with such slight modulation of the voice that they seemed to be speaking rather than chanting' (*Confessions*, x, 33).

The synagogue also gave rise to the refrain-forms represented in Western chant by the antiphon and respond, as well as to 'direct' or continuous psalmody. These forms were later associated with 'antiphonal' singing (from side to side of a choir) and 'responsorial' singing (in which the choir or congregation replies to a cantor or small group of singers) respectively. It is unlikely that either the synagogue or the early Christian congregations employed antiphonal chant in the former sense; but the Hellenistic-Jewish sect known as the Therapeutae employed an alternation between men and women in the first century, and the practice may have been more widespread. A response, of course, can mean a repetition as well as a refrain, and it is clear that the Church inherited a wide variety of usages. St Augustine mentions some of the fourth-century possibilities in his sermons. Elsewhere, like St Jerome, he describes the *jubilus*, probably to be identified with the melisma sung to the final syllable of the word 'Alleluia'.

To the rite of the Jewish synagogue the Christians added only one permanent element: the commemoration of the Last Supper which is the essential feature of the Mass or Eucharist (in the East 'liturgy' in its technical sense). The same rite, without the eucharistic element, provided the basis of the Offices or hours of prayer. In the West it was the Mass which eventually gave rise to the greatest musical elaboration, while in the East it was the Office which provided the framework for the great hymnological repertories of the Byzantine and other Eastern churches: Syrian, Coptic, Abyssinian and Armenian. These repertories, important though they are both for their intrinsic interest and for comparative study (insofar as they can be deciphered) lie outside the scope of this book.

The new-found freedom of the Church under Constantine enabled the liturgy (in its general sense of formal public worship) to develop without inhibition. Constantine's building programme included the construction of sanctuaries in Jerusalem and its environs at the places where the events of Our Lord's life were supposed to have occurred. Around these grew a complex liturgy, which was described at the end of the fourth century by the Galician abbess Etheria in her account of her pilgrimage to the Holy Land (Duchesne, *Origines*, pp. 510–42). The daily round of Offices included Matins with Lauds, Sext, None and Vespers; in Lent Terce was added. On Sundays the night Office is extended and Lauds is merged with the weekly Mass. The great feasts are characterized by visits to the holy places associated with the original events.

Etheria refers to hymns as well as to antiphons and to responsorial psalms. The nature of her antiphon is uncertain; it may have been a choral psalm with refrain, or merely a free composition with alternating choirs. 'Hymn' at this date could mean merely a psalm or a composition in psalmodic style (such as the Te Deum); there are also early hymn-texts in Greek and Latin which use classical metres. The earliest surviving hymn with music is a third-century fragment in Greek alphabetical notation, setting a Greek anapaestic text to a neumatic melody with oriental affinities (*NOHM*, ii, p. 4). The isosyllabic hymn (with an equal number of syllables in each line) was cultivated in Syriac by St Ephraem (306–73) as a popular form for the opposing of heresy, and in the West by St Hilary of Poitiers (d. *c.* 367), St Ambrose (d. 397) and Prudentius (d. *c.* 405). It is in St Ambrose and Prudentius that we first find the concept of hymns for specific hours of the day, though it is not until St Benedict in the sixth century that there is evidence for the regular use of Latin hymns in the daily Office. The isosyllabic form permitted the repetition of the same melody unaltered from stanza to stanza—a popular practice which in turn may have contributed to the eventual transition from scansion by quantity to scansion by stress.*

The liturgy of Rome was evidently modelled in some important respects on that of Jerusalem. Particularly significant are its stational character, represented by visits to specific churches in the city, and the close integration of the monastic and lay elements in the Christian community. It is of course a papal liturgy, the pope as bishop of Rome being the central figure in all major events. There is evidence that, following the introduction of the liturgy of Jerusalem to Rome under Pope Damasus I (reigned 366–84), a number of popes including Gregory I (reigned 590–604) concerned themselves with the 'editing' of the cycle of chants for the whole year (Apel, *Gregorian Chant*, pp. 46–8). While Gregory's precise musical role will always remain uncertain (see below, p. 19) there is no doubt that in his time the Roman Mass had achieved its basic form as exemplified in Table I (p. 18); many of its elements are said to have been introduced by Gregory himself, and the Agnus Dei is the only important later addition.

As for the Office, it was finally codified by St Benedict in his *Rule* as an eight-fold cycle, consisting of Matins (*Vigiliae* or *Nocturna laus*), Lauds (*Matutini*), Prime, Terce, Sext, None, Vespers and Compline. He prescribed all the psalms and canticles for the day hours, contrasted the singing of psalms with antiphons with their performance 'sine antiphona in directum',† and specified the singing of responds after lessons and the singing of hymns. At the same time he relates his own purely monastic rite to the existing customs of the Roman Church ('sicut psallit Ecclesia Romana', ch. xiii).

While St Benedict's *Rule* became the foundation of Western monasticism, the Roman rite as such, and particularly its formularies and chants for the Mass, did not make such easy headway. It did however make considerable progress in Britain, where the original British Church was gradually being supplanted by that of Rome. Bede records the success of John, archcantor under Pope Agatho and abbot of Saint Martin, in promoting the Roman chant in Monkwearmouth and elsewhere in the north (*Eccl. Hist.*, iv, 18), and there are numerous other indications from the eighth and ninth

---

* The entire subject of medieval scansion is complex and controversial. The view taken here is that the classical *ictus*—a kind of regular notional stress analogous to the bar-line in music—remained a significant factor both in vernacular and in non-quantitative Latin verse. The transition is therefore not so much one of kind as of degree, an actual correspondence of stress and *ictus* often taking the place of the rhythmical impetus formerly given by the long syllable. For further remarks on the relation of musical to verbal rhythm see below, pp. 87f., 132.

† 'straight through without an antiphon'.

centuries (see *NOHM*, ii, pp. 99–100). On the continent progress was more difficult. Milan with much of northern Italy possessed a different rite regarded by Duchesne as the parent of the other two principal rites of Western Europe, Gallican and Mozarabic. Eventually the Roman rite was accepted in Gaul under the Frankish kings; but it is not at all certain that the intended musical reform was complete, or even that it had any permanent effect at all. The Mozarabic rite remained until 1076 (it has always persisted in Toledo, though its original music cannot be transcribed), while the Milanese or 'Ambrosian' rite has remained intact with its medieval chant until the present day.

## The Latin liturgies and their chant repertories

All Christian liturgies have as their basis a dual calendar which has its roots in the Jewish year but also incorporates the pagan calendar of Julius Caesar. Its starting point is the Jewish Passover, the feast of the spring full moon, Easter Day being the Sunday immediately following this day (Council of Nicaea, 325). The fiftieth day thereafter is the feast of Pentecost, and in the Latin rites the number of Sundays after Pentecost varies to allow for four Sundays in Advent (six in the Ambrosian rite) before Christmas Day on 25 December. Before Easter a fixed period of nine weeks begins with Septuagesima, before which there is a varying number of Sundays after Epiphany (6 January, originally the oriental Christmas). This is the *temporale* or *proprium de tempore*: its details have varied from time to time but from the fourth century it has had as its points of departure the movable Easter and the fixed Christmas. Opposed to it is the *sanctorale* or cycle of feasts of the saints, based entirely on the secular calendar; but it should be noted that early medieval manuscripts combine the *temporale* and *sanctorale* in one continuous sequence—the present arrangement did not come about until the thirteenth century.

The somewhat complex history of the daily Office (see Van Dijk, *Origins*, pp. 15–26) need not concern us here, as it has little bearing on the musical differences between the chant repertories. The public Mass is another matter. We are to think essentially of a Sunday-by-Sunday routine, with special solemnity for Easter and Pentecost, and of course Masses for Christmas, Epiphany and other great feasts. The week before Easter acquired its own special solemnity, and certain of its days acquired particular ceremonies. Gradually the weekdays of Lent were filled up with special Masses; and as the *sanctorale* was gradually enlarged many other days in the year acquired their own Masses. By the ninth century the Mass was a daily routine, any vacant days being filled by votive Masses for special intentions or by repeating the Mass of the previous Sunday.

Each Mass—and this is also true of the Office—contains some elements which are variable, or 'Proper', and some which are permanent, or 'Ordinary' (ultimately from the phrase *ordo missae*), as well as some which do not fall clearly into either category. We now give in tabular form (overleaf) the order of events (i.e. the 'public' events as distinct from private prayers added by the priest) in the Gallican, Mozarabic and Roman-Frankish Mass of the seventh to the tenth centuries. Such a table can indicate the shape of the liturgy only in its broadest outlines; to a certain extent it is conjectural, and it does not altogether compare chronologically equivalent rites (for example the Gallican Mass, placed first in the table, was supplanted in Gaul by the Roman Mass, placed fourth). Liturgical distinctions are indicated typographically: bold type for proper chants, capitals for ordinary chants, italics for proper readings and prayers, and roman type for ordinary (or substantially invariable) prayers and other formulae. Round brackets enclose items occasionally omitted, and square brackets enclose items occasionally inserted, e.g. during Lent.

With these four rites are associated five chant repertories: Gallican, Mozarabic, Ambrosian, 'Gregorian' and 'Old-Roman'. The connection between the first three and their complementary rites is obvious. The extent to which they have survived depends on the date at which the rite was suppressed. The Gallican rite was abolished before liturgical music was normally written down, and its chant has disappeared except for isolated specimens preserved by chance in later manuscripts. Mozarabic chant survives only in heighted neumes (see p. 22f.), which cannot be accurately deciphered; again a few simple chants have survived in later copies, but it is not clear why readable copies have not come down to us from Toledo, where the rite remained in force. Ambrosian chant survives mainly in readable manuscripts from the twelfth century onwards, though there are earlier fragments. The loss of complete Ambrosian manuscripts in neumatic notation is another unexplained mystery.

**Table 1**: Outline of Latin liturgies

| Gallican | Mozarabic | Ambrosian | Roman-Frankish |
|---|---|---|---|
| **Antiphona ad praelegendum** | **Officium** | **Ingressa** | **Antiphona ad introitum** |
| (AIUS)[1] | GLORIA IN EXCELSIS[2] | GLORIA IN EXCELSIS[2] | KYRIE ELEISON |
| KYRIE ELEISON[4] | [TRISAGION] | KYRIE ELEISON[4] | (GLORIA IN EXCELSIS) |
| (BENEDICTUS DOMINUS)[5] | [BENEDICTUS DOMINUS][5] | [Preces] | |
| *Collectio* | *Collectio* | *Collectio* | *Collecta* |
| *Lectio* | *Lectio* | *Lectio* | *Lectio* |
| | (BENEDICTUS ES)[6] | (BENEDICTUS ES)[6] | |
| | **Psallendum** and **Clamor** | **Psalmellus** | **Responsum graduale** |
| *Lectio* | *Lectio* | *Lectio* | [*Lectio*] |
| BENEDICTUS ES[6] and **Respond** | (**Laudes**) | **Alleluia** or **Cantus** | (**Alleluia**) or [**Tractus**] |
| *Evangelium* | *Evangelium* | *Evangelium* | *Evangelium* |
| (Homily and Prayers of the Faithful) | | | (Homily) |
| (CREDIMUS IN UNUM DEUM) | | | (CREDO)[7] |
| **Sonus** | **Laudes** | **Antiphona post Evangelium** | |
| **Laudes** | **Sacrificium** | **Offerenda** | **Offertorium** |
| *Oratio* | TRISAGION and *Oratio* | *Oratio* | *Oratio* |
| Commemoration of Saints, Prayer and Prayer 'ad pacem' | **Ad pacem** | | |
| *Immolatio* | *Illatio* | *Prefatio* | *Prefatio* |
| SANCTUS | SANCTUS | SANCTUS | SANCTUS |
| Eucharistic Prayer | Eucharistic Prayer | Eucharistic Prayer | Eucharistic Prayer |
| **Fractio panis** | **Ad confractionem panis** | **Confractorium** | PATER NOSTER and Libera nos |
| PATER NOSTER | PATER NOSTER | PATER NOSTER | Fractio and Pax |
| *Benedictiones* | *Benedictiones* | *Benedictiones* | AGNUS DEI[8] |
| **Trecanum** | **Ad accedentes** | **Transitorium** | **Communio** |
| *Post communionem* | *Post communionem* | *Post communionem* | *Post communionem* |
| | | KYRIE ELEISON and conclusion | Ite missa est and DEO GRATIAS |

18

1. The Byzantine *Trisagion*, also preserved in the Roman *Improperia* (*LU*, pp. 737–8) in bilingual form.
2. Imported into the Mass from Rome. Originally a Greek text, it survives with parallel Greek and Latin texts in a ninth-century Frankish MS with fragmentary notation (Parrish, pl. I).
3. Nine-fold.
4. Three-fold.
5. Canticle of Zachary (Luke 1: 68–79).
6. Canticle of the Three Holy Children (Daniel 3: 52–56: cf. *LU*, pp. 348–50).
7. Not introduced in Rome itself until 1014.
8. Introduced by Pope Sergius I (reigned 687–701).

'Gregorian' and 'Old-Roman' chant, however, pose problems in connection with their antiquity and their relationship to what is known of the history of the Roman rite. Gregorian chant, which is often still identified quite simply as the contemporary musical accompaniment to St Gregory's Roman Mass, survives in complete manuscripts from the tenth century onwards, at first in neumes and later in fully readable notation. The earliest manuscript of Old-Roman chant dates from 1071 and is in heighted neumes; there is a handful of later sources up to the thirteenth century, when the repertory disappears altogether. If Gregorian chant is Roman, what is Old-Roman?

The earliest investigators regarded this repertory as merely a decadent version of Gregorian, but this was difficult to equate with its apparently more primitive style and its disappearance after the thirteenth century. It was subsequently regarded as pre-Gregorian (hence 'Old-Roman'), possibly even fourth-century and so contemporaneous with what was often regarded as an Ambrosian chant which actually dated from the time of St Ambrose himself. As a matter of fact it is highly dangerous to assume that any of these repertories had achieved anything like their final form before the ninth century, i.e. a hundred years before the earliest complete Gregorian manuscripts. The half-dozen surviving manuscripts of chants from that century are all without musical notation, and it is difficult to accept the idea of an oral tradition lasting for more than a hundred years: indeed it is easier to imagine that the idea of fixity in the chant melodies arose only shortly before 900. This is not to say that certain basic melodic elements in the chant are not much older, nor that the principles on which highly melismatic chants were improvised do not go back many centuries—this is proved by the comparisons with Jewish melodies already mentioned; but it does follow that St Gregory and the other popes who are said to have 'edited a cycle of chants for the whole year' cannot have been composers in the accepted sense—their activities were almost certainly confined to establishing the texts on which the musicians could work.

Another important point concerning the earliest musical manuscripts is that they are all of Frankish origin. This leads one to suspect even the Roman, let alone the Gregorian, origin of the chant which bears that name. Liturgical developments in Rome and Gaul may help to shed light on this and on the Old-Roman problem.

It has been established beyond reasonable doubt that in Rome from the second half of the seventh century onwards the papal liturgy began to diverge from that of the monasteries and basilicas, which retained the original rite. It is also known that when a hundred years later the Roman rite supplanted the Gallican in the Frankish kingdoms there was a good deal of confusion as a result. Partly this was because Old-Roman, rather than papal, books were sometimes sent (e.g. to Corbie, *c.* 825), and partly because the papal books themselves required modification to suit local conditions. In the eleventh century a succession of German popes brought the modified books back to Rome with them, and this liturgy became the basis of the papal court liturgy, in its turn the forerunner of the modern Roman rite. Meanwhile the Old-Roman rite declined in favour, but it was retained in some places, and it is from the eleventh to the thirteenth centuries that the few surviving musical sources are dated. By the end of the thirteenth century Old-Roman in its pure form was virtually extinct, and the use of the papal court emerged triumphant though not unscathed.

The problem for the musical historian is to know at what stage along the line Gregorian chant emerged as a separate repertory from Old-Roman. Laying aside theories which assert a purely chronological relationship between them, two hypotheses appear to deserve consideration.

According to the first, the musical separation began in Rome itself with the emergence of the separate papal liturgy, the latter corresponding to Gregorian chant (though some would reverse the position). We are not, of course, expected to believe that the two repertories had already reached the form in which we know them by, say, 700, but rather that the process which ultimately resulted in the sharp differentiation found in the sources of the eleventh century and later, began in Rome in the second half of the seventh century, and more particularly under Pope Vitalian (reigned 657–72).

The second hypothesis would equate the emergence of Gregorian chant with the modifications made to the papal liturgy in Gaul. Though equally impossible to prove, this theory presents distinct advantages to the musician. It is easier to imagine a process whereby Frankish singers, attempting to preserve what they could of their ancient traditions and yet at the same time seeking to conform to Roman customs, ended up by creating a basically new repertory of their own, than it is to imagine a musical division taking place within the confines of a single city. It is also reasonable to regard Gregorian chant as exhibiting a mean between what we may conjecture to have been the exuberance of Gallican chant (as represented by its Ambrosian cousin) and the austerity of Old-Roman (see Example 18 below). Finally, it is the theory which accords most closely with the evidence of the manuscripts themselves.

## Notation and performance

Broadly speaking two main systems of notation grew up in connection with Christian chant; they are usually called 'ecphonetic' and 'neumatic' respectively. The former, however, was not normally used for psalms, which as we have seen came to be chanted according to the principle of ecphonesis or recitation on a single note, while the term 'neumatic' is in the wider sense applicable to both systems. The simplest and most logical of the ecphonetic notations was the Syrian, in which a system of points served to indicate the outline of the various punctuating melismas (see *NOHM*, ii, pp. 10–11), itself related to the Old-Palestinian dot-system of the Jews (see P. Kahle in Bauer-Leander, *Historische Grammatik der hebräischen Sprache des Alten Testaments*, 1922, pp. 130–54). Ecphonetic notation reached great complexity in the East and among the Jews during the first millennium; but in the West only a few basic signs were used, although they differed from the Syrian in their use of the point. The mature Latin system, found in manuscripts from the twelfth century onwards, is as follows (there is a distinction between the name for the signs, *positurae*, and the types of division which they denote, *pausationes*):

**Table 2:** Latin ecphonetic notation

| Positura | Pausatio | Sign |
|---|---|---|
| Punctus circumflexus | Flexa | ? |
| Punctus elevatus | Metrum or Mediatio | ↲ |
| Punctus versus | Punctum or Versus | ; or · |
| Punctus interrogativus | Interrogatio | ↗ |

The signs for the *metrum* and *versus* are first found in the eighth century, for the *interrogatio* or question in the ninth century, and for the *flexa*, which represents a less important subdivision than the *metrum*, about 950. Their relationship to signs of punctuation in general is a complex matter which cannot be entered into here, but it may be stated that they have the appearance of neumes added to the points devised by the grammarians to indicate divisions of the sentence. However, the musical interpretations given from the twelfth century onwards differ according to the liturgical status of the reading—Office lesson, Epistle or Gospel (see below, pp. 31–34).

Neumatic notation proper is derived from the accents applied by Alexandrian grammarians to the Greek language. However, the very name 'accent' (Greek *prosōdia*) implies a musical origin, and it may be more accurate to speak of a common parentage for accents and neumes. These accents are the *acutus* ('), *gravis* (`), *circumflexus* (^) and, in theory at least, *anticircumflexus* (ˇ), corresponding to the Latin neumes, *virga, tractulus, clivis* and *pes* respectively. But just as Latin ecphonetic notation makes use of signs other than the point, so neumatic notation uses signs other than those derived from accents, in particular the point and the apostrophe.

The Latin neumes attained a peak of complexity at the Frankish (now Swiss) monastery of St Gall in the tenth century. Not only are these the most elaborate of all neumes, but they are almost the earliest to have survived, and there are only fragments extant which are demonstrably earlier than the famous *Cantatorium* (St Gall, Stiftsbibliothek, MS 359; facsimiles in *PM*, II, i) of the early tenth century. In addition to the usual neumes, the St Gall manuscripts include episematic forms (i.e. with modified shapes or additional elements to indicate lengthening) and Notkerian letters or *litterae significativae*, described by the St Gall monk Notker Balbulus (d. 912) amongst others. These indicative variations of rhythm or pitch, e.g. *c* (*celeriter*, quickly), *t* (*tenere*, hold), *e* (*equaliter*, unison with preceding note) and *iv* (*iusum*, below).

In order to cope with all the meaningful variants in the notation a special method of transcription has been devised (see Table 3). According to this, only those notes which are physically attached together in the sources are joined by a slur. The 'virga-element' is represented by ♩ and the 'punctum-element' by • . This enables the forms to be distinguished without implying a specific rhythmic relationship between the two. The 'episema-element' is represented by – (hence *tractulus* = ﹍ ), the 'apostropha-element' by , , the 'oriscus-element' by ♫ and the 'quilisma-element' by ♫♫ (for their meaning see below). Again, no specific rhythmic relationships are intended. Liquescence is indicated by a smaller note-head, and a broken bracket is used for single neumes formed from separate elements (e.g. *climacus*, ⌐• = ┌• •⌐ ; *scandicus*, ⌐ = ⌐• •┌ ). The actual pitches are obtained by comparison with later manuscripts.

Peter Wagner's theory that the main neumes are derived from combinations of the *punctum* and *virga* has been accepted, but not his contention that these represent short and long note-values respectively. Ninth- and tenth-century theoretical sources which refer to long and short notes in the ratio 2:1 are concerned mainly or solely with syllabic chant; and while it may be possible to demonstrate such a relationship in the note-forms employed in these circumstances it is not possible to make generalizations which are applicable to the whole body of Latin chant. The *episemata* and Romanian letters are also unlikely to represent proportional modifications of rhythm. Their character appears rather to be that of subtle nuances, and for that reason they are not translated into specific time-values.

**Table 3:** Neumatic elements and their transcription

| Name (liquescent name in brackets) | Sign | Transcription | Episematic Forms: Sign | Transcription | Liquescent Forms: Augment. Sign | Transcr | Dimin. Sign | Transcr |
|---|---|---|---|---|---|---|---|---|
| Virga (cephalicus) | | | | | | | | |
| Punctum | | | | | | | | |
| Tractulus (epiphonus) | | | | | | | | |
| Clivis (ancus; celaphicus) | | | | | | | | |
| (ancus)[1] | | | | | | | | |
| Pes (pinnosa; epiphonus) | | | | | | | | |

| Name (liquescent name in brackets) | Sign | Transcription | Episematic Forms: Sign | Transcription | Liquescent Forms: Augment. Sign | Transcr | Dimin. Sign | Transcr |
|---|---|---|---|---|---|---|---|---|
| Porrectus | | | | | | | | |
| Torculus (—; pinnosa) | | | | | | | | |
| Apostropha | | | | | | | | |
| Oriscus | | | | | | | | |
| Franculus | | | | | | | | |
| Pes quassus | | | | | | | | |
| Quilisma with pes | | | | | | | | |

1. With this meaning the *ancus* is a diminutive of the *climacus* (/·), not of the *clivis*.

25

Liquescent notes or *semivocales* may either prolong a neume (augmentative) or reduce the quality of its final member (diminutive). There is no difference in appearance between a liquescent *virga* (augmentative) and a liquescent *clivis* (diminutive); but whereas the former prolongs the pitch of the main note the latter consists of two pitches like the *clivis* itself. The correct interpretation can be deduced only by comparison with later sources. Liquescents occur in certain well-defined phonetic contexts, and always immediately before a change of syllable. In 1891 the monks of Solesmes published an exhaustive analysis of the liquescents found in the tenth-century manuscript St Gall 339 (*PM*, I, i–ii). Reducing the Solesmes classification of four broad cases (which is open to criticism in detail) to two, we find that liquescent notes occur either on certain consonants or on the second of two vowels (including the *i* in *eius*, *huius*, etc.). The Solesmes theory, which has been followed by most writers, supposes an additional vowel of indeterminate quality between two consonants (e.g. *in$^e$uenit, ad$^e$ te*). In that case it is not clear what happens when an *m* or a *g* occurs between two vowels. Rather more attractive is the idea that the consonants themselves are to be vocalized, *t* and *s* being softened to *d* and *z* respectively when they are treated in this way (e.g. in such contexts as 'fiat pax', 'nobis Domine'). In this way they become completely analogous to the second vowel in *aula, eius*, etc., where the effect is to divide a diphthong into its component vowels (note the non-classical treatment of the *i* in *eius* here).

The remaining neumes all appear to involve some special manner of performance, such as the use of chromaticism, microtones and *glissandi*. The *apostropha* is normally found in groups of two or three, when they are classed as *repercussa*, although a change of pitch may occur (e.g.  ,”  ). It is possible that the sign indicates a rapid repercussion characterized by the use of the glottal stop, or even the rough breathing or letter *h*. On the other hand later manuscripts, which may interpret the *tristropha* ( ,,, ) in different ways (e.g. at the conclusion of the psalmodic formula in Introits of the first mode as *fff* or *fef*), suggest that originally a quarter-tone (here the one between *f* and *e*) may have been denoted. In French neumes the *tristropha* is represented by three short strokes, the apostrophe being reserved to denote a downward leap.

The *oriscus* appears to represent an upward or downward *glissando* or *portamento*, or sometimes a downward and upward motion in succession. In addition to the forms shown in the table it is combined with the *punctum* to form the *pressus* (e.g. $\ulcorner$ = $\ulcorner$ $\subset\!\!\!\iota$ $\cdot$ ) and as the middle note of an upward group of three to form the *salicus* ( $\underset{\cdot}{!}$ = $\overset{\cdot}{.}$ $\mathcal{J}\mspace{1mu}\overset{\cdot}{\rho}$ or $\underset{\sim}{\jmath}$ = $\overset{\cdot}{.}$ $\mathcal{J\!\!J}\mspace{1mu}\overset{\cdot}{\rho}$ ) which is clearly a variant of the *scandicus* mentioned above (p. 23). The *quilisma* is always attached to a *virga* or other neume and probably indicates an upward chromatic ascent or slide. Finally the *trigon*, a group of *puncta* appearing in some such form as .ˑ. , also appears to involve chromaticism (see Example 22).

The method of transcription put forward here may be called a 'narrow' transcription as distinct from the 'broad' transcription currently in use and which is suitable for most purposes. In this all single notes except liquescents are transcribed as untailed full-sized black notes. The narrow transcription is suited primarily to neumatic notations of the cheironomic or non-heighted variety to which the St Gall neumes belong, and is used in the following pages only for pieces transcribed directly from such sources.

The other principal early method of notation consists of neumes which are carefully heighted according to the relative pitch of the individual notes, and is called 'diastematic'. The most important schools of diastematic notation are the central Italian (Beneventan) and southern French (Aquitanian). The former is a continuous script embodying many subtle nuances, while in the latter the single notes have become detached into separate symbols, mostly resembling a rather fat *punctum*. Both soon evolved into a primitive staff-notation, and from the former ultimately developed the characteristic later German *Hufnagel* (hob-nail) or Gothic notation. The latter grew into the standard French square notation of the thirteenth century, which however also retained some features of cheironomic notation. But before the staff could become anything more than a vague help in establishing relative pitches it had to be harnessed to one of the medieval systems of letter-notation.

The ancient Greeks had used two letter-notations, transmitted to the Latin West by Boethius, who describes them (and indeed the whole idea of notation) as a now unfamiliar device used by 'veteres musici' (*De Institutione Musica*, iv, 3). He himself used roman letters to illustrate various points of acoustics, but did not set up a regular new system. From the tenth century onwards we find various letter-notations in use, of which the commonest represented the two-octave series *A–a'* by the letters A–P (omitting J) or by A–G plus a–g plus å. To this the author of the *Dialogus* (see p. 41n) added the note G, represented by the Greek gamma (Γ). At the same time the note *b* flat (but not *B* flat) was recognized as an independent diatonic note, as it had been in the Greek system, usually represented by b (*rotundum* or round) as opposed to ♭ (*quadratum* or square) for *b* natural. Other systems included a curious one invented by Hermannus Contractus (1013–54), using symbols to denote the intervals between one note and the next; and an equally curious one using symbols based mainly on the Greek symbols for rough breathing or *prosōdia daseia* (hence 'Daseian' notation). The latter was used extensively in a treatise of *c.* 900, the anonymous *Commemoratio brevis* which records the psalm-tones and a few antiphons in unequivocal form, as well as for the notation of the earliest sources of polyphony (see Chapter 4).

Another important source for establishing the exact readings of the chants is the eleventh-century MS Montpellier (Faculté de Médecin, H 159;—introduction and facsimile in *PM*, I, vii–viii). It is one of a small group of manuscripts which record both neumes and letters. The letter-notation is particularly interesting, for it supports some of the hypotheses previously made about chromaticism and microtones. It is based on the letters a–p, with an italic *i* to represent *b* flat. There are signs which appear to indicate the quarter-tones between *B* and *c*, *e* and *f*, *a* and *b* flat, *b* and *c'*, and *e'* and *f*. The complete series is as follows:

In addition the *cephalicus* is marked, e.g. m̂l , and the *epiphonus*, e.g. lm̃ . The *pressus* is shown as h̑kh , the *quilisma* as d̃ef and the *franculus* as gf̃e . These last three all seem to imply some kind of *portamento* or *glissando*. The manuscript, which contains the chants of the Mass arranged according to their tonality, is a vital document for the study of the melodies in their original form.

Eventually it was the 'A–G' letter-notation which proved to be the most suitable for the purpose of relating diastematic neumes to a fixed point of reference. This was done by means of the clef, which is simply a letter attached to the beginning of a staff-line The development of the staff and its attendant clefs underwent many vicissitudes, but by the thirteenth century a completely un-ambiguous international notation had emerged, the square notation of northern France. All the original subtleties of rhythm and nuance had been lost except for some of the liquescents; but the development was a vital one for the history of Western music, and the new note-shapes were the ancestors of our modern ones.

Something must be said of the system of solmization codified by Guido of Arezzo (d. 1050). The entire system was divided into hexachords or six-note major scales starting on G, C and F. These were known as the hard, natural and soft hexachords respectively, according to the presence of B natural (hard), B flat (soft) or neither (natural). Each scale was denoted by the symbols *ut, re, mi, fa, sol, la,* derived from the initial syllables of each line in turn of the first stanza of the hymn 'Ut queant laxis', one of the tunes of which started each line on a successively higher degree of the scale. The object was to enable the singer to calculate the position of the semitone, which always came between *mi* and *fa*. The system came to be called the gamut, from its lowest note, *gamma*, and its solmization syllable, *ut*. It has no connection with the modal system described below (pp. 39–42).

The following discussion of the music is intended to be confined to melodies deemed to have been in existence by about the year 950. Some of them may be very much older, and a few may go back to the earliest Christian times, as is shown by the comparative studies mentioned earlier. Inevitably attention is centred on Gregorian chant, the manuscripts of which demonstrate a uniform tradition from *c.* 900 onwards. In the case of Ambrosian and Old-Roman chant there is a gap between the concluding date of this chapter and the earliest manuscripts: as has been stated, the earliest source of Old-Roman chant is dated 1071, while the earliest Ambrosian manuscript apart from a few fragments (London, British Museum, Add. MS 34209) is of the twelfth century. Yet there is every reason to believe that these repertories had acquired a substantial degree of fixity at least as early as Gregorian chant. More serious is the virtual inaccessibility of Gallican and Mozarabic chant, though their antiquity is unchallenged. A final difficulty concerns the formulae for the recitation of the lessons, Epistles and Gospels: the earliest document to give the interpretation of the signs dates only from the late twelfth century. Yet any thorough description of early medieval chant must include this topic, and for our purposes it is best to begin with it, always bearing in mind the fact that the evidence is of a less satisfactory nature than for the bulk of the repertory.

## The recitation of prose texts

The essential features of recitation, or cantillation, are the reciting note and the punctuating formulae. In Hebrew, in which the stress normally falls on the final syllable of a word, this would naturally give rise to a series of melismas; but in the recitation of Latin prose the notes of such formulae are distributed among the final syllables of a phrase according to its stress-pattern. This may not always have been so, and some classes of Latin chant, especially the more ornate ones, give ample evidence of the persistence of the melismatic treatment of final syllables. As examples we may cite some of the endings to the psalm-tones; the standard *neuma* or melisma attached to some chants on the final syllable; the extended melismata of the Tracts and Alleluias (especially on the final syllable of the Hebrew word *Alleluia* itself); and, as a curiosity, the Ambrosian 'Gloria in excelsis' (*LU*, p. 91, *GR*, p. 89★). Here a very simple recitation is punctuated by long melismas on final syllables:

**Example 1**

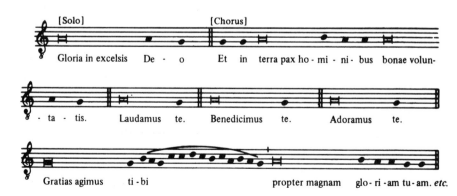

30

*Translation* Glory be to God on high, and on earth peace to men of good will. We praise thee, we bless thee, we worship thee, we glorify thee, we give thanks to thee for thy great glory.

1. The prose readings comprise the lessons for the Office, and the lessons and Gospels for the Mass. The earliest manuscript to give the interpretation of the ecphonetic signs is the important Cistercian exemplar of the late twelfth century now in Dijon, Bibliothèque Publique, MS 114. In view of the Cistercian anxiety to restore old customs, its readings must be taken very seriously. Its interpretation for the lessons of the Office, in particular Matins, takes the form of a model sentence defining the melodies of the *flexa*, *metrum* and *punctum* (after Wagner, *Einführung*, iii, p. 38):

**Example 2\***

Sic facies        flex   am?   sic   ve - ro   me - trum?   sic   au - tem   pun- ctum.

*Translation* Thus will you make the *flexa*, thus the *metrum* and thus the *punctum*.

The formulary for the lessons at Mass is indicated by the melody given for the preliminary announcement (Dijon, MS 114, f. 102v):

**Example 3**

Lectio  epistolae     be - a - ti  Pau-li  a - po-sto- li.  ad     Ro - ma - nos.

ad     Co-rin -thi - os....   Lectio    li - bri Ge - ne -sis....   In  di - e - bus  il - lis.

\* In Example 2-6 the medieval punctuation is used

*Translation* The reading from the epistle of blessed Paul the apostle to the Romans. to the Corinthians. . . . the reading from the book of Genesis. . . . In those days,

The clef is not given, but another conservative source, the fourteenth-century Carthusian manuscript Basle, BV 29, confirms that this formula, like those of the Office lesson and the Gospel at Mass, was originally recited on *a*. The question arises as to whether the *b* should be flattened or the *f* sharpened, but this question cannot be answered with any certainty. The epistolary in the Dijon MS begins at the vigil of the Nativity, a service which required two lessons, one from each testament. The following is an interpretation of the first lesson of the epistolary (f. 103). The interpretation of the conclusion, marked by neumes above the text in the manuscript, is conjectural:

**Example 4**

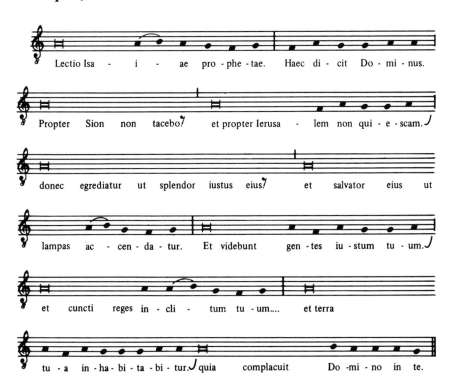

*Translation* The reading from Isaiah the prophet. Thus saith the Lord: For Sion's sake will I not hold my peace, and for Jerusalem's sake I will not rest, until the righteousness thereof go forth as brightness, and the salvation thereof burneth as a lamp. And the gentiles shall see thy righteousness, and all kings thy glory:.... and thy land shall be inhabited, for the Lord delighteth in thee.

The tone of the Gospels in the Dijon MS (f. 114v) is indicated as follows; we add the first sentence of the first Gospel, also for the vigil of the Nativity:

**Example 5**

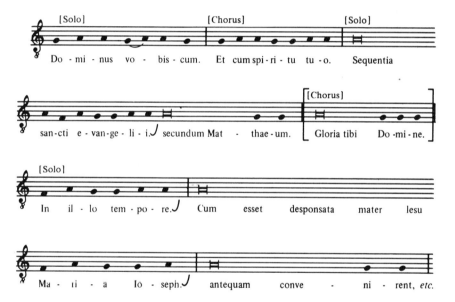

*Translation* The Lord be with you. And with thy spirit. The continuation of the holy gospel according to Matthew. [Glory be to thee O Lord.] At that time, when Mary the mother of Jesus was espoused to Joseph, before they came together, *etc.*

The Carthusian manuscript amplifies the instructions required in particular contexts, and adds a formula for the interrogation in all three tones (Wagner, op. cit., iii, pp. 40, 43, 47), e.g.:

**Example 6**

*Translation* (a) Amos, what seest thou? (b) O God, who justifieth thee? (c) What is truth?

Note the change of reciting-note for the interrogation in the Epistle and Gospel.

The sub-tonal structure of the formulae as preserved in these and other manuscripts is generally replaced in later sources by a sub-semitonal formula based on *f* or *c*.

2. Simple prayers were sung in exactly the same way as the lessons, i.e. with *flexa*, *metrum* and *punctum*. More complex are the tones for the 'Pater noster' and the Preface and Canon of the Mass. The Mozarabic form of the 'Pater noster' appears to be the oldest of these. It is clearly psalmodic in structure, and the melody closely resembles that of the oldest known version of the 'Gloria in excelsis' (see below, p. 59). It may be set out in schematic form as follows (Wagner, op. cit., iii, pp. 58–9):

**See Example 7 opposite**

Closely connected with the tone for the 'Pater noster' is that of the Preface, since both are part of a continuous sequence of prayers and chants framing the consecration (see p. 18). At one time, possibly the period we are now considering, the entire sequence from the prayer after the Offertory to the 'Pax Domini' (to the 'Pater noster' in the Gallican rites) was sung by priest and congregation. Later the first prayer, the eucharistic prayer, and in the Roman rite the 'Libera nos', were to be said in an undertone, with only the conclusion of each surviving as a sung formula. In all rites the basic musical material was retained from beginning to end. It is best illustrated in the Roman rite from the twelfth-century Cistercian manuscript already referred to. The quotation begins with the conclusion of the first prayer, by now known as 'Oratio secreta' (f. 134r) (overleaf):

**Example 7**

[Solo]

Pa - ter no - ster:

1. qui     es   in   cae - lis.     A - men.
2. Sanctificetur     no - men   tu - um.     A - men.
3. Adveniat     re - gnum   tu - um.     A - men.
4. Fiat vo - lun-tas tu - a:     sicut in caelo     et   in   ter - ra.     A - men.
5. Panem nostrum quo - ti - di - a - num:     da     no - bis   ho - di - e.     Qui - a Deus es.
6. Et dimitte nobis de - bi - ta no - stræ:     sicut et nos dimittimus debito - ri - bus   no -stris.     A - men.
7. Et ne nos in - du - cas:     in ten - ta - ti - o - nem.     Sed li - be - ra nos a malo.

[Chorus]

*Translation* Our Father, who art in heaven, Amen. Hallowed be thy name, Amen. Thy will be done, on earth as it is is in heaven, Amen. Give us this day our daily bread, for thou art God. And release us from our debts as we release our debtors, Amen. And lead us not into temptation, but deliver us from evil.

35

**Example 8**

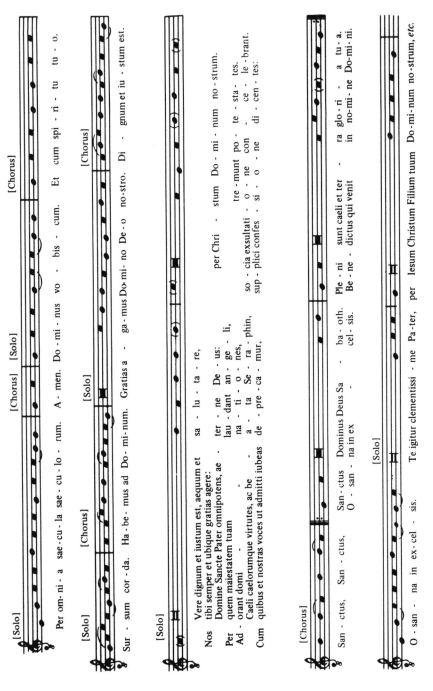

*Translation* Throughout all ages of ages, Amen. The Lord be with you. And with thy spirit. Lift up your hearts. We lift them up unto the Lord. Let us give thanks unto the Lord our God. It is meet and right. It is indeed meet and right, fitting and healthful, that we should always and everywhere give thanks to thee, O Lord, Holy Father almighty, eternal God, through Christ our Lord; through whom the angels praise, the dominations adore, the powers fear, the heavens and the heavenly virtues and the blessed Seraphim together in exultation celebrate thy majesty; with whom we pray that our voices too may be admitted, saying with humble confession: Holy, Holy, Holy is the Lord God of hosts. The heavens and the earth are full of thy glory. Hosanna in the highest. Blessed is he that cometh in the name of the Lord. Hosanna in the highest. Thee therefore O most clement Father, through Jesus Christ thy Son our Lord, *etc.*

This is the Common Preface used on ferial days. The Sanctus is quoted after the earliest known melody (see below, p. 59), which is clearly designed to lead on from the Preface. The phrase of the second 'Hosanna in excelsis' provides a musical rhyme with the 'per omnia saecula saeculorum. Amen' formula at the beginning of Example 8. By the twelfth century the Canon was said silently, but it may originally have begun somewhat as shown (cf. the melody for 'Libera nos' below). The Canon concludes as follows (Wagner, op. cit., iii, pp. 62, 65, 68–9):

**Example 9**

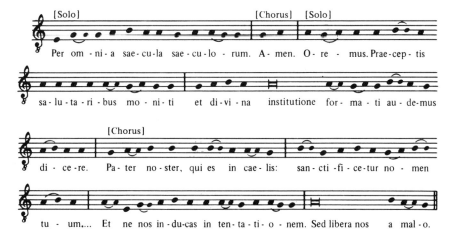

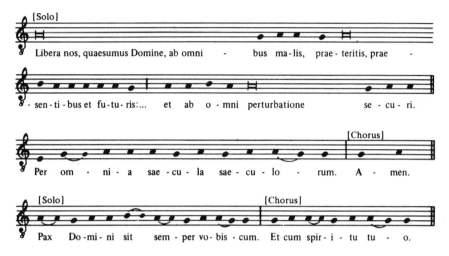

[Solo] Libera nos, quaesumus Domine, ab omni - bus ma-lis, prae-teritis, prae -

-sen-ti-bus et fu-tu-ris:... et ab o-mni perturbatione se-cu-ri.

[Chorus] Per om-ni-a sae-cu-la sae-cu-lo-rum. A-men.

[Solo] Pax Do-mi-ni sit sem-per vo-bis-cum. [Chorus] Et cum spir-i-tu tu-o.

*Translation* Throughout all ages of ages. Amen. Let us pray. Warned by saving precepts and taught by divine example we are bold to say, Our Father, who art in heaven, hallowed be thy name.... And lead us not into temptation, but deliver us from evil. Deliver us from all evils, past, present and to come:...and from all disturbance of quiet. Throughout all ages of ages. Amen. The peace of the Lord be always with you. And with thy spirit.

The source here is the eleventh-century Benedictine MS known as the Sacramentary of Desiderius (Montecasino, MS 339). This represents an even earlier stage than the Cistercian MS, and its Beneventan notation retains much of the flexibility of the earliest neumes. An elaborate formula for the Preface for Sundays and feasts is quoted by Wagner, op. cit., iii, p. 70.

### Psalmodic forms

1. Some of the music quoted above comes close to psalmody. The distinction between the recitation of psalms and of prose texts lies in the greater regularity of the former. Each verse of a psalm or canticle in Gregorian chant contains a *mediatio* or *metrum* at the half-way point, and a formula for the *punctus* at its close. The first, or all, of the verses may begin with an 'intonation'.

The simplest application of this principle is to be found in the antiphonal psalmody of the Office. With a very few exceptions Office psalms were performed with an antiphon, sung by all, originally between each verse but later at the beginning and end of the psalm only. The psalm itself would be sung in alternation from side to side of the monastic choir. The main musical problem was the reconciliation of the tonality of the antiphon with that of the psalm. In Ambrosian chant the antiphons were classified into four 'families' according to their final note (*d*, *e*, *f*, or *g*; *a*, *b*, *c′* or *d′* in transposition). Within each family the tenor of the psalm-tone was selected to correspond to the note said to predominate in the antiphon, though this could be a matter of opinion. Finally an ending or *clausula* was chosen to lead into the repeat of the antiphon. It should be added that the Ambrosian psalm-tones lacked the *mediatio*.

Clearly this system admitted of great flexibility. The psalm-tones, characterized by intonation, tenor and ending, bore a fluid relationship to the four families of antiphons. This would have been characteristic of psalmody generally in the East and West prior to the Roman-Frankish rationalization of the ninth and tenth centuries, which took the form of a fixed relationship between the *tenor* of the psalm-tone and the mode of the antiphon.

In order to explain the Western concept of mode it is necessary to digress a little. There are basically two ancestors: the ancient Greek *tonoi* and the Byzantine *oktoēchos*.

The *tonoi* of the Greeks were not modes, but rearrangements or *species*, always preserving the same serial order, of the intervals constituting a basic scale form (most characteristically a two-octave descending melodic minor scale in our terminology). Thus, taking our A minor (*a′* to *A*) as the norm, B minor would still appear to cover the same range, but with C and F sharps. At the same time the note defined functionally as, for example, the 'middle' (*mesē*) would have moved up from *a* to *b*. The Greeks were quite clear that in the second case the note *a* was the 'middle' only *kata thesin*, i.e. by virtue of its position; had the *tonoi* been modes it would have remained the 'middle' *kata dunamin*, according to its force or function. The object of the exercise was to accommodate a melody of any *tessitura* within a theoretical two-octave range by transposing it to an appropriate key. (However, some theorists presented the transposed scales in fully extended form, e.g. B minor as *b′–B*). Since the Greek octave, like ours, contained seven intervals, the logical number of different *tonoi* was seven.

The same principles were also applied to the central octave *e'–e* of the complete two-octave *tonoi*. To the seven *tonoi* Boethius (supposedly following Ptolemy) added an eighth, an octave higher than the first according to the position of the (functional) *mesē*. Example 10 shows these eight *tonoi* in ascending order (M = *mesē*) with the central octaves distinguished by black notes. Below them are shown the corresponding octaves as purely diatonic scales over the two-octave range, with the names applied to them from the tenth century onwards in brackets (these names can be explained in more than one way, but they amount to a confusion between the order of the *tonoi* and the necessarily opposite order of the diatonic octaves):

**Example 10**

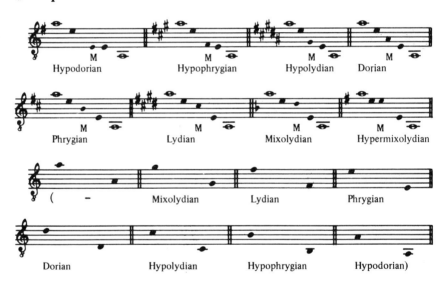

The medieval theorists also required an eighth scale, but for entirely different reasons which had to do with the modal system of the East known as the *oktoēchos*.

The *oktoēchos* was a cycle of chants in the Byzantine liturgy for the eight Sundays from Easter Day to Pentecost. Each group of chants was in one of the eight Eastern modes or *ēchoi*. These are characterized not by a particular scale but by formulae particular to each one. The eight modes are divided into two groups of four each:

authentic (*kurioi*) and plagal (*plagioi*). Although there is no theoretical link between each mode and a particular *finalis* it does emerge in transcription that melodies of the first mode will end on *d* or *a*, those of the second on *e*, those of the third on *f* and those of the fourth on *g*. The four plagal modes have the same *finales*, although *a* does not appear as *finalis* in mode 1. In fact Byzantine musicians defined their modes according to their starting notes rather than according to their *finales*, each melody being prefixed by a short formula which linked the 'correct' starting-note to the actual beginning of the melody. Authentic modes had relatively high starting-notes, plagal modes relatively low ones. Western musicians appear to have toyed with this idea for a time, but eventually abandoned it in favour of a definition according to range and *finalis*. However, they retained the notion of an appropriate introduction to their antiphons in the shape of alternative endings to the psalm-tones.

The medieval Latin theorists did not initially relate the *ēchoi* to the *tonoi*. Aurelianus of Réomé, writing about 850, refers to four authentic and four plagal modes, which he calls 'toni', and describes some of their melodic characteristics. (When, earlier, he refers to the ancient Greek system, it is to one of fifteen *tonoi* transmitted to the West by Cassiodorus.) In the anonymous *Commemoratio brevis de tonis et psalmis modulandis* (*c.* 900) these are numbered 1, 3, 5, 7 and 2, 4, 6, 8 respectively, the *finales* in each group being *d e f* and *g* respectively. The earliest attempts to link the scale-ranges of the *tonoi* to the modes occur in Hucbald's *De harmonica institutione* (*c.* 900) and in an anonymous treatise of composite authorship which is attached to it and called simply *Alia musica*. In one of the five or so sections into which the *Alia musica* can be divided is found for the first time the bracketed terminology of Example 10, and in another section the scales are equated with the characteristic formulae of the several *ēchoi*. Ultimately the following scheme resulted, in which each scale is divided into a fifth plus a fourth or vice versa, and allotted a *finalis* (F) and a *tenor* (T). The bracketed notes outside the octave were recognized in the tenth century\*, though the name and scale-construction of the eighth mode were finalized only by Hermannus Contractus in the eleventh:

\* More specifically in the *Dialogue de Musica* formerly attributed to Odo of Cluny but now recognized to be by an Italian monk of *c.* 1000. See Huglo in *Revue de Musicologie*, lv (1969), 119–171.

**Example 11**

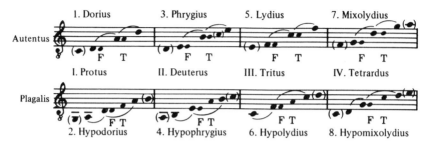

It will be seen that the normal distance between the *finalis* and the *tenor* (the latter more properly a characteristic of a psalm-tone than of a mode) was a fifth in the case of the authentic modes and a third in the case of the plagal modes. However in the *Commemoratio brevis*, our earliest source of the actual psalm-tones (apart from the laborious and ambiguous verbal descriptions of Aurelianus), the *tenor* of the eighth mode is already *c′* instead of *b* while those of the third and fourth modes oscillate between *b* and *a* and *g* and *a* respectively. In the final system the *tenor* of the fourth mode settled on *a* and that of the third mode moved up to *c′*. Here are the eight psalm-tones as given in the *Commemoratio brevis*, set to the first eight verses of Ps. 118 (A.V. 119):

**Example 12**

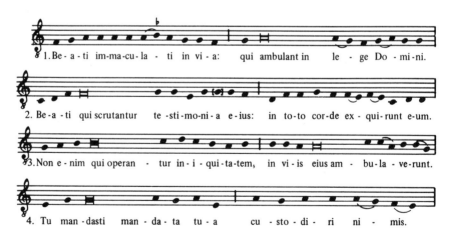

5. Ut-i-nam dirigantur vi-ae me-ae, ad cu-sto-diendas iustifi - ca-ti-o-nes tu-as.

6. Tunc non confundar, dum per-spi-ci-o in omni man - da - ta tu - a.

7. Con-fi - te-bor tibi Domine in directi - o-ne cor-dis: quod didici iu - di -ci-a tu-a.

8. Iu-sti-fi - cationes tuas cu-sto-di-am: non me de-re-lin-quas us - que-qua-que.

* Gerbert *f*

*Translation* 1. Blessed are the undefiled in the way, who walk in the law of the Lord. 2. Blessed are they that keep his testimonies, and that seek him with the whole heart. 3. For they who do iniquity have not walked in his ways. 4. Thou hast commanded us to keep thy commandments diligently. 5. O that my ways were directed to keep thy statutes. 6. I shall not be ashamed when I have respect unto all thy commandments. 7. I shall praise thee O Lord in uprightness of heart because I have learnt thy judgments. 8. I will keep thy statutes: O forsake me not utterly.

The importance of the *Commemoratio brevis* lies in its use of Daseian notation (see above, p. 28) to notate the psalm-tones and a selection of antiphons with precision at a time when neumatic notation could do no more than indicate their general outline. It gives no scales, but the mode of an antiphon can be recognized from its *finalis* and its range as compared with the standard *neuma* of the mode (see below). Its whole attitude to psalmody is more flexible than that shown in modern manuals such as the *Liber Usualis*. The terminology is different, too: the *tonus* is what we should call the mode, i.e. the tonality; the psalm-tone is called 'modulatio psalmi', while *modus* is a 'method' of interpreting the *mediatio* in any one *tonus*. After enumerating the eight *toni* with their psalm-melodies as above, the author points out that some antiphons require special psalm-melodies, or even an alternation of two such melodies. As an example of the latter he quotes the antiphon 'Benedicta tu' with the first two verses of the canticle 'Benedictus Dominus' (to the Daseian notation of the *Commemoratio brevis* we add the neumes of the Hartker Codex, St Gall, 390–1):

**Example 13**

Be - ne - di - cta  tu in  mu - li - e - ri - bus,  et  be - ne - di - ctus fru - ctus

ven - tris  tu - i.  Be - ne - dictus  Domi - nus

De - us  Is - ra - el,  qui - a  visitavit  et  fecit  redemptionem  ple - bis su - ae.

Et  e - rexit cornu sa - lu - tis no - bis  in do - mo David  pu - er - i  su - i.  Be - ne - di - cta *etc.*

*Translation* Blessed art thou among women, and blessed is the fruit of thy womb. Blessed is the Lord God of Israel, for he hath visited and redeemed his people, and hath raised up a horn of salvation for us in the house of David his servant. Blessed *etc.*

The melisma at the end of the antiphon is an example of a *neuma* (there was one for each *tonus*) to reinforce the tonality or to provide a festive note. A special psalm-melody was also required for the *tonus novissimus*, as exemplified by the antiphon 'In templo Domini':

**Example 14**

In  tem - plo Do - mi -  ni om - nes  di - cent  glo -  ri - am. [Ps] Af - ferte Domino

fi - li - i  De - i:  af - fer - te  Do - mi - no  fi - li -  os  a - ri - e - tum.

*Translation* In the temple of the Lord all will declare his glory. Bring to the Lord, O sons of God, bring to the Lord the young of rams.

In modern parlance this psalm-melody is known as the *tonus peregrinus*; but the term *tonus novissimus* does not refer to the psalm-melody itself, which is in fact very old and of Jewish origin, but to the tonality, which appears to be characterized by a range of *c* to *b* (flat?) with *finalis g*.

The method of matching a psalm-melody to the beginning of an antiphon by means of various endings (*diversitates* or *differentiae*) is covered in greater detail in the medieval tonaries. A tonary is a list of chants in a particular category (Office-antiphons, Introits, Communions, and sometimes Offertories and Office-responds), arranged according to their mode and, within each mode, according to the psalm-tone ending required to match the opening of the chant itself. The earliest surviving tonary is that of St Riquier (late eighth century), a tonary of chants for the Mass; a Carolingian tonary can be recognized in three sources from the late ninth and early eleventh centuries. Other famous early examples are those of Regino of Prüm and one of Italian origin (formerly believed to be by Odo of Cluny). But our author alone illustrates the ways of treating the middle of a psalm-verse for the purposes of matching the music to the words, or for the sake of euphony. Some verses are given two mediations. Most of his examples are of isolated verses; nevertheless the fifth mode is illustrated by two complete psalms (137 and 96), of which we shall give a somewhat hypothetical reconstruction of the first in connection with the antiphon 'Solvite templum hoc':*

## See Example 15 overleaf

The *Commemoratio brevis* is also noteworthy for a section on rhythm, in which performance according to the quantity of Latin syllables is advocated. But the application of this principle is uncertain in many details; and it should be remembered that it is mentioned by the author only in connection with simple psalmody (see above, p. 23).

* The repetition of the antiphon after every verse is confirmed by a remark at the beginning of the penultimate paragraph of the *Commemoratis brevis*.

## Example 15

Sol-vi-te tem-plum hoc, di-cit Do-mi-nus; et post tri-du-um re-ae-di-fi-

-ca-bo il-lud: hoc au-tem di-ce-bat de tem-plo cor-po-ris su-i. [Fine]

cor-de me - o, quo-ni-am audisti verba o - ris me-i.

| | | | | |
|---|---|---|---|---|
| Con-fi-tebor tibi Domine in toto | cor-de me - | o, | quo-ni-am audisti verba | o - ris me-i. |
| In con-spectu angelorum psallam tibi, adorabo ad templum | sanc-tum tu - | um, | et con-fitebor | no-mi-ni tu-o. |
| Su-per misericordia tua et veri | ta-te tu - | a, | quo-ni-am magnificasti super omne nomen sanc-tum tu-um. | |
| In qua-cunque die invocavere te | ex-au-di me, | | mul-ti-plicabis in anima | me-a vir-tu-tem. |
| *Con-fi-teantur tibi Domine omnes | re-ges ter - | rae, | quo-ni-am audierunt omnia verba | o-ris tu-i. |
| †Et can-tent in vi | is Do-mi-ni, | | quo-ni-am magna est | glo-ri-a Do-mi-ni. |
| **Si am-bulavero in medio tribulationis vivi-fi-ca-bis | ma-num tu - | am, | et su-per [iram] inimi - vum me fecit | dex-te-ra tu-a. |
| corum meorum extendes | | me, | et sal- | |
| Do-mi-ne re | tri-bu-e pro me, | | Do-mi-ne | |
| misericordia tua | in sae-cu-lum, | et | o-pe-ra manuum tuarum | ne de-spi-ci-as. |
| Glo-ri-a Patri et Filio et Spiri | tu-i Sanc - | to, | sic-ut | |
| erat in principio et | nunc et sem - | per, | et in saecula saecu - | lo - rum. A-men. |

[D.C. al Fine after each verse]

* Gerbert *Confitebor.*

† Gerbert gives the second half of the verse only. The following verse of the psalm is omitted in his text, so it is also left out here. In other respects too his text differs from the Vulgate but is followed here.

** Gerbert *Si ambulabis.*

*Translation* Destroy this temple, saith the Lord, and after three days I shall rebuild it; but this he spake concerning the temple of his body. I will praise thee, O Lord, with my whole heart, for thou hast heard the words of my mouth. In the sight of the angels will I sing praise unto thee; I will worship toward thy holy temple, and praise thy name concerning thy loving-kindness and truth, for thou hast magnified thy holy name above every name. Whenever I cry unto thee, hear me; thou shalt increase the strength in my soul. Let all the kings of the earth praise thee O Lord, for they have heard all the words of thy mouth, and shall sing in the ways of the Lord, for great is the glory of the Lord. If I walk in the midst of trouble thou wilt revive me; thou shalt stretch forth thine hand against the wrath of my enemies, and thy right hand shall save me. O Lord take revenge on my behalf; thy mercy O Lord endureth for ever; despise not the works of thine own hands. Glory be to the Father and to the Son, and to the Holy Ghost, as it was in the beginning, is now, and ever shall be, world without end, Amen.

The growth in the style of the antiphon may be traced from the simple one- or two-phrase antiphon with Biblical words, usually taken from the psalm or canticle to which it is joined, to the more elaborate, melismatic type of the later Middle Ages. Examples of the former may be seen in the antiphons to the five psalms for Sunday Vespers, including the antiphon 'Alleluia' for use in Eastertide only (*LU*, pp. 251–6), and in the antiphon 'Lumen ad revelationem gentium' for the 'Nunc dimittis' at Candlemas (*LU*, pp. 1357–8), where the antiphon is still found repeated after each verse (the verse used for the antiphon itself being omitted). Even in these simplest of antiphons, however, the lyrical principle, as opposed to the recitation of the psalm itself, is clearly apparent. The next stage was the expansion of the antiphon in length and in choice of text, firstly non-psalmodic and finally non-Biblical words being chosen. The melodies are now normally of three or four phrases and have a certain regularity of structure, as in 'Solvite templum hoc' above. Though many hundreds of such antiphons were composed, they nearly all conform to one of about fifty melodic types, more or less evenly distributed among the eight tones. Though this classification is a modern one, pioneered by Gevaert (*La Mélopée antique*) and Frere (*AS*), it has a close parallel in the method employed in the medieval tonaries, where the aim was the purely practical one of grouping antiphons together according to their opening phrase, each group corresponding to a particular psalm-ending.

Melismatic antiphons for the Office are a development of the later Middle Ages and will be discussed in the following chapter. A more melismatic type, however, is found in the antiphonal psalmody of the Mass in the earliest manuscripts.

2. The antiphonal chants of the Roman Mass are the Introit and Communion. Originally the Offertory also belonged to this category. It is significant that all these chants are designed to accompany liturgical actions. At one time they all consisted of a complete psalm (or a substantial portion), with the antiphon between each verse. The papal rite called for additional verses after the 'Gloria Patri' of the Introit and Communion, the so-called *versus ad repetendum* which are still found in a few early musical manuscripts. Later the number of verses was reduced to one, while at around the time of the earliest musical documents the Offertory was provided with an elaborate verse like that of a respond (see below). A little later the Communion lost its verse altogether, and later still the Offertory joined it.

The psalm-tones for the Introit and Communion were rather more elaborate than those of the Office, and those for the Offertory may have been similar. The Gregorian Introit-antiphon is a lightly-melismatic, lyrical melody of carefully balanced proportions:

**Example 16**

St Gall, Stiftsbibl., 339, p. 1.

Pitch-interpretation from Montpellier, Faculté de Médecine, H 159, p. 86.

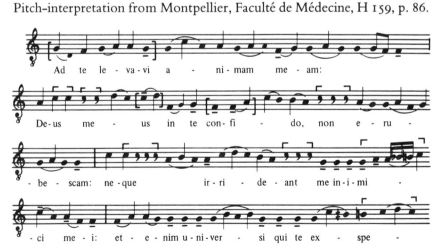

- ctant    non con - fun    den - tur. Ps. Vi - as   tu - as Domi - ne de - mon -

stra mi - hi:    et   se - mi - tas tu    as    do - ce me.

[] = missing in St. Gall

*Translation* Unto thee have I lifted up my soul; my God, in thee do I put my trust and shall not be ashamed; neither let my enemies laugh me to scorn; for all those who wait for thee shall not be confounded. *Ps.* Show me thy ways, O Lord, and teach me thy paths.

The Communion was similar in style; the Offertory, which will be discussed with responsorial forms, rather more elaborate. Neither in Ambrosian nor Old-Roman chant are the antiphonal chants of the Mass so well proportioned; in the former the psalm-verse is completely missing.

3. The principle of response is found at every level of complexity in Latin chant. A response may complete a phrase already begun, as in litanies, or it may add a complementary phrase to one already sung; it may consist of a partial or total repetition of a verse, or it may be an independent refrain. Initially, and characteristically, it is the response of a congregation to a precentor; but the refrain principle was extended to antiphonal chant, and in its classical form responsorial chant also is a matter for trained singers, the *schola cantorum*.

All the Offices contain various types of response, but it is the *responsoria prolixa* or great responds of Matins which claim our particular attention. The form consists of the respond proper, sung (after the opening phrase) by the choir, and one or more verses, sung by soloists except for the closing phrase, interspersed with repetitions of the respond between and after the verses. In Old-Roman chant these repetitions are performed in full, but in Gregorian they are often abbreviated by omitting a portion of the opening. The 'Gloria Patri', when it is sung, is performed only as far as the words 'Spiritui Sancto', indicating a very archaic origin for the form. The verses are usually highly elaborated psalm-tones, as in the following respond of the eighth mode from Matins of Christmas Day: note the change of reciting note to the *finalis* in the second half, a characteristic of the responsorial tones for the plagal modes:

**Example 17**

St Gall, Stiftsbibl., 390, f. 45.

*Translation* To-day true peace has descended upon us from heaven; to-day throughout the whole world the heavens are made sweet. V. Glory be to God on high, and on earth peace to men of good will.

A few later compositions, however, have freely-composed verses. The Invitatory at Matins (Ps. 94) is a responsorial chant with a complete psalm.

4. The form in the Mass which corresponds most closely to the Office respond is the Gradual. Here, however, only a single,

complete repetition of the respond was performed, while the verses are freely composed according to the method of centonization described below in connection with the Tracts.

We now give extracts from the Gradual 'A summo caelo' in its Ambrosian, Old-Roman and Gregorian forms, in order that a comparison can be made between the different versions of a highly melismatic chant (cf. *PM*, I, ii, pp. 6–8. The transposition of this second-mode melody up a fifth in copies written in staff or letter notation permitted the transcription of its lowest note, the theoretically non-existent *B* flat, as *f*, as well as the inclusion of *b* flats, which would otherwise have become *e* flats. Chants were often thus presented a fourth or fifth higher than the strict modal system would allow in order to obviate the appearance of notes outside the system):

**Example 18**

London, Brit. Mus., Add. 34209, p. 7.

Ambrosian (Psalmellus)

Rome, Bib. Vat., lat. 5319, f. 7.*

Old-Roman

Einsiedeln, Stiftsbibl., 121, p. 15.
Montpellier, Faculté de Médecine, H 159, p. 153†.

Gregorian

A  sum - mo cae  -  -  lo  e - gres  -

si  -  -  o  e  -  ius:  *continued*

(Ambrosian)

* Readings checked from *MMMA*, ii, page 88
† Montpellier lacks letters for the verse *Caeli enarrant*
** London *annunciant*; Einsiedeln *adnunciat*

*Translation* From the highest heaven is his going forth . . . V. The heavens declare [the glory of God]; the firmament announces [the works of his hand].

The Alleluia ultimately derives from the use of this Hebrew word in psalms, when it could be provided with a long *neuma* or *jubilus* on the final syllable. (This may also be the origin of the separate *neuma* which could be attached to other chants; see above, p. 44). St Gregory sanctioned the performance of the Alleluia, sung by itself, as a Mass chant; but by the ninth century it was provided with one or more freely-composed verses:

## Example 19

Einsiedeln, Stiftsbibl., 121, p. 1.
Pitch-interpretatin from Montpellier, Faculté de Médecine, H 159, p. 115.

[Solo, repeat Chorus]

Al - le - lui - a.

[Chorus]                                                          [Fine]

[Solo]

℣ O - sten - de no - bis Do - mi - ne

mi - se - ri - cor - di - am tu -

-am: et sa - lu - ta - re tu - *continued*

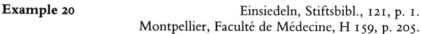

[D.C. al Fine senza rep.]

*Translation* Alleluia. V. Show us they mercy O Lord, and grant us thy salvation.

The Offertory was also provided with one or more freely-composed verses during the ninth century (see Apel, *Gregorian Chant*, p. 512). As a responsorial chant it came to be grouped amongst solo chants performed after a lesson (in this case the Gospel), rather than amongst the chants which accompany an action. The Offertory verses, unfortunately discarded soon afterwards, are the most elaborate of all chants in the standard repertory, with their extended range, word-repetitions, long melismas, and complete emancipation from the recitation principle. (It is possible that in many cases, the respond-sections were also re-composed at about the same time, since they betray some of the same characteristics). The verses were published by C. Ott (*Offertoriale*), but with unwarranted departures from the manuscript readings. The following extracts include the second verse of the Offertory for Advent I in full; this is another example of a second-mode melody transposed up a fifth, this time for the sake of the accidentals and extended range of its verses:

**Example 20**                    Einsiedeln, Stiftsbibl., 121, p. 1.
                    Montpellier, Faculté de Médecine, H 159, p. 205.

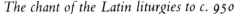

\* in Montpellier 159 the section from here to the end is repeated a fifth higher.

*Translation* Unto thee O Lord have I lifted up [my soul] . . . *etc* V. Direct me in thy truth . . . *etc* V. Look upon me and have mercy upon me O Lord; keep my soul and deliver me; I shall not be confounded for I have called upon thee.

5. The Tracts, corresponding to the Ambrosian *Cantus*, demand separate treatment. In the first place, they set only the text of the psalm. But instead of an elaborated recitation we find the most thoroughgoing application in Latin chant of the Eastern principle of centonization, or patching together of standard melodic phrases. In Byzantine chant this method is applied to hymnody, but in the Tracts to the psalmody itself. Tracts are found only in the 2nd and 8th modes, and E. Werner has pointed out that the cadential formulae in the two modes are identical (*The Sacred Bridge*, p. 531), namely:

**Example 21**

(a) at half-verse        (b) at the end of the verse

(for the notational peculiarities of these cadences in the earliest MSS see next example)

One must however distinguish between such short motives and the standard phrases (often also called formulae) on which entire compositions are built. The stock of such phrases does of course differ according to the two modes. An interesting point is that, within each mode, most of the older Tracts end with the same standard phrase, thus disposing of the idea that they are abbreviated from longer pieces. Tracts vary in length from two to fourteen verses, and each verse may contain three or four phrases.

Various methods of analysing Tracts have been used, but the following will be found to illuminate all the essential aspects of the construction. Each phrase is marked by a letter at the beginning (A, B, C etc.) and at the end (Z, Y, X etc.), the standard last phrase being MN. The resulting half-phrase may overlap with identical material (e.g. $A\overset{\frown}{Z}$) or be separated by free material (e.g. B–Y). Subscript numerals denote successively shorter versions of a standard phrase (e.g. Y, $Y_1$, $Y_2$); small letters denote short motives associated with the longer phrases. The method is here applied to the four verses of a single Tract, although analysis of all the older Tracts in any one mode would yield fuller results (see e.g. Apel, *Gregorian Chant*, p. 319).

**Example 22**

Einsiedeln, Stiftsbibl., 121, p. 82.
Montpellier, Faculté de Médecine, H 159, p. 132.

1. De pro-fun - dis cla - ma - vi ad te

Do - mi - ne:

Do-mi - ne ex-au - di
vo cem me - - - am
2. Fi - ant au-res tu - - ae:
in - ten - den - tes
in o - ra - ti - o - nem
ser - vi tu - - - i.
3. Si in-i-qui-ta-tes ob - ser - va - ve - ris,*
Do - mi - ne:
Do-mi - ne quis sus - ti - ne - *continued*

\* Einsiedeln *obseruaberis*

57

bit?    4. Qui - a   a - pud   te

pro - pi- ti - a - ti - o   est,

et pro - pter le - gem   tu - am

sus- ti - nu - i   te, Do -

mi- ne.

*Note* The letter-notation in Montpellier is incomplete. However, its interpretation of the four-note *trigon*, given here as

is $c'c'c'g'$; our interpretation attempts to preserve the apparent pitch-direction of the Einsiedeln neumes. The interpretation of the other forms of *trigon* as

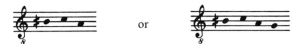

follows as a natural consequence.

*Translation* 1. Out of the depths have I cried unto thee O Lord; Lord, hear my voice. 2. Let thine ears be attentive to the prayer of thy servant. 3. If thou, Lord, shouldest mark iniquities, O Lord, who shall stand? 4. For with thee there is forgiveness; and for the sake of thy law have I upheld thee, O Lord.

The form may therefore be tabulated as AZ $BY_1$ CX DW; EV FY GX DW; HU IY CW; H JY$_2$ GX MN.

*Other forms*

1. First to be considered are the items of the Ordinary of the Mass, the Te Deum, and some other prose texts. The oldest of these is the Sanctus of the Mass (Isa. 6: 3) with Benedictus (Matt. 31: 9). Its original melody is quoted above in Example 8. This three-fold Sanctus is not to be confused with the *Trisagion* which opened the Gallican rite (see p. 18), sung in Greek.

Either the Kyrie or the 'Gloria in excelsis', or both, occur near the beginning in all Latin rites. The Gloria was originally a Greek hymn, while the Kyrie was never translated. Neither was initially part of the Mass. The Kyrie was originally a three-fold invocation, as it still is in the litany (see especially *LU*, p. 838) and in the Ambrosian rite, where it follows the Gloria. The concluding Kyrie of the litany for Rogationtide (*LU*, p. 838) has the form AAB; and the simplest way of expanding this to the Roman ninefold form is seen in the following very similar twelfth-century version (Wagner, op. cit., p. 440):

**Example 23**

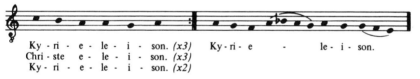

Ky - ri - e - le - i - son. *(x3)*   Ky - ri - e   -   le - i - son.
Chri - ste   e - le - i - son. *(x3)*
Ky - ri - e - le - i - son. *(x2)*

*Translation* Lord have mercy. Christ have mercy. Lord have mercy.

As Wagner observed, this leads naturally into the archaic Gloria XV of the Vatican edition, which may be compared with Example 1 above:

**Example 24**

Glo - ri - a                                    in ex   -         cel - sis  De - o.
Et   in            terra  pax  ho - mi - ni - bus  bonae            vo - lun - ta - tis.
                   Lau - da   -                          -        mus  te.
Be - ne   -  di - ci   -                                 -        mus  te.
Ad - o   -   ra        -                                 -        mus  te.
Glo   -      ri           -                              -        fi - ca - mus  te.
Gra - ti   -     as a - gi - mus  ti - bi        propter magnam glo - ri - am  tu - am.

*Translation* Glory be to God on high, and on earth peace to men of good will. We praise thee, we bless thee, we worship thee, we glorify thee, we give thanks to thee for thy great glory.

Its actual melodic shape is very similar to that of the fourth psalm-tone (see Example 12), and still closer to the Mozarabic 'Pater noster' (Example 7).

The Gallican and Mozarabic rites employed as Ordinary chants both the 'Benedictus Dominus Deus Israel' (Canticle of Zachary, Luke 1 : 68) and the 'Benedictus es, Domine Deus patrum nostrorum' (Daniel 3 : 52). A version of the latter can be found in the archaic Roman rite for Saturday in Ember Week of Advent (*LU*, p. 348; *GR*, p. 16).

The Agnus Dei, like the Kyrie, is also a litany chant, and was apparently introduced to the Roman Mass by Pope Sergius I (687–701). The Credo (Nicene Creed, approved by the Council of Nicaea, 325) was not sung in the Mass in Rome until 1014, although it had appeared in Spain from 589 and later in France and Germany in the form 'Credimus in unum Deum'. A Mozarabic melody, similar to the Vatican Credo I, has survived, while the Ambrosian melody (*AMM*, p. 611) is even simpler.

The Te Deum resembles the Gloria in being a quasi-psalmodic text. Its place is at the end of Matins. Two psalm-tones are employed and a more extended, antiphon-like melody for the verses 'Aeterna fac', 'Salvum fac', 'Et rege eos' and 'In te Domine speravi' (*LU*, p. 1832).

2. The Latin metrical hymn was originally a popular form which gained a liturgical foothold through monasticism, especially that of St Benedict. In the process of adaptation to liturgical use, many long hymns were divided into sections for separate use, each section being provided with a doxology; many textual corruptions set in, and were incorporated into the standard medieval versions. The most significant of the earlier authors are St Ambrose (d. 397), Prudentius (d. after 405), Sedulius (fifth century), and Venantius Fortunatus (d. after 600). The principle of versification is normally one of an equal number of syllables in each line (isosyllabism) with a dependence on classical scansion by quantity which varies from one writer to

another. In the later Middle Ages scansion by stress replaced scansion by quantity almost universally (see note on page 15).

The earliest hymnaries with music are those of Moissac and Kempten, both of *c.* 1000 (see *MMMA*, i), although a few hymns sung in special Masses are found in Graduals of the tenth century; while a melody for 'Aeterna Christi munera' is found in the *Musica Enchiriadis*. The Moissac hymnary is written in staffless, though heighted, neumes, while that of Kempten uses alphabetic notation. Two melodies in the Moissac MS for Fortunatus' 'Pange lingua', different from any in later medieval or present-day use, and different again from the version sung on Good Friday (*LU*, p. 742; *GR*, p. 236), reinforce the point that we are far from being able to reconstruct the original melodies to these poems:

**Example 25**

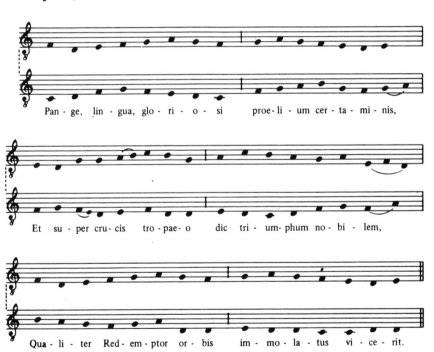

*Translation* Sing, my tongue, of the fighting in the glorious contest, and tell of the splendid triumph of the victory of the cross, how the Redeemer of the world was sacrificed and gained the victory.

Since in fact the bulk of the readable sources are of later date and contain a different repertory, the hymns will be discussed more fully in the next chapter.

3. As in the case of the hymns, the musical evidence concerning tropes and sequences comes mainly from a later period than that covered by this chapter. But the historical development began well within its scope, and for that reason a discussion of their origin is desirable at this point.

A trope may be a purely musical addition, a purely verbal addition, or a combination of the two, to an existing musico-liturgical entity. Its origin in Latin chant is very remote, for what is an antiphon (unless it is merely a single verse of the psalm with which it is sung) but a trope to a psalm? This reminds us that the Byzantine *troparion* is a short chant similar in character and function to the Latin antiphon (Wellesz, *Byzantine Music*, p. 171). Latin *tropus* is found in Cassiodorus and Fortunatus (sixth century) in the general sense of a melody, but its more specific sense of trope or liturgical intercalation may be due to Byzantine influence. The exact transliteration of *troparion* (*troparium*) was reserved for a troper or book of tropes.

A sequence is a particular kind of trope, associated with the Alleluia of the Mass.* *Sequentia* or *sequela* originally meant the *jubilus* or *neuma* on the last syllable of the word 'Alleluia', either in its original form or as modified and extended. In its final medieval form a sequence consisted of a lengthy text, in verse or 'poetic prose', to a new melody or to a modification of the original *jubilus*, serving as a substitute for the repetition of the Alleluia after its verse. Since this repetition, after the first phrase, was performed chorally, the sequence, though often extremely elaborate, was itself a choral chant.

That the sequence was originally a purely melodic variant and extension of the Alleluia on its repetition after the verse is now

---

* It has recently been pointed out by P. Evans (*The Early Trope Repertory*) that the term *tropus* is reserved in musical manuscripts for additions in which new words and new music (usually in neumatic or melismatic style) appear simultaneously. But there is need for a word in English to denote the entire phenomenon of accretions—verbal, musical or both—to an existing chant, and 'trope' has been widely accepted in this sense. There is no suggestion, of course, that tropes in the narrow technical meaning preceded the sequences historically: the earliest are those ascribed to Tuotilo of St Gall (d. 913).

generally accepted.* The initial phrase (sung by a soloist) was normally left unchanged, and was followed by a series of repeated phrases (double versicles) with a short single phrase to conclude, though many variants of this basic structure exist. It is melismas of this kind, and not the original *jubili* of the Alleluia, which are the *melodiae longissimae* to which Notker Balbulus, monk of St Gall (d. 912), added texts on the principle of one syllable to a note. (Although syllabic texts on original Alleluias, as well as on their verses, are also found, they are of later date and are irrelevant to the origin of the sequence: see below, p. 77.)

Notker did not claim to have originated the practice of setting words to sequences; he obtained the idea from a monk fleeing from the Abbey of Jumièges after its devastation by the Normans in 851 or 862 and received advice from his teacher Yso (d. 871). Several factors would seem to indicate the priority of France in the evolution of the sequence as a literary form: French sequences frequently retain the initial word 'Alleluia' for the initial phrase; they make frequent use of rhyme or assonance with its final syllable (*–a, –am, –as,* etc.); and there is an intermediate stage documented, in which some, but not all, pairs of phrases are provided with words (e.g. 'Adest una', 'Adorabo major', 'Fulgens praeclara' in A. Hughes, *Anglo-French Sequelae*, nos. 2, 3, 23). Sequences originating in Germany and Italy tend to ignore these points. When a German sequence can be shown to correspond to an Anglo-French *sequela* its melody sometimes diverges from it in detail, suggesting that at one time there was a

---

* Many authorities describe the sequence (wordless or otherwise) as following, rather than replacing, the repetition of the Alleluia after its verse. Though this may occasionally have been done, it would normally result in a tautological repetition of the word 'Alleluia' and of the music to its opening phrase, and there can be no doubt that originally the sequence was intended as a substitute. The Sarum Missal specifically states that, when a sequence is to be sung, only the opening phrase of the Alleluia must be sung after the verse; and since the word 'Alleluia' has been detached from the sequences which originally began with it, no tautology results. When a sequence did not originally begin with the word 'Alleluia', a musical tautology does then exist, though not a verbal one. I do not believe that even this purely musical tautology was originally intended; it may have crept in when the texts of both French and German sequences were combined into a single cycle and the word 'Alleluia' detached from the former.

A particular problem is raised by a number of early sequences related to no known 'Alleluia'. An interesting case is that of 'Stans a longe' (Hughes, *Anglo-French Sequelae*, no. 51; text in Raby, *Oxford Book*, no. 85 and *AH*, liii, no. 93), which is related in both text and melodic opening to the antiphon of that title (*AS*, pl. 337; *AM*, p. 601). But even these are settings of the word 'Alleluia' in their (presumably original) 'textless' form.

common stock of melodies which suffered local corruptions before the words were added.

The following sequence illustrates a melody adapted to texts of both kinds. It is based on the Alleluia quoted above, Example 19. The original version (Hughes, no. 41) is entitled 'Ostende major', after the Alleluia verse, and to distinguish it from a shorter *sequela* based on the same Alleluia. We give extracts from this sequence (a) in its wordless form, (b) as set to the Anglo-French text 'Salus aeterna', and (c) as set to the Notkerian 'Clare sanctorum':

**Example 26**                    Oxford, Bod. Lib., Bodl. 775, f. 127.

Ibid., f. 167v.

- pti - o ve - re no - stra,     Con-do-lens huma-na per-i - re sae-cla per tem-ptantis  nu-mi-na, *etc.*

Ibid., f. 130.

(c) [Solo]

Cla - re san -cto-rum se - na -tus a - po-sto- lo - rum, prin - ceps or - bis ter - ra - rum

[Chorus]

re - ctor-que reg- no - rum,   Ec - cle - si - a - rum mo - res    et vi- tam mo-de-ra-re,

Quae* per doc - tri - nam tu - am    fi - de - les  sunt   u - bi - que.

An - ti - o - chus et Re-mus† con - ce - dunt ti - bi,  Pe - tre, reg - ni so - li - um; *etc.*

\* MS *qui*
† MS *Romus*

*Translation* (b) Alleluia. Eternal salvation, unfailing life of the world, light everlasting, and truly our redemption, grieving that the human race perishes through the tempter's might *etc.*
(c) Illustrious council of the holy apostles, Lord of the world and Ruler of kingdoms, govern the ways and life of the churches, which through thy doctrine are everywhere faithful. Antiochus and Remus concede to thee, O Peter, the throne of the [heavenly] kingdom; *etc.*

The ultimate home of this body of melody is indeed a much more interesting question than that of the sequence as a literary form.

The general principle of melodic enrichment of a standard repertory by repetition, variation and extension is found in other responsorial forms, generally though not always in connection with repetitions of the respond-section. There is evidence that it occurred in Gallican and Mozarabic chant; most interesting of all are the varied repeats of the Alleluia in Ambrosian chant (see *NOHM*, ii, pp. 131–6). This principle is one source of troping; and it was in the sequence, a highly specialized species of trope, that it reached early maturity.

# Bibliography

## Musical sources

For Jewish chant see Idelsohn, *Thesaurus*; Byzantine chant can be studied in facsimile and transcription in *MMB*. The Old-Roman Gradual is printed in *MMMA*, ii; for Ambrosian chant see *PM*, I, v–vi (facsimile and transcription) and the modern editions *AMM* and *LVM*. The Visigothic Antiphonary is given in facsimile in *MHS*, vi. Gregorian chant is available in facsimile in numerous volumes of *PM*, supplemented by *AS* and *GS* for the Sarum rite; the standard modern editions include *LU*, *GR*, *AR*, *AM* (for the monastic rite) and other publications of Solesmes. A selection of Offertories with their verses is in Ott, *Offertoriale*; for Alleluias see *MMMA*, vii; for hymns *MMMA*, i; for sequences Hughes, *Anglo-French sequelae*. A recent comprehensive selection of Latin chant is given in *Anthology of Music* ( = *Das Musikwerk*), xviii (Oxford and Cologne, 1960).

## Literary sources

The standard editions of the Greek theorists are those of Meibom, Jan, Macran (Aristoxenus), and Düring (Ptolemy). Church Fathers in *PG*, *PL*, *CSEL*; English translations in the editions of Roberts and Wace. St Augustine, *De musica* in *PL*, xxxiv; German translation by C. J. Perl (Strassburg, 1940); with French translation by G. Finaert and J.-J. Thonnard (Bruges, 1947); English summary by W. Jackson Knight (Orthological Institute). Boethius, *De Inst. Musica* in *PL*, lxiii and ed. Friedlein; German translation by Oskar Paul (Leipzig, 1872). Cassiodorus, *Institutiones* in *PL*, lxx and ed. Mynors; bk. ii, 5, 'De musica' in Gerbert, *Scriptores*, i, pp. 15–19. Isidore of Seville: *Etymologiae* in *PL*, lxxxii and ed. Lindsay (extracts in Gerbert, op. cit., i, pp. 19–25); *De ecclesiasticis officiis* in *PL*, lxxxiii. Benedict, *Regula*, Ed. McCann (with English translation). Bede, *Historia Ecclesiastica*, ed. Colgrave and Mynors (with English translation); of many separate translations note especially that by L. Sherley-Price, rev. R. E. Latham (Penguin Classics, 1968). Amalar of Metz, *De ecclesiasticis officiis* and *De ordine antiphonarii* in *PL*, cv and ed. Hanssens.

Liturgical texts: Brightman, *Liturgies*; Leonian Sacramentary, ed. Feltoe; Gregorian and Gelasian Sacramentaries, ed. Wilson. Spanish texts in *MHS*; six early Graduals without music, ed. Hesbert. Hymns and sequences especially in *AH*; also in many collections of Latin verse including that of Raby. Tropes in *Corpus Troporum* (Stockholm, 1975–).

Musical theory, eighth to tenth centuries: Gerbert, *Scriptores*, i, gave texts of Aurelianus (*Musica Disciplina*), Remigius of Auxerre, Hucbald (*De Musica*), the so-called *Alia Musica* of composite authorship, the so-called *Musica Enchiriadis* and *Scholia Enchiriadis* by Otgerus, the anonymous *Commemoratio brevis* (the last four of which were printed under Hucbald's name), Regino of Prüm (*De Harmonica Institutione*) and the *Dialogus* and other works attributed to Odo of Cluny but in reality anonymous. More recent editions include one of *Alia Musica* by J. Chailley (Paris, 1965), of Aurelianus by L. Gushee (*CSM*, xxi); one of the *Musica Enchiriadis* by H. Schmid is promised. A translation of Aurelianus has been published by J. Ponte (Colorado College of Music Press, 1968). Of the tonaries, Coussemaker, *Scriptores*, i, published those of Regino of Prüm and one attributed to Odo of Cluny but in fact Franciscan (note also that the *Proemium tonarii* printed by Gerbert, i. 248, is not a preface to the tonary printed by Coussemaker, but to an Italian tonary of the eleventh century); for recent work on tonaries see below. For a survey of older literature and editions, see Reese, *Music in the Middle Ages*, pp. 125–7; for an excellent account of recent work, see A. Gallo in *AcM*, xliv (1972), pp. 78–85.

*Studies*

On the liturgy: A. Baumstark, *Liturgie comparée* and *Nocturna Laus*; Denis and Boulet, *Eucharistie*; Duchesne, *Origines*; Hanssens, *Nature et Genèse*; Jungmann, *Missarum Sollemnia*; Van Dijk, *Origins*.

Jewish and Eastern chant: Idelsohn, *Jewish Music*; Werner, *The Sacred Bridge*; Wellesz, *Eastern Elements*, *Byzantine Music* and in *NOHM*, ii.

Latin chant, general: Anglès in *NOHM*, ii; Apel, *Gregorian Chant*; Corbin, *L'Église*; Ferretti, *Esthétique*; Gastoué, *Origines*; Gevaert, *La Mélopée antique*; Reese, *Music in the Middle Ages*; Stäblein and others in *MGG*; Wagner, *Einführung*.

Palaeography and interpretation: E. Cardine, 'Sémiologie grégorienne' in *EG*, xi (1970), pp. 1–158, and 'Le Chant grégorien est-il mesuré?' ibid., vi (1963), pp. 7–38; Fleischer, *Neumenstudien*; Suñol, *Introduction*; Vollaerts, *Rhythmic Proportions* (but see Cardine in *EG*, vi); Wagner, *Einführung*, ii. Note also plates and commentaries in Bannister, *Monumenti*; *EBM*, iii; Parrish, *Notation*; Staerk, *Les Manuscrits latins*; Thibaut, *Monuments*.

Chant repertories: A. Gastoué, 'Le Chant gallican' in *Revue de Chant grégorien*, xli–xliii; Thibaut, *L'Ancienne liturgie gallicane*; studies of the Mozarabic rite in *MHS*; Ambrosian chant in Huglo, *Fonti e paleografia*; R. Jesson, 'Ambrosian Chant' in Apel, *Gregorian Chant*, pp. 465–83; R. J. Snow, 'The Old-Roman Chant' ibid., pp. 484–505; M. Huglo, 'Le Chant

"Vieux-Romain" ' in *Sacris Erudiri*, vi (1954), pp. 96–124; S. J. P. Van Dijk, 'The Old-Roman Rite' in *Studia Patristica* (Berlin, 1962), pp. 185–205; J.-M. Canivez, 'Le Rite Cistercien' in *Ephemerides Liturgicae*, lxiii (1949), pp. 276–311.

Tonaries, etc.: on the tonary of St Riquier see Huglo in *Revue grégorienne*, xxxi (1952), pp. 176–86, 224–33; the Carolingian tonary of Metz was described by W. Lipphardt in the *Kongressbericht Köln 1958* (Kassell, 1959), pp. 179–81 and later published by him as *Der karolingische Tonar von Metz*. See also Huglo in *AnnM*, iv (1956), pp. 7–18 and in *AcM*, xl (1968), pp. 22–8 and his recent comprehensive work, *Les Tonaires*. The same author has published a study of Byzantine and Western tonal systems in *Studies in Eastern Chant*, iii (Oxford, 1972). See also Gallo, op. cit.

Special aspects: P. Bohn, 'Das Liturgische Recitativ und dessen Bezeichnung in den Liturgischen Büchern des Mittelalters' in *MMg*, xix (1887), pp. 29–36, 45–52, 61–8, 78–80; P. Dronke, 'The Beginnings of the Sequence' in *Beiträge zur Geschichte des Deutschen Sprache und Literatur*, lxxxvii (1965), pp. 43–73; J. Froger, *Les Chants de la Messe*; N. de Goede, 'Origin and Development of the Sequence' in *MMN*, vi, pp. ix–lxiv; J. Handschin, 'Trope, Sequence and Conductus' in *NOHM*, ii, pp. 128–74; H. Husmann, 'Alleluia, Vers und Sequenz' in *AnnM*, iv (1956), pp. 19–53, 'Sequenz und Prosa' in *AnnM*, ii (1954), pp. 61–91, and 'Die St Galler Sequenztradition bei Notker und Ekkehard' in *AcM*, xxvi (1954), pp. 6–18; R. Weakland, 'The Beginnings of Troping' in *MQ*, xliv (1958), pp. 477–88; Crocker in *MQ*, lii (1966), pp. 183–203; Evans, *The Early Trope Repertory*. The standard work on Notker is W. Von den Steinen, *Notker Der Dichter* (Bern, 1948). On versification see Norbert, *Introduction*.

# 2 Later Latin chant and derivative forms

As the requirements of the Roman liturgy expanded through the provision of new feasts with their proper texts it became necessary to supply them with music. The simplest way of doing this was to adapt existing melodies to the purpose. The earliest example of this procedure in the context of the Mass is to be found in the Proper of the Mass for Trinity Sunday. Trinity Sunday is simply the first Sunday after Pentecost, which like the other three Sundays following an Ember Week originally had no Mass of its own. In this case the gap was filled up by the votive Mass of the Holy Trinity; but in some places an alternative procedure, whereby the Masses of the succeeding Sundays were moved back one week *en bloc*, had already been adopted. This resulted in the confusing situation found in the modern Roman Gradual, in which the now superfluous Mass for the first Sunday after Pentecost is retained for use on the first vacant feria (*GR*, p. 311). The text of the Mass of the Holy Trinity is first met with around 850; but the earliest musical source, in which the Mass now heads the series of Sundays after Pentecost, is the tenth-century Gradual, St Gall 339. The sources from which the musical adaptations were made have been summarized by Apel (*Gregorian Chant*, p. 68).

Apart from such adaptations, the term 'Gregorian' has even less relevance to the liturgical melodies of the tenth to the thirteenth centuries than to those of the preceding era. Under this heading, nevertheless, we consider items belonging to categories traditionally so regarded in four divisions: simple recitation formulae, Proper of the Mass and Office, Ordinary of the Mass, and hymns.

1. It has already been explained that the tones for lessons and prayers survive in readable form only in later medieval sources, and that only in certain cases can they be assumed to be of early medieval date. The later Middle Ages saw the substitution of $c'$ or $f$ for $a$ as reciting note, and the growth of special tones for lamentations, passions and genealogies. It is from such formulae that most of the readings of the modern liturgical books are derived, though the genealogies (Matt. 1: 1–17 and Luke 3: 23–38) have disappeared (for their music see *AS*, pls. 51, 88 and Wagner, *Einführung*, iii, pp, 253–7). The psalm-tones underwent a simplification as compared with the methods of the *Commemoratio brevis*, and the tenors of the eight tones became standardized as $a, f, c', a, c', a, d'$ and $c'$ respectively. The *tonus peregrinus* melody was retained, but not the other special tones, although the more elaborate formulae for the Gospel canticles and for the Introit verses were kept. Again, modern books reflect later medieval custom (but cf. *AM*, pp. 1212, 1219).

2. The Proper of the Mass did not see a large amount of new composition, since additions to the liturgy were catered for largely by borrowing existing texts and by adaptation of old melodies to new texts. A considerable exception to this exists, however, in the case of the Alleluias, many of which betray stylistic features which can hardly have been current before the tenth century: extended range, repetitive melismatic structures, long descending scale-passages, etc. Even more than the Offertory verses of the later ninth century (see p. 54), these melodies herald the freedom of the later Middle Ages. As an example we give the Alleluia 'Multifariae olim Deus', later assigned to the feast of the Circumcision but first found in the tenth century in an appendix to the Gradual with the vague heading 'De Nativitate Domini'. It is transcribed here from Einsiedeln, Stiftsbibl., MS 121 (facsimile in *PM*, I, iv). With its range of an eleventh and repetitive organization it represents a distinct advance on the older type shown in Example 19 (the transcription is to a certain extent conjectural: for the more usual later version see *LU*, p. 441 or *GR*, p. 49):

**Example 27**

Einsiedeln, Stiftsbibl., 121, p. 358.

[In later versions the melisma, $ al Fine, is added; the *Alleluia* would then be sung again, but without the chorus repeat of the initial solo phrase. For the Sequence based on this *Alleluia*, see the upper part of Example 47.]

*Translation* Alleluia. V. God, who at sundry times spake by the prophets, hath in these last days spoken unto us by his Son.

The Office provides many more examples of new composition. As examples of the new melodic spirit we may cite the four antiphons of the Blessed Virgin Mary (*LU*, pp. 273–6), or the antiphon 'O Christi pietas' for the Office of St Nicholas, later adapted to 'O quam suavis' for Corpus Christi (*LU*, p. 917) and Sanctus VIII:

**Example 28**

AS, pl. 361.

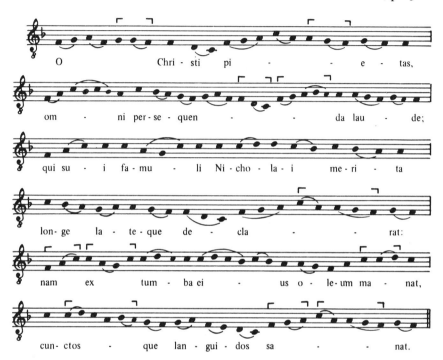

*Translation* O compassion, worthy of all praise, of Christ, who declares the merits of his servant, Nicholas, far and wide; for oil flows from his sepulchre and heals all those who are weak.

New or adapted music was also required for the many 'rhythmical' ('governed by stress') and rhymed Offices which were provided for new or reformed feasts; e.g. those by Pierre de Corbeil, first archbishop of Sens (1200–22), for the Circumcision, and by Julian of Spires for the feast of St Francis of Assisi (composed probably 1231–2). Their music, however, does not partake of the rhythmic character of the texts, being commonly in the style of ordinary neumatic chant (see above, p. 13) and not infrequently resembling or even adapted from actual plainsong. None of these rhymed

Offices is retained in the modern service-books, but there are 'unofficial' modern editions of some of them (see Bibliography).

3. The additions to the Ordinary are best considered in the order in which they occur in the Mass. An enormous number has survived (e.g. over 200 for the Kyrie, about 300 each for the Agnus and Credo), only a tiny fraction of which are given in the modern books. The form of the Kyrie quoted in the previous chapter (Example 23) was AAA AAA AAB. Other forms found in the Vatican edition (i.e. *LU*, pp. 16–94; *GR*, pp. 4*–93*) are AAA BBB AAA$_1$; AAA BBB CCC$_{(1)}$ and ABA CDC EFE$_1$ (a numeral after a letter indicates a lengthened version of a phrase). This crude method of analysis, however, ignores numerous subtle cross-references within the sections, and instances of musical rhyme where the beginning of the phrase is different. A variant of the last of these forms equates the second 'Christe' with the second 'Kyrie' (ABA CBC DED$_1$), or nearly so, as in the following 'Kyrie Rex summe' from English sources:

**Example 29**

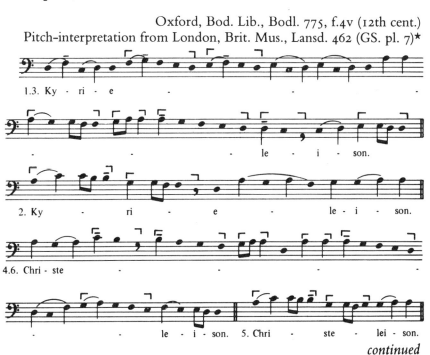

Oxford, Bod. Lib., Bodl. 775, f.4v (12th cent.)
Pitch-interpretation from London, Brit. Mus., Lansd. 462 (GS. pl. 7)*

*continued*

73

7.9. Ky - ri - e - lei - son. 8. Ky - ri - e - le-i - son.

*Translation* Lord have mercy. Christ have mercy. Lord have mercy.

Later melodies of the 'Gloria in excelsis' largely abandon the psalmodic structure of Example 24, though various forms of repeat structure are usually retained. An exception is the unusually free melody for Gloria I in the 'cantus ad libitum' section of the Vatican edition. The later chants for the Credo are very poorly represented in the Vatican edition, but its melodies for the Sanctus and Agnus may be studied with profit (the process of adaptation as applied to the Ordinary of the Mass has been mentioned above in connection with the Sanctus, p. 72).

The grouping together of the items of the Ordinary is a product of the later Middle Ages. Kyrie-Gloria and Sanctus-Agnus pairs are found in twelfth-century manuscripts, and groupings of all four items date from the thirteenth century: the 'Ite, missa est' or 'Benedicamus Domino' was added in the fourteenth. Originally such groupings were of musically dissimilar material, except that the Ite or Benedicamus might be related to the Kyrie. Something of an exception exists in the case of Mass VIII, known as 'de Angelis', however, inasmuch as to the related Kyrie and Ite is added a musically related Gloria and Credo (Credo III), though the latter is assigned only to the seventeenth century. The Credo has usually retained its isolated position even in modern publications.

4. It has already been explained (p. 61) that there are no sources giving incontrovertibly early melodies for the hymns. The standard edition of the melodies is that of *MMMA*, i, though it is by no means complete. The later Middle Ages saw numerous additions to the corpus as well as variants which brought the melodies more into conformity with the artistic canons of the period. This can be well illustrated from the thirteenth- and fourteenth-century English

versions of the hymns collected in *Plainsong Hymn Melodies and Sequences* and utilized in modern hymnals such as the *English Hymnal* (2nd ed., 1933). One cannot help feeling that in its Sarum version such a marvel of simplicity and economy of means as 'O lux beata Trinitas' has found its perfect form (cf. the version in *AM*, p. 533):

**Example 30**

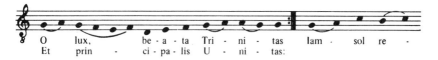

(3 stanzas)

*Translation* O light, blessed Trinity and primal Unity: now that the fiery sun goes down, pour thy light into our hearts.

Few of the melodies are as tautly constructed as this, but the best of them show the same well-balanced neumatic style which neither destroys nor exaggerates the textual rhythm.

*Tropes*

The general character and remoter origin of the trope have already been discussed (p. 62), and the early sequence singled out for special discussion. It is more convenient in this chapter to consider trope and sequence in their logical order, according to which the sequence is a specific kind of trope.

Both forms seem to have originated in the practice of adding melismas to established chants. There is, however, an essential difference between melismas added internally and those added at the end of a chant. The latter kind is for all practical purposes confined to the sequence, for it is only on the word 'Alleluia', which can tolerate a long melisma on the final syllable, that a truly open-ended development can occur. Even added melismas which occur towards the end of a respond are internal, in that their conclusion is identical

75

with the original cadence, though the later development of this form produced something which is akin to the latest stage of the sequence. An example of this is in the respond 'In medio ecclesiae', with its *triplex neuma* referred to by Amalar of Metz. Here the melisma on the last word ('intellectus') is expanded on the two repetitions, but the last nineteen notes are identical each time (*NOHM*, ii, pp. 143–4).

The melismas of Alleluias and responds are the main evidence for the theory that tropes (including the sequence) were originally purely a musical addition. As soon as verbal additions come into consideration, three distinct situations must be recognized: new words to old ('Gregorian') melismas; new words to non-Gregorian but nevertheless pre-existent music; and new words to completely new music. It is not always easy to decide to which of these categories a particular trope belongs; nor is it possible to be dogmatic about their respective chronological priority. Finally, many tropes exhibit a combination of either the first and second or the first and third methods.

1. The first method applies to forms which are already melismatic in character, including the Kyrie from the Ordinary and the Alleluia and Offertory from the Proper of the Mass. In the case of the Kyries, however, the priority of the music cannot be proved in every case. Some manuscripts show the troped and untroped texts in alternation (Apel, op. cit., pp. 431–2). The words 'Kyrie eleison' (or 'Christe eleison') in the troped form may be replaced completely, or 'eleison' only retained; or they may be separated by the troped text. In the case of the responsorial chants the trope may concern either the respond or the verse. An Alleluia trope of this kind is of course quite distinct from a sequence, since it does not involve new melodic material (but see below, p. 77). Normally the new text takes one or more words of the original as a starting-point.

2. The second category contains, apart from a large number of sequences, those responds in which melismas had occurred, which were demonstrably not part of the original version, and which are found elsewhere with syllabic texts: e.g. the respond 'In medio ecclesiae' already referred to (*NOHM*, ii, p. 142).

3. A number of responds take an existing melisma as a starting-point for syllabic setting, but extend it before closing with the original conclusion, thus combining our first and third methods (cf. the sequence below, p. 78). Apel (op. cit., pp. 436–7) has analysed a respond treated in this way, 'Concede nobis', with its prose 'Perpetua mereamur gaudia'. (The Latin word *prosa*, diminutive *prosula*, refers specifically to the text of any trope, including the sequence, even if it is in verse.) The musical form of this prose is *A BB* CC . . . FF *G*, like that of a regular sequence. The italicized letters correspond to the original respond material.

The usual types of chant to which new musical material may be added are of course the less melismatic ones, e.g. the Gloria, Sanctus, Agnus, Introit. Handschin has pointed out an important distinction between the types, represented by the first three and the latter respectively, since the original Ordinary chants correspond much more closely to the style of the tropes themselves than do those of the Proper (*NOHM*, ii, p. 165). Wagner (*Einführung*, iii, p. 511), followed by Apel (op. cit., p. 439) quotes an interesting trope to the Christmas Introit 'Puer natus est', which remains obstinately centred on *a* while the Introit itself, being in the seventh mode, is on *g*. Many Introit tropes, such as the trope 'Hodie cantandus est nobis puer' to the same Introit, ascribed to Tuotilo (d. 913; Wagner, iii, pp. 511–12) are merely introductions. This particular one is in dialogue form—which lands us right on the doorstep of liturgical drama (see below, p. 80).

*Sequence*

If our subdivision of tropes with texts is applied to sequences, it will be seen that technically the first category (new words to old melismas) is not applicable. It is true that the 'original' music to the word 'Alleluia' is sometimes underlaid with a syllabic text; but to qualify even remotely as sequences such settings would have to be shown to be placed after the verse, whereas in the extant examples they come beforehand, usually either preceded or immediately followed by the untroped Alleluia melisma. On the other hand a very large number of sequences fall into the second, or first and second, category, of which latter Example 26 above is an example (p. 64; see also the upper line of Example 47 below, p. 117, in which only the briefest reference is made to the parent Alleluia, Example 27).

An example of transitional style is the well-known Easter sequence 'Victimae Paschali' retained at the Council of Trent (*LU*, p. 780; *GR*, pp. 242–3). The melody is apparently new, and coeval with the words, which are by Wipo (d. *c.* 1050). It follows perfectly the irregularity of stress and rhyme shown in the text. The full maturity of the later sequence is seen in the works of Adam of St Victor (ed. E. Misset and P. Aubry, Paris, 1900), who lived in the first half of the twelfth century. Here a regular trochaic metre is firmly established (though not to the exclusion of other metres), usually in the form 887 887 with a rhyme-scheme aab, ccb for each stanza or pair of versicles. In later stanzas the pattern might be extended to 8887 or 88887 with a corresponding rhyme-scheme aaa(a)b, ccc(c)b, or otherwise varied. In some cases such variants occur from the beginning; and indeed the metrical variety of his work as a whole should not be under-estimated. Each pair of versicles was normally sung to the same melody, the old single versicle at the beginning and end being now abandoned; but the principle was sometimes applied to pairs of stanzas instead. The music (which is not certainly known to be by Adam himself) is also more varied than is sometimes supposed; the style may be illustrated by a few verses from his sequence for the Circumcision, in which there is only one 'normal' stanza (not quoted here):

**Example 31**

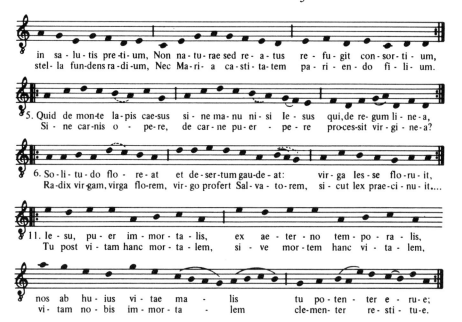

in sa - lu - tis pre -ti - um, Non na - tu - rae sed re - a - tus re - fu - git con - sor - ti - um,
stel - la fun-dens ra -di -um, Nec Ma - ri - a ca - sti - ta-tem pa - ri - en - do fi - li - um.

5. Quid de mon-te la - pis cae-sus si - ne ma-nu ni - si Ie - sus qui, de re- gum li - ne - a,
Si - ne car-nis o - pe- re, de car - ne pu- er - pe - re pro-ces-sit vir - gi - ne-a?

6. So - li - tu - do flo - re - at et de - ser-tum gau-de - at: vir - ga Ies - se flo -ru - it,
Ra -dix vir -gam, virga flo-rem, vir- go profert Sal- va - to-rem, si - cut lex prae-ci - nu- it....

11. Ie - su, pu - er im - mor - ta - lis, ex ae - ter - no tem- po - ra - lis,
Tu post vi - tam hanc mor - ta - lem, si - ve mor -tem hanc vi - ta - lem,

nos ab hu - ius vi - tae ma - lis tu po -ten - ter e - ru - e;
vi - tam no - bis im - mor - ta - lem cle-men- ter re - sti - tu-e.

*Translation* Glory is sung on high to the new-born King, through whom concord is restored to earth and heaven. Rightly is the birthday of Christ worshipped, by whose birth is born the grace of the new law. The mediator, given to us as an earnest of salvation, shrinks from the partnership not of nature but of sin. The star does not lose its brightness in pouring forth its radiance; neither does Mary lose her chastity in bearing a Son. What is a stone cut from a mountain without human aid but Jesus who, coming from a line of kings, proceeded without the working of the flesh from the childbearing flesh of a virgin? Let solitude flourish and the desert rejoice: the stem of Jesse has flowered. The root produces the stem, the stem the flower, and a virgin has produced the Saviour, just as the law foretold...Jesus, immortal child, born into time out of eternity, powerfully deliver us from the evils of this life; after this mortal life or living death, mercifully restore to us immortal life.

The sequences retained in the modern service-books (except for 'Victimae Paschali') are similar to the most regular of Adam's sequences; indeed St Thomas Aquinas's 'Lauda Sion Salvatorem' for Corpus Christi (*LU*, p. 945; *GR*, p. 315) uses one of Adam's tunes (cf. Example 76).

*Conductus*

The conductus differs from the sequence and trope in that it is in no way linked to an existing melody. It may however from the textual point of view be a trope. It is in origin a solemn processional song, generally preceding a benediction or some other liturgical act. Its use in the procession preceding the reading of the Gospel links it to the sequence, and its frequent use of trochaic metre (in terms of stress-pattern, not quantity), provides another parallel. (Perhaps both the conductus and the sequence in its later form are derived from the so-called rhythms: sacred or secular verses with no liturgical function using the 87 trochaic metre. A collection of these with music occurs in the St Martial MS Paris, Bibl. not., lat. 1154.) Its text is always in equal stanzas, and unlike the processional hymn it is without a refrain. Musically there are two main kinds: melismatic and syllabic. A fine example of the former is Perotinus' 'Beata viscera Mariae virginis' (ed. Thurston, pp. 124–5; for Perotinus see below, pp. 137–9), though it has a refrain and its rhythm is iambic. Examples of the latter occur in the *Ludus Danielis* (see below). But the highest development of the conductus is as a polyphonic form (see pp. 122–7).

*Liturgical drama*

This term has sometimes been felt to be inappropriate; but in fact the works to be discussed under this heading are strictly tied to the liturgy and were performed by clerics at liturgical services. The origin of the form lies in the following processional antiphon for Easter Sunday:

| *Int[errogatio]*: | Quem quaeritis in sepulchro, Christicolae? |
| *R[esponsum]*: | Jesum Nazarenum crucifixum, o caelicolae. |
| | Non est hic, surrexit sicut praedixerat; ite, |
| | nuntiate quia surrexit de sepulchro.* |

* 'Whom do you seek in the sepulchre, O Christian ones?
Jesus of Nazareth who was crucified, O heavenly ones.
He is not here, he has risen as he foretold; go,
proclaim that he has risen from the sepulchre.'

This text is usually described as the introductory trope to the Introit 'Resurrexi'; but its appearance in St Gall, Stiftsbibl., MS 339 as a processional antiphon is strong evidence that this was its original function.

It was not until this little dialogue had been moved to Matins and somewhat extended, however, that it became a true drama with action, costumes, etc. Clearly a dramatic version of the Easter story, which begins 'very early in the morning', was more appropriate to the conclusion of the night Office than to the Mass of Easter Day, celebrated in broad daylight. Having moved to Matins, there the genre apparently stayed: not only at Easter and Christmas, when it is entirely appropriate there, but also on many other occasions when such plays were performed. Almost always the concluding rubric instructs that the Te Deum be performed, this being the final chant of Matins on all feasts.

The earliest 'dramatic' source of the Easter play is probably that found in one of the two early eleventh-century tropers from Winchester (Oxford, Bodleian Library, Bodl. 775), where however it is curiously placed between the tropes for Palm Sunday and Holy Saturday.* The original dialogue is enlarged here by familiar antiphons put into the mouths of the characters. Its liturgical position is clarified, and its brief stage-directions, amounting to no more than who is to sing which phrases, are supplemented by a passage from the tenth-century English Benedictine Customary known as *Regularis Concordia*. In the following transcription a summary of the latter is combined with a transcription of the neumes from the Bodleian manuscript, obtained partly by comparison with other, more readily decipherable sources (cf. *ML*, xxvii, pp. 5–7):

**See Example 32 overleaf**

The summit of artistic development in the sphere of the sepulchre play is probably to be found in the version of the 'Fleury play-book' (Orléans, Bibliothèque Municipale, MS 201), written in the thirteenth century in the famous monastery of St Benoît-sur-Loire at

---

* The companion troper (Cambridge, Corpus Christi College, MS 473) has only an abbreviated text without music.

## Example 32

Oxford, Bod. Lib., Bodl. 775, f. 17

*During the third responsory three brethren (representing the holy women), wearing capes and carrying censers, approach the sepulchre, where a fourth brother (the angel) has previously placed himself. The three appear to be looking for someone.*

Angel:
Quem quae - ri - tis in se - pul - chro, Chri-sti - co - lae?

Women:
Ie - sum Na - za - re-num cru-ci - fi - xum, o cae - li - co - la.

Angel:
Non est hic, sur - re - xit sic - ut prae - di - xe - rat:

i - te nun-ti - a - te qui-a sur - re - xit di - cen - tes:*

Women *(to the clergy)*:
Al - le - lui - a, re - sur - re - xit Do - mi - nus ho - di - e,

le - o for - tis, Chri-stus Fi - li - us De - i.

De - o gra - ti - as, di - ci - te ei a.

Angel:
Ve - ni - te et vi - de - te lo - cum u - bi po - si - tus

e - rat Do - mi - nus, al - le - lu - ia, al - le - lu - ia.

* *Regularis Concordia* has *a mortuis* for *dicentes*, which makes better dramatic sense.

## Later Latin chant and derivative forms

*They enter the sepulchre and see the cloth in which the Cross (representing Christ) was wrapped. This they display to the assembled clergy.*

Angel:

†Ci - to e - un - tes, di - ci - te di - sci - pu - lis qui - a sur - re - xit

Do - mi - nus. Al - le - lu - ia, al - le - lu - ia.

Women:

Sur - re - xit Do- mi - nus de se - pul - chro, qui pro no - bis

pe - pen - dit in li - gno. Al - le - lu - ia.

Then the Prior intones *Te Deum*.

† *Regularis Concordia* omits this antiphon.

*Translation* **Angel**: Whom seek ye in the sepulchre, followers of Christ? **Women**: Jesus of Nazareth who was crucified, O heavenly one. **Angel**: He is not here; he has arisen as he had foretold. Go and proclaim that he has arisen, saying\*: **Women** (*to the clergy*). Alleluia, the Lord has risen to-day, the strong lion, Christ the Son of God. Thanks to be God, say 'eia'. **Angel**: Come and see the place where the Lord was laid, alleluia, alleluia. Go quickly, tell the disciples that the Lord has risen. Alleluia, alleluia. **Women**: The Lord has risen from the sepulchre, who for our sakes hung on the wood [of the cross]. Alleluia.

\* or 'from the dead'.

Fleury (for eds. see Bibliography). Apart from Lenten sermons, it contains ten music-dramas in the order of the liturgical year. The seventh of these is a sepulchre play. Its core is a revised version of the 'Quem quaeritis', but it is enormously expanded. The familiar dialogue is preceded by a processional item for the three Marys. After it Mary Magdalen alone remains behind and meets Peter and John, who enter the tomb. When they leave, there follows her encounter with the supposed gardener. The other two Marys then reappear and there is general rejoicing; finally Christ himself enters in glory and the Te Deum is sung. The music is a combination of new melody to new words and old plainsong antiphons where these are appropriate, as well as the original antiphon.

The contents of the Fleury play-book reveal the extent to which drama had permeated the liturgy by the thirteenth century. The next item in the manuscript is a *Peregrinus* play, dealing with Christ's appearance to the two disciples on the road to Emmaus, which is the subject of the Gospel for Easter Monday. It also adds the incident of doubting Thomas (Low Sunday, the octave-day of Easter). Its concluding rubric directs the singing not of the Te Deum but of 'Salve festa dies', a processional hymn customarily sung at the beginning of Mass on a variety of feasts with a similar refrain but with different stanzas. Its use here suggests a performance before Mass on Easter Day or Low Sunday rather than on Easter Monday. The twelfth-century version of this drama edited by Smoldon ends with a direction to sing 'Christus resurgens', a processional antiphon also sung before the Easter and Low Sunday Masses, as well as after Vespers on Easter Day and during the week. A fourteenth-century version from Saintes ends with the Magnificat.

The fifth and sixth of the Fleury dramas are for the Christmas season. The original Christmas drama arose from a trope in dialogue form to the Introit of the third Mass on Christmas Day ('Puer natus est nobis'), similar to that of Easter. It too was transferred to Matins and became the *Officium Pastorum*. It characteristically begins with the angels' 'Nolite timere' (Luke 2: 10–12) and 'Gloria in excelsis'; in the dialogue the questioners are two midwives. The Fleury version is called *Ordo ad representandum Herodem* and is enormously extended. The adoration of the shepherds is followed by the arrival of the *magi* at Jerusalem, their encounter with Herod, their journey to Bethlehem (where they meet the shepherds), their adoration and offering of gifts, their dream and their departure 'per aliam viam'. The next item in the manuscript is an [*Ordo a*]d *interfectionem puerorum*, or Massacre of the Innocents, including the flight into Egypt and ultimately the return of the Holy Family. This play possesses a convincing emotional climax in Rachel's long lament for her children, interrupted periodically by two *consolatrices*. Her outburst after their first intervention deserves quotation:

**Example 33**

*Translation* Ah! how shall I rejoice, while I see these dead limbs?...O grief! O changed joy of fathers and mothers.

The first four plays in the manuscript deal with legends of St Nicholas, whose feast falls on 6 December. The ninth is *Ad representandum conversionem beati Pauli apostoli*, the celebration of which is on 25 January; but the play may have been intended for the commemoration of St Paul on 30 June. The last play relates the raising of Lazarus, which is the subject for the Gospel on the Friday in the fourth week of Lent. But a play would have been considered an unsuitable adornment for this period of the year, and in any case it could not then have ended with the Te Deum as the manuscript directs. The last two plays, therefore, do not necessarily violate the principle of chronological order mentioned earlier.

Only a few plays dealing with the Passion story have survived, and the only two complete texts that are known are from the manuscript collection known as *Carmina Burana* (see Chapter 3, pp. 94–5), the music of which cannot be transcribed. More common are the various *planctus,* or laments, sung by one or more characters at the foot of the Cross. One of these, from Cividale, has been edited by Smoldon. Mary the mother of the Lord is joined here by the other two Marys and by John; the source states that the 'play' is to be performed on Good Friday but neither states nor implies its liturgical context. Smoldon has suggested the ceremony of *Improperia* as a possibility; and this is supported by the position of a similar lament in the fourteenth-century processionals from Padua edited by Vecchi, which also include dramatic pieces for Christmas, the Purification, the Annunciation, Easter, Ascension and Epiphany. These are all closely linked to the liturgical ceremonies attached to the Mass of the day, where their true significance is much more readily appreciated than in the context of Matins.

The last of the dramas we have to consider, the Play of Daniel (*Danielis Ludus*) is of a rather different kind, though its source still suggests a liturgical context. Only a few such dramas on Old Testament subjects have survived, and this Play of Daniel is the only one with decipherable musical notation. A somewhat similar play by Hilarius, a travelling scholar of the twelfth century, survives without music. The manuscript containing our 'Daniel' (Brit. Mus. Egerton 2615) was written for Beauvais Cathedral between 1227 and 1234. There is some reason to suppose, however, that the play itself was originally written at about the same time as the Hilarius drama, that is around 1140. The manuscript clearly indicates a performance in the context of Matins of the Circumcision (1 January), one of the days on which the subdeacons were accustomed to rule the services, especially in the secular cathedrals of northern France. In the course of time their rule had led to various excesses, and a movement of reform, represented by Pierre de Corbeil's new Office for the Circumcision at Sens (see above, p. 72), separates the date of composition of 'Daniel' from the date of its source. It may therefore have undergone various modifications during this period. In spite of this the work as we have it is unique among surviving dramas of the period in its greater length, the originality and variety of the music and the strength of the characterization. The syllabic choral conductus is widely employed to accompany the entrances and exits of characters. The text implies the use, at times, of both men's and boys' voices ('turba virilis et puerilis') and of instruments ('Simul omnes gratulemus, resonent et tympana; citharistae tangant chordas, musicorum organa resonent ad eius praeconia').* Although in general one must be wary of transferring poetical imagery into actual performing practice, there is considerable justification for assuming instrumental participation in a feast so conspicuously marked in other respects by a truly astonishing freedom.

We have come a long way from the earliest sepulchre play, with its pre-existent music and immediate liturgical relevance. Medieval

---

* 'Let us all rejoice together, and let the drums resound;
  let the harpists strike the strings, let the musicians' instruments
    resound in his praise.'

drama, however, was destined not to develop further in this direction; instead, it moved outside the church and became a vernacular, largely spoken form.

## Methods of performance

This is a convenient point to consider various problems of performance in early medieval music. Once the actual pitches can be deciphered (either directly or by comparison with other sources) the main problem is rhythmic. This problem is a recurrent one in all music up to about 1225, though the points at issue change from one period to another. It has already been explained (pp. 23, 45) that the few references to longs and shorts in ninth- and tenth-century theorists do not permit a rigorous application of the principle to early Latin chant as a whole; nor does its notation give clear indications of precisely measured rhythm. It is generally agreed, however, that from the eleventh to the thirteenth centuries the more complex rhythms of earlier centuries gave way to a slower-moving *cantus planus*. From the middle of the thirteenth century once again, however, we find an attempt to quantify the rhythmic values of Latin chant, beginning with the rules of Hieronymus de Moravia (summarized by Reese, *Music in the Middle Ages*, pp. 145–6). In the later Middle Ages the diamond-shaped *punctum* was used, in syllabic chants, to indicate short syllables; and this, together with the retention of the liquescent *virga* in its augmentative significance, led to the use, in England at least, of plainsong symbols as an alternative notation for simple polyphony in the late fifteenth and early sixteenth centuries.

Meanwhile a totally different approach to rhythm had arisen in connection with twelfth- and thirteenth-century polyphony. For the purposes of ensemble all rhythm was in ternary metre, and regulated according to one of six rhythmic modes. This system will be described more fully later (pp. 131–7); but it concerns us here because it has been applied by some modern scholars to monophonic music of the same period. According to their theory the mode of a piece can be determined by the versification of its text: trochaic metre will yield mode 1 ( $\downarrow$ $\downarrow$ ), iambic metre will yield mode 2 ( $\downarrow$ $\downarrow$ ), etc. But the stress-pattern of the second mode in polyphonic theory is the opposite of that of the iambic foot (or its equivalent) in verse (the same is true of mode 4 and the anapaestic foot); and in their alternation of long and short values such transcriptions, dubious enough when applied to such examples of classical versification as the iambic hymns of St Ambrose, lose all theoretical justification when applied to non-quantitative verse. A further objection to the modal theory is that it results in much slower speeds in monophonic song of the twelfth and early thirteenth century than are appropriate in contemporary polyphony: in other words they are made to conform to a stage in the development of rhythmic style later than that which had actually been reached. Some transcriptions even impose late thirteenth-century notions of rhythm on songs, such as those of Marcabru (fl. 1129–48) or Jaufré Rudel (fl. 1130–47), whose texts were written before any kind of modal theory can have existed. The only possible justification for this would be that such transcriptions at least conform to the style of music current when the manuscripts containing the music of such songs were compiled, i.e. in the late thirteenth or early fourteenth centuries; and this view is to a certain extent upheld by the rhythmic versions of the *Chansonnier Cangé* (see p. 105 and Example 41).

A certain amount of thirteenth-century monophony, not excluding settings of Latin texts, can be quite convincingly rendered in triple metre, though the choice of mode is better determined by purely musical considerations: for example whether melismas occur more frequently on the stressed or unstressed syllables, as well as by less definable factors. This would yield the following results for two well-known sequences:

**Example 34**

*Translation* (a) Come, Holy Spirit, and shed the ray of thy heavenly light. (b) Day of wrath, that day; the earth shall be reduced to ashes, as David and the Sybil have foretold.

But of course there is no need to keep to triple rhythm in monophony, and indeed it is often abandoned by recent editors. When a text offers clear evidence of quantitative scansion, for example in dactyls, it may be possible to give a literal equivalent, as in the following conductus from the Play of Daniel, where a binary rhythm seems preferable to the triple metre usually imposed on it:

**Example 35**

*Translation* The crowd of men and gathering of boys applauds the holder of the stars, the all-powerful.

But equally there may be instances where the 'official' scansion is better ignored; and indeed there is no reason why the mode should not be changed during the course of a piece, or indeed altered out of all recognition. And as has been said, scansion by stress provides no logical basis for choice of mode at all.

Having arrived at this point, we are compelled to ask what is the evidence that this music is to be put into any kind of regular rhythm whatsoever. Here the theorist Johannes de Grocheo comes to our help with his reference to music which is neither unmeasured nor measured but 'non praecise mensurata'. Of course it is clear that some monophonic pieces are indeed strongly metrical; and this is sometimes confirmed by their appearance in polyphonic settings. Others are not at all metrical in character: few people would want to impose a regular rhythm on Example 30, for instance. But a very great deal of monophony, both sacred and secular, seems to fall into Johannes de Grocheo's special category. Modern transcriptions, though not necessarily strictly modal, are usually shown in precise note-values, with the implication that a certain degree of *rubato* is permissible, depending on the character of the piece. In the next chapter, however, the music will be shown in non-committal rhythm as hitherto, but with suggestions for rhythmic interpretation above the staff. Some of the later sources are in fact in measured notation; and indeed they confirm the idea of the distinction between strongly measured and less strongly measured styles, as one may see by comparing, for example, certain lyrics by Adam de la Halle with some of the *Cantigas de Santa María* (see Example 42 below and *NOHM*, ii, pp. 261–6).

The other main problem in modern performance concerns instrumentation; again certain aspects of this cannot be fully entered into before the discussion of early polyphony, but some points may be made here. All the music discussed in this chapter would have been sung by males, of course; but boys' voices were available in secular (as opposed to strictly monastic) institutions and may have been used for female parts in plays performed in those circumstances. They are quite inappropriate to the early, monastic, sepulchre plays, or to those in the Fleury play-book, for instance. As for profane music, it all depends upon what social conditions one is trying to recreate; it would be absurd to suppose that women never sang in company, but it is not necessary to assume that a poem put into the mouth of a woman may not be sung by a man.

The most prominent of medieval instruments is the organ. Just when the classical instrument, the *hydraulis* in which the air pressure is regulated by water, died out is uncertain; but the instrument reintroduced to the West from the East in the eighth century was a bellows-organ, and subsequent references to the *hydraulis* are either learned reconstructions or inexact uses of the word to mean a bellows-organ. The latter is first found in churches in the tenth century, usually in a monastic milieu; it eventually attained enormous size although smaller instruments, called positives, continued in use. In the thirteenth and fourteenth centuries the portative organ, blown and played by the same person and therefore capable of monophonic music only, became extensively used.

Apart from the organ, the only other instruments widely admitted to church use were small bells or *cymbala* (Gk. *kumbalon* from *kumbē*, cup). These were suspended in a row above the performer and struck with a hammer; their use, like that of the organ, was regulated by liturgical custom. Apart from accompanying the voices in written or unwritten polyphony, they were also used, from the thirteenth century, in alternation with them.

Of the enormous variety of other medieval instruments only brief mention can here be made. It should be emphasized that any use of instruments with voices, or in combination with each other, implies some kind of primitive polyphony: heterophony (simultaneous varying of the melody), drone or the use of parallel intervals. It is impossible to imagine a medieval player slavishly following a given line, even if there was one to follow. (For the earliest written monophonic dances, see the next chapter, and for the earliest written polyphonic dances, Chapter 8.) We know that vocal polyphony was improvised in haphazard fashion in the twelfth to fourteenth centuries, and evidently instrumentalists could do the same. Some instruments, like the organ, could provide their own polyphony: the bagpipe with its drone, the hurdy-gurdy, and the psaltery.

The study of the instruments has to be carried out by matching the terminology of the literary sources with the evidence of the iconography (paintings, miniatures, sculpture, carvings, etc.). There are virtually no actual survivals. There is an uninterrupted trail of references to profane music with its instruments from classical times until the supplanting of Latin by the new vernaculars. Blanket terms like *cithara* and *lyra* could mean any plucked instrument, and *tibia* any blown instrument. Their classical prototypes vanished as did the *hydraulis*, and were replaced by harps, lutes and the psaltery (a square or triangular harp covered on one side and laid on the knee) as regards plucked instruments, and by recorders and shawms in the case of blown instruments. Celtic and Germanic cultures made their contributions. Bowed instruments, the ancestors of the viol, made their appearance. Latin words (*chrotta, fidicula,* etc.) were invented for or reapplied to the new phenomena, and in turn gave rise to new vernacular words.

Among genuine classical survivors the bagpipes occupy an important place. Indeed they are still to be heard in their primitive form in the remoter parts of Europe. The *organistrum, symphonia* or hurdy-gurdy, on the other hand, is a genuine medieval instrument, the strings of which are actuated by a wheel and stopped with keys; there is normally a drone. Percussion instruments existed in great variety: small cymbals (*crotali*) and many kinds of drum (*tympana*) were prominent. The appropriate use of all these instruments is possibly the most taxing problem of all for those who seek to recreate the actual sound of medieval music outside the immediate orbit of the church.

# *Bibliography*

*Musical sources*

Modern editions of chant in *LU, GR, AR, AM*; facsimiles in *AS, GS, PM, EBM,* iii; Loriquet, *Le Graduel.*

Sequences in Hughes, *Anglo-French Sequelae*; Misset and Aubry, *Les Proses d'Adam de Saint Victor*; *MMN,* vi (the Utrecht *Prosarium*); *MMS,* i–iv.

Tropes and later Latin chant in *MMMA,* i (hymns), iii (Introit-tropes) and vii (Alleluias); the St Martial repertoire in Evans, *The Early Trope Repertory.* English versions of hymns and sequences in *Plainsong Hymn-Melodies and Sequences.*

Rhymed and rhythmical offices: Villetard, *Office de Pierre de Corbeil* and *Office de Saint Savinien et de Saint Potentien*; Wagner, *Die Gesänge der Jakobusliturgie.*

Liturgical drama: Smoldon, *Officium Pastorum* (Paris, Bibliothèque Nationale, f. lat. 904), *Peregrinus* (Paris, Bibl. Nat. n.a. lat. 1064), *Planctus Mariae* (from Cividale), *The Play of Daniel* (London, Brit. Mus., Eg., 2615), *The Play of Herod* (Fleury play-book, nos. 5 and 6), *Sponsus,* and *Visitatio Sepulchri* (Fleury play-book, no. 7). The complete Fleury play-book is published in facsimile and in modal transcription in Tintori, *Sacre*

*Rappresentazioni*; the fifteenth-century dramas from Padua are in Vecchi, *Uffici Drammatici Padovani*; facsimile of *Carmina Burana*, ed. B. Bischoff, in *PMMM* ix. See also Smoldon in *ML* (1946) below.

## Literary sources

Note especially Johannes Affligemensis (John Cotton), *De Musica* (*CSM*, i; Gerbert, *Scriptores*, ii, pp. 230–65); Guido of Arezzo, *Micrologus* (*CSM*, iv; Gerbert, op. cit., ii, pp. 2–24); Hieronymus de Moravia (Coussemaker, *Scriptores*, i, pp. 1–94; also ed. S. M. Cserba); Johannes de Grocheo, *De Musica*, ed. J. Wolf in *SIMG*, i (1899–1900), pp. 69–130 (cf. H. Müller in *SIMG*, iv (1902–3), pp. 361–8), also ed. Rohloff. Texts of hymns and sequences esp. in *AH*. Tropes in *Corpus Troporum* (Stockholm, 1975–). *Regularis Concordia* ed. Symons.

## Studies

On later Latin chant: B. Stäblein, articles in *MGG*; Apel, *Gregorian Chant*; Wagner, *Einführung*.

Tropes and sequences: J. Handschin, 'Trope, Sequence and Conductus' in *NOHM*, ii, pp. 128–74; P. Evans, *The Early Trope Repertory*; P. Dronke (see Bibliography, Chapter 1), N. de Goede in *MMN*, vi (see Musical Sources above); Wellesz, *Eastern Elements*, esp. pt. iv; Husmann, (see Bibliography, Chapter 1).

Liturgical drama: W. L. Smoldon, 'Liturgical Drama' in *NOHM*, ii, pp. 175–219, and 'The Easter Sepulchre Music-Drama' in *ML*, xxvii (1946), pp. 1–7; K. Young, *The Drama of the Medieval Church* (2 vols., Oxford, 1933; reprinted 1951; Dolan, *Le drame liturgique*.

Instruments: E. A. Bowles, 'The Role of Musical Instruments in Medieval Sacred Drama' in *MQ*, xlv (1959), pp. 67–84, and 'Were Musical Instruments Used in the Liturgical Service during the Middle Ages?' in *GSJ*, x (1957), pp. 40–56; G. Hayes, 'Musical Instruments' in *NOHM*, iii, pp. 468–502, and bibliography pp. 528–9; H. Panum, *The Stringed Instruments of the Middle Ages*, rev. and trans. J. Pulver (London, [1941]); J. Perrot, *The Organ*; Munrow, *Instruments*.

# 3 Profane and vernacular monophonic song

*Latin song*

Latin secular song is no doubt the form in which we should expect to find the earliest remnants of a purely European art, untouched by oriental elements. Unfortunately very little of this music can be transcribed, as it survives mostly in unheighted neumes. It is a curious fact that even the famous collection known as *Carmina Burana*, which was compiled as late as *c.* 1230, is notated in this fashion. Such music can only be recovered, in most cases, either by comparison with versions having alternative, sacred, texts (*contrafacta*), or if they survive in polyphonic pieces. In the latter case the setting sometimes, though not always, indicates a specific rhythm.

An example of the former case exists in the 'O admirabile Veneris idolum', perhaps of the tenth century, which shares its tune with a religious song, 'O Roma nobilis' (*NOHM*, ii, p. 221; both texts in Raby, *Oxford Book of Medieval Latin Verse*, nos. 101, 103). Several songs in *Carmina Burana* can be identified in polyphonic settings in the Florence manuscript of Notre-Dame polyphony (see below, pp. 139–48); these include the very first song in the manuscript, 'Fas et nefas ambulant' (which however did not originally have that position). The polyphonic setting is on f. 225 of the Florence manuscript; and since it is in non-mensural notation one should not be dogmatic about the rhythm of its melody in monophonic form.

**See Example 36 opposite**

It can be seen from this that there is no essential difference in style between sacred and profane Latin song at this period; and indeed the whole repertory of twelfth- and thirteenth-century monophony is

**Example 36**

Munich, Staatsbibl., Clm 4660, f. 1.

Fas et ne - fas am - bu - lant Pas - su fe - re pa - ri; Pro - di - gus non red - i - mit Vi - ti - um a - va - ri; Vir - tus tem - pe - ran - ti - a Qua - dam sin - gu - la - ri De - bet me - di - um Ad u - trum - que vi - ti - um Cau - te con - tem - pla - ri

(5 stanzas)

*Note* this transcription is based on a consideration of the neumes of all five stanzas of the Munich MS. It necessarily differs in many respects from the Florence version of the melody.

*Translation* Right and wrong walk almost step by step; the spendthrift does not redeem the vice of the miser; virtue should aim carefully for the mean between each vice with a certain particular moderation.

drawn together by stylistic links which transcend the boundaries of language and function.

Although there is written evidence for the appearance of

Romance languages from as early as the ninth century, it is only with the close of the eleventh century that any of them was used as a vehicle for artistic song. The first of these was the language of Provence and the surrounding area of southern France.

### Troubadours

The music of the troubadours was, as far as the surviving music is concerned, an exclusively lyrical art. There are no examples of epic or dramatic music extant, although the epic as a literary form was known and may have been sung. What has come down to us is a fairly small number of manuscripts, some of which also include trouvère song. But this is not to say that it lacks variety. The style ranges from elaborate solo songs of elegiac character to boisterous choral dances.

In this repertory can be found in its purest and simplest form the essence of the whole of medieval lyricism. Arising in part from the courtly art of Guilhem IX of Aquitaine (1071–1127), whose poems are recorded without music except for one fragment, it permeated all classes of society. The standard subject of the verse was courtly love, but there are also religious and popular poems, and there were no specific limitations on subject matter. The melodies are generally assumed to be the work of the poets themselves; and in the absence of any indication to the contrary the conventional ascriptions are retained here, though there are examples (as in the case of the trouvères) of a single tune doing duty for more than one poem.

The characteristics of these songs include great formal variety within the context of a somewhat formalistic approach, and a melodic style which often approaches that of Latin chant, especially late Latin chant of the kind represented by the Marian antiphons (see above, p. 71).

A proper appreciation of medieval song-forms depends on a sound approach to classification. We must be prepared for the fact that medieval terminology often refers to the subject-matter or general character of the songs rather than to their form properly speaking. Modern terminology often creates confusion and suggests inappropriate derivations from liturgical genres. It would be well to begin by looking at the verse. Is there a refrain? If so, is it internal (recurrent within each stanza), or external, or both? Are there several stanzas, and if so are they uniform? The structure of a single stanza may now be analysed in terms of scansion and rhyme-scheme; are the actual rhymes repeated from stanza to stanza? Finally the melody itself may be analysed and its structure related to that of the poem.

Logically a refrain is recognizable as such only upon repetition, so that an external refrain can be discerned only when more than one stanza is available for inspection. It is true that in northern France a *chanson avec des refrains* was cultivated in which each stanza had a different 'refrain'; but these so-called refrains were merely snatches of popular tunes tacked on to the end of each stanza—they do not contradict our general statement. An external refrain may be discerned in Marcabru's famous 'Pax in nomine Domini', a crusader song apparently composed in 1137, where the sixth line of every nine-line stanza ends with the word 'lavador' (Gennrich, *Troubadours*, p. 12, and *Lo Gai Saber*, no. 4; *HAM*, i, no. 18a; *NOHM*, ii, p. 229). In the equally famous *alba* or dawn-song 'Reis glorios', by Guiraut de Bornelh (d. *c.* 1220) the last line of the stanza is 'Et ades sera l'alba' ('and soon will come the morning'; printed Gennrich, *Troubadours*, p. 14, and *Lo Gai Saber*, no. 24; Reese, *Music in the Middle Ages*, p. 215; *HAM*, i, no. 18c: the last stanza, ending with a different refrain, is spurious).

Each of the seven stanzas of 'Lanquan li jorn son lonc en may' by Jaufré Rudel (fl. 1130–47) has the word 'lonh' at the end of lines 2 and 4 (Gennrich, *Troubadours*, p. 12, and *Lo Gai Saber*, no. 5). This song also has a *tornada* (French *envoi*, Italian *commiato**) corresponding to the last three lines of a stanza and sung to that part of the melody. Its last few words repeat those of the last complete stanza, but the piece is not a ballade in the later French sense. A piece which actually bears the title *balada* is the anonymous 'A l'entrada del tens clar', where there is an internal refrain in the word 'Eya' at the end of lines 1, 2 and 3 of each stanza and an external refrain consisting of its last two lines (Gennrich, *Troubadours*, p. 22, and *Lo Gai Saber*, no. 49; *NOHM*, ii, p. 241). This is a lively spring song and the refrains are probably intended to be sung chorally.

The songs are normally provided with uniform stanzas, though the *tornada* is fairly common. Some, e.g. 'Per solatz d'autrui chant

* The Italian *ritornello* differs in always being provided with new music: see page 186.

soven' by Aimeric de Peguilhan (fl. 1195–1230) have two (Gennrich, *Troubadours*, p. 19). Rhyme-schemes are often complex and highly repetitive, and assonance is also employed. 'Quant Amors trobet partit', a *tenson* or debate by Peirol (fl. 1190–1220), uses the rhyme-scheme ababbccdd, and the actual rhymes are repeated in each stanza. There is no refrain, but there are two *tornadas* (Gennrich, *Troubadours*, p. 18, and *Lo Gai Saber*, no. 41). 'Lo ferm voler' by Arnaut Daniel (fl. 1180–1210), whom Dante placed higher than Guiraut de Bornelh and to whom he paid the compliment of writing eight lines in Provençal (see *Purg.*, xxvi, 115–148), is a *sestina* in which the final words of each line are retained in each stanza but in a different order (Gennrich, *Troubadours*, p. 16, and *Lo Gai Saber*, no. 32). Finally the poets show an astonishing variety in the length and number of the lines in their stanzas.

In settings of the single stanza the tunes vary from closely-knit structures to melodies involving virtually no repetition. To illustrate the former we may cite 'Be m'an perdut' by Bernart de Ventadorn (fl. 1145–95; Gennrich, *Troubadours*, p. 13, and *Lo Gai Saber*, no. 8), whose melodies have survived in greater number than those of any other troubadour:

**Example 37**

Paris, Bibl. Nat., f. fr. 22543, f. 57.

en s'a - mor me de - leih e·m so - jorn; Ni
de ren als no·s ran - cu - ra ni·s cla - ma.

*Translation* Truly all my friends in the region of Ventadorn have lost me, since my lady loves me not; and it is right that I should never return there, since now she is wild and cruel towards me, which is why she gives me a bitter and gloomy look; for in her love I take delight and dwell; nor has she any further cause for rancour or complaint.

As written out in this way it looks like a simple binary form, with two *pedes* and a *cauda* (AAB), to use Dante's terminology (*De vulgari eloquentia*, ii. 10. 3–4). But the second half of the *pes* is repeated intact at the end, giving ababcdb as a more accurate diagram, corresponding to the rhyme scheme ababaab. Finally there are two extensive quotations from the *pes* in the body of the *cauda* (x and y), and two smaller motives (w and z), the latter of which occurs seven times altogether in the stanza, with or without its final note, and contributes much to the character of the melody. The poem has six stanzas without a refrain, and a *tornada* repeating the last three lines.

Many examples of this form are less subtle and merely repeat the end of the *pes* at the end of the *cauda*. This device was still in use in the fifteenth-century French ballade. Still others have no repetition at all beyond that of the two *pedes*. In the case of melodies without *pedes* we have examples where only one line is repeated, or even where there is no repetition at all: a type described by Dante as *oda continua* (op. cit., ii. 10. 2). As an example of the latter we take a song by Folquet de Marselha, whose activity as a song-writer dates from 1179–93, but who later became bishop of Toulouse and founder of its university; he was a learned man whose poetic style is described by Gennrich as being 'rich in aphorisms, maxims, abstract comparisons and antitheses'. His melodic style covers a wide range and is a little obscure:

**Example 38**                                            *Lo Gai Saber*, no. 29.

En chan - tan m'a - ven a mem - brar So qu'eu cug
chan - tan o - bli - dar; E per so chant qu'o -
- bli - des la do - lor E·l mal d'a - mor; Et
on plus chan plus m'en so - ve, Que la bo -
- ca en al re non a - ve Mas en 'mer -
- ce!, Per qu'es ver - tatz e sem - bla be Qu'ins
el cor port, dom - na, vos - tra fais - so Que·m
chas - ti - a qu'ieu no vir ma ra - zo.

*Translation* In singing it befalls me to remember what I seek to forget in song; and this is why I sing, to forget the grief and pain of love; and the more I sing the more I remember it, for my mouth finds no other word save 'mercy!'. Wherefore it is truth, and well it appears, that in my heart, lady, I bear your image, which prevents me from changing my mind.

Here there are no repetitions beyond the merest casual resemblances. Even more than in the case of Example 37, the music seems to defy a metrical interpretation which does not destroy its charm. There are five stanzas and two *tornadas*, each of the latter corresponding to the last four lines of the stanza.

Many of the troubadours' songs are dance-like in character and imply a strong rhythm. An example of this is the well-known 'Kalenda maya' (Gennrich, *Troubadours*, p. 16), said to have been written by the poet Raïmbaut de Vaqueiras on an existing *estampida* or dance-tune. Here each twenty-line stanza has the musical form AA BB CC$_1$. A dance-like piece by Guiraut d'Espanha de Toloza, 'Ben volgra, s'esser poges' (Gennrich, *Troubadours*, p. 20), is a good deal more complicated. There is a four-line refrain (A) followed by three ten-line stanzas having the form BB$_1$A, B having 3 lines. There are then three *tornadas* of four lines each, which can only be sung to the music of A; finally a cue indicates repetition of the refrain. The whole thing can be thought of as being in one large stanza (*A* BB$_1$A BB$_1$A BB$_1$A AAA *A*) and, in its widest sense, a rondeau; it is written in mensural notation in the manuscript and may be laid out as follows:

**Example 39**                    Paris, Bibl. Nat., f. fr. 844, f. 186.

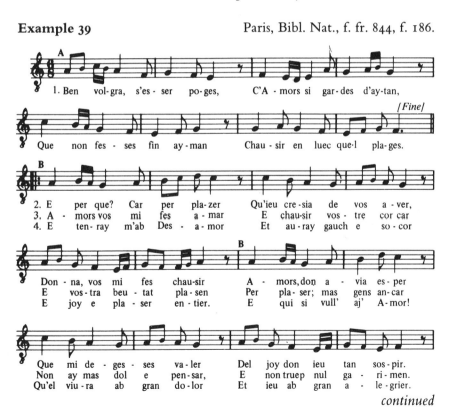

*continued*

| | | | | | | | | | | | | | |
|---|---|---|---|---|---|---|---|---|---|---|---|---|---|
| | Ar | m'a - ves | a | tal | punch mes, | | Que | tot | jorn | vauc | de - si - ran | | |
| | E | pos per | pla - | ser | ay pres | | Pe - | na, | do - lor | et | af - fan, | | |
| | E | si | d'ays - so | suy | re - pres, | | Sap - | cha ma | ra - | son | e - nan: | | |
| 5. | Mon | de - liech, | non | vos | vuell ges, | | Mas | mon des - | pla - | ser | de - man; | | |
| 6. | E | mal a·n, | pues | qu'es - ser | m'es, | | Qui | A - mors ser - | vi - | ra | tan | | |
| 7. | Dan - | sa, car | ieu | ay | a - pres | | Qu'el | Reys Kar - les | fay | gent chan, | | | |

| | | | | | | | | | | | |
|---|---|---|---|---|---|---|---|---|---|---|---|
| La | mort, don ay | do - | lor gran; | | Car | non faitz so | | c'A - mors fes. | | |
| A - | mors me - ti | a | mon dan, | | Qu'a - | re - bu - sa·m | a | pa - les. | | |
| C'A - | mors va·n con - | tra - | ri - an, | | Per | so ay·l con - | tra - | ri pres. | | |
| E | si as el | mi | co -man, | | Ieu | au - ray tot | cant | obs m'es. | | |
| Con | a fah, de | say | e - nan; | | Car | non fa·n so | que | dretz es. | | |
| Per | a - quo as | el | ti man; | | Car | de fin pres | es | a - pres. | | |

After the end of 4, repeat from 𝄋 only, three times, for 5, 6, 7; then *D.C. al fine*.

*Translation* I would, if it might be, that Love would refrain so far as not to make the true lover choose a love that wounded him. And why? Because for the pleasure which I thought to have of you, Lady, Love made me choose you, wherein I had hope that you could profit me in the joy for which I so often sigh. Now you have brought me to the point where always I desire death, whence I have much grief; for you do not what Love did. Love made me love you and choose your beloved heart and your pleasing beauty for pleasure's sake; but so far I have nought but pain and torment, and I find no cure; and so then instead of pleasure I have received pain, grief and suffering; I count Love as my loss since he openly rejects me. So I will side with Dislove and will have happiness and relief and joy and all pleasure. Let him who will have Love! For he will live with great grief and I with great gaiety. And if I am reproved for it let him know my mind henceforth: Love is contrary, and so I have become contrary too. My delight, I want no more of you, but I ask for my displeasure; and if I commend myself to it I shall have all I need. And woe to him, since it is to be so with me, who serves Love as much as he has done, henceforth; for he does not what is right. Dance, since I have learned that King Charles* makes a fine song, on that account I send you to him; for he is well versed in the ways of art.

* Charles of Anjou

Only one example is known, however, of a Provençal rondeau in the narrower sense of the word—that is in which the music of the refrain provides the entire material of the song (*NOHM*, ii, p. 245).

The songs of the troubadours were widely known outside Provence. In Spain, Catalonia and northern Italy they were imitated in the same tongue, though the music has not survived. In southern Italy, especially Sicily, a school of Italian poetry arose in which Provençal and northern French themes were imitated. But it was in northern France itself that the influence of the troubadours found its ripest fulfilment.


## Trouvères

The formative influences on trouvère style included not only that of the troubadours but also that of popular music. The jongleurs, whose counterparts existed under various denominations in other parts of Europe, were the poor relatives of the goliards or travelling scholars, lacking their clerical status and knowledge of Latin. They provided a rough-and-ready popular entertainment at the places they visited, and were the first professional musicians (outside the Church) of modern Europe. They were often instrumentalists as well as singers, actors and entertainers, and their repertoire included *chansons de geste* and, later, the songs of the trouvères themselves. Undoubtedly their status increased, until in Colin Muset (early thirteenth century) their number included a genuine poet and composer.

The *chanson de geste* was an epic poem (of which the earliest example is the famous *Chanson de Roland* of *c.* 1100, dealing with an episode in the reign of Charlemagne) written in verse paragraphs or *laisses* of unequal length. Each line was sung to the same melodic fragment except, apparently, the last line of each paragraph, which was sung to a different tune. This is the principle employed in *C'est d'Aucassin et de Nicolete*, called by its author a 'cantefable' in which however the verse alternates with sections of prose narrative. The music is extant (see *NOHM*, ii, pp. 223–4, for reference to sources and for a transcription of one of the verse sections). *Chansons de toile* were short narrative poems in uniform stanzas with a refrain, sung in a similar way.

The trouvères were originally noble amateurs, including at the summit of society such a figure as Thibaut IV, Count of Champagne and King of Navarre; but their art was soon cultivated by representatives of other classes, amongst them the burghers who formed *puis* or musical societies of which that at Arras was the most notable. As the social orbit of trouvère song widened its scope increased, until in variety of subject-matter and treatment it exceeded that of its model, as it did indeed in melodic charm and individuality, though hardly in sophistication.

One of the most important of the early trouvères was Blondel de Nesle, who was a contemporary of Bernart de Ventadorn. Like the latter he could manage subtle musical structures, and his melodic style is largely stepwise and reminiscent of Latin chant (cf. Example 37). The following song has the melodic structure $ababcc_1b_1$, and there are five stanzas with an *envoi* of three lines:

**Example 40**

Paris, Bibl. Nat., f. fr. 844, f. 141.

A l'en-trant d'es-té, que li tans com-men-ce Que
Sui sou-pris d'a-mours ou mes cuers ba-lan-ce. Diex

j'oi seur la flour les oi-siauz ten-tir, Ou
m'en doint a-voir joie a mon plai-sir,

au-tre-ment cuit mo-rir sanz fail-lan-ce, Car

je n'ai el mont au-tre sou-ste-nan-ce, Qu'a-

-mours e[s]t la rienz que je pluz de-sir.

*Translation* At the beginning of summer, when I first hear the song of the birds resounding on the spray, I am surprised by a love which overturns my heart. May God grant me joy at my pleasure, or else I believe I shall die without fail; I have no other sustenance in the world, for love is the thing which I most desire.

That first generation also included such figures as Conon de Béthune, Huon d'Oisi, Guiot de Provins, Gace Brulé and the Chastelain de Coucy (Gui II).

Thibaut IV, who died in 1253, was not a very distinguished melodist, except in a few isolated examples (see, e.g., *NOHM*, ii, p. 231); but he cultivated a variety of types, including the *chanson avec des refrains* and the *lai*, and appears as a character in several *jeux partis* or musical debates. The *lai* was originally a narrative poem indistinguishable from the *roman*, with its octosyllabic rhyming couplets; but later it acquired greater freedom of form and subject-matter and sometimes resembled the sequence in having a double-versicle structure (see above, p. 63). The following example by Thibaut IV has a sacred subject and has the formal peculiarity that almost every section takes as its point of departure a phrase from the preceding one. It is also characterized by genuine depth of feeling and has the advantage of being written (in one source) in a primitive form of mensural notation. It is too long to quote in full but the following extracts will give an idea of its style:

**Example 41**  Paris, Bibl. Nat., f. fr. 846, f. 23.
(Ibid., f. fr. 844, f. 66).

*continued*

de bon - tez, Vos - tre douz moz sa - vo - rez Ne soi-
- ent pas o - bli - ez; Proi - ez por nos. Ja - més ne se -
- rons res - cous, Se ne le su - mes par vous, De
voir le sai. Ci lais - se - rai: Dex nos doint
sanz de - lai A - voir son se - cors ve - rai.

*Translation* I will begin to compose a *lai* about the best of women; but I greatly fear that I have known too much suffering, so that my melodies will turn into weeping. Mother and most sweet virgin, if you make any delay in praying to the most high Lord, I must indeed have great fear of the devil, of the evil one . . . Lady, full of bounty, may your gentle sweet words not be forgotten; pray for us. We shall never be rescued if not by you, I know it for a truth. Here will I leave the matter; God grant us his help without delay.

Songs of a popular nature are more numerous than in the troubadour repertoire. There are a number of rondeaux, of which the standard form is *abaaabab*, the italicized letters standing for the internal refrain. The refrain was certainly sung chorally in these early examples of the form, which originally had several stanzas (for a rondeau reconstructed from the middle voice of a motet see *NOHM*, ii, p. 245). This character stands out clearly in the lyrics for Adam de la Halle's pastoral play *Li Gieus de Robin et de Marion*, apparently performed at court in Naples in 1283. Adam was the son of a burgher of Arras and became a member of its *pui*. The two best songs from *Li Gieus* have often been reprinted (e.g. Gennrich, *Trobadours*, p. 38; *NOHM*, ii, p. 232; complete edition of the play with its music by Gennrich, *Le Jeu*). Many of his separate lyrics, which like *Li Gieus* survive in mensural notation, are livelier in rhythm than those of his contemporaries and anticipate the innovations of the fourteenth century:

**Example 42**

Paris, Bibl. Nat., f. fr. 25566, f. 11.

Il ne muet pas de sens che - lui qui plaint
Pour chou ne puis ve - oir que chiex bien aint

Paine et tra - vail, qui a - quiert a - van - ta - ge.
Qui, pour go - ir, d'a - mour souf - fran-che ga - ge.

Qui n'est souf - frans et d'es - ta - ble co - ra - ge,

Il ne se doit en - tre - mes - tre d'a - mer,

Car cuers ne puet en a - mour pour-fi - ter

Qui est a - com - pa - gniés a cuer vo - la - ge.

(5 stanzas and four-line *envoi*)

*Translation* It is not folly to have to complain of woe and misery provided a man reaps some benefit from it. Wherefore I cannot see that he loves well who puts love's suffering in pawn in order to have his enjoyment. He who is not patient and of stable intent should not meddle with love; for a heart cannot profit in love if it is coupled with a fickle one.

Though monophonic music continued to be composed in France after his death in *c.* 1288, and underwent a striking resurrection in the hands of Machaut, Adam is in a very real sense the last of the trouvères.

## English song

The songs of both southern and northern France were heard in
England as a natural result of their political affiliations; indeed the
strength of this influence is supposed to have stifled any native
English tradition. The few survivals include the songs of St Godric
(d. 1170), which partake of the character of vernacular tropes to
plainsong melodies, and a few thirteenth-century secular—but at the
same time moralistic and gloomy—songs to English words. There is
also evidence that the Anglo-Saxon tradition of sung epic poetry
continued until the fourteenth century; but of its musical nature we
are wholly ignorant.

## Minnesinger

The German counterparts to the troubadours and trouvères were the
Minnesinger, whose subject was courtly love (*Minne*). The melodies
of the earliest of the Minnesinger have not survived; but as their
songs were sometimes written on the model of troubadour and
trouvère songs whose melodies are extant, these at least can be
reconstructed. The earliest surviving melody, to a song by Walther
von der Vogelweide (*c.* 1170–1230; Gennrich, *Troubadours*, p. 51;
*NOHM*, ii, p. 253) is itself a variant of an older Provençal tune. The
second phase is represented by Neidhart von Reuental (*c.* 1180–
1250), by whom songs with melodies survive in fair numbers.
The third period is that of Heinrich von Meissen, known as
Frauenlob, or 'praise of ladies' (d. 1318). In later years the French
tradition of the *pui* was adopted, and eventually assumed great
importance in German provincial life. The Meistersinger, as the
denizens of these guilds came to call themselves, survived into the
sixteenth century and preserved the traditions of the fourteenth-
century *Geisslerlieder* or penitential songs and of German religious
song in general, as much as of the Minnesinger; and they fitted
naturally enough into the scheme of things at the time of the
Lutheran Reformation.

The Germans adopted one of the favourite troubadour forms, that
of two *pedes* and *cauda*, with or without repetition at the end; the
*pedes* were known as *Stollen* (props), the *cauda* as *Abgesang* and the

whole form as *Bar*. As an example we give a song by Neidhart which illustrates his simple, homely style:

**Example 43**

Berlin, Staatsbibl., germ. fol. 779, f. 234.

"Sinc an, gul - dîn huon! ich ·gibe dir wei - ze",
Al - sô vreut den tum - ben guot ge - hei - ze

(Schie - re dô Wart ich vrô) Sprach si,
Durch daz jâr. Würde ez wâr, Sô ge -

nâch der hul - den ich dâ sin - ge:
- stuont ni man - nes muot sô rin - ge,

Al - sô mir der mî - ne dan - ne wae - re.

Mac si durch ir gei - lic - heit Mî - niu leit

Wen - den? ja ist mîn kum - ber kla - ge - bae - re.

(rhythm conjectural)

*Translation* 'Sing up, golden cock! I'll give you corn', (how I rejoiced!) spake she whose praises I sing; thus the fool is happy with vain expectations the whole year through. Were it true, no man's spirits would stand as high as mine would then be. Will she in her careless gaiety change my sorrows? Truly my grief is lamentable.

Not all German songs are as syllabic as this; nor should duple rhythm be regarded as especially appropriate to German song. But simplicity was also a characteristic of the *Leich*, the equivalent of the *lai*, which was cultivated by a number of thirteenth-century composers including Frauenlob (for an example see *NOHM*, ii, p. 258; facsimile in Runge, *Die Sangweisen* and Parrish, *Notation*, pl. XVIII).

## Spanish and Italian song

We have already referred to the cultivation of the troubadours' art in Italy and Spain (p. 103). But the music from these countries which survives is, apart from a few unimportant fragments, entirely religious in character. The Spanish contribution consists essentially of the *Cantigas de Santa María* collected by Alfonso X, 'el Sabio', written in the Galician dialect. The preferred form is similar to that of the French *virelai* and the Italian *ballata*: a refrain is sung at the beginning, between each stanza, and at the end of the song; part of the music for the refrain may be retained in the verse. The notation is mensural and both triple and duple rhythms are found, sometimes in alternation.

The Italian songs are called *laudi spirituali* and are an outcome of the penitential movement which also resulted in the *Geisslerlieder* in Germany. Though many of them resemble the latter in being simple and 'congregational' in style, the *laudi* are often elaborate songs requiring skilled artistry. In form they are similar to the *cantigas*; and as in them it is treated with considerable freedom. But the notation is non-mensural and the style often resembles the more ecstatic kind of plainchant.

It is impossible to do justice to these collections in a few short examples. The reader is referred to the quotations in *NOHM*, ii, pp. 261–9, and to the complete editions by Anglès and Liuzzi.

## Instrumental dances

This is perhaps the place to mention the few items of instrumental monophony which have come down to us. The most important survival is a set of eight *estampies royales* and one *dansse real* in the *Manuscrit du Roi* (see above, p. 101), of which the first *estampie* is imperfect. The form of the *estampie* resembles that of the sequence and *lai* in having a series of repeated sections, in the case of the *estampie* with varied endings which are sometimes marked 'ouvert' and 'clos'. There is a good deal of repetition altogether, because the repeated sections or *puncti* are usually identical after the first phrase. The most attractive of this set is probably the fourth (*HAM*, i, no. 40b).

There is also an English dance of the thirteenth century which embodies the same principles, though with greater freedom; it also includes a short passage of three-part counterpoint which appears to be intended as a conclusion. Some of the details of its notation, which is a curious mixture of modal and mensural, are far from certain; but at all events it is a lively piece (*HAM*, i, no. 40c; facsimiles in *EEH*, i, pl. 24).

Finally one should mention the fourteenth-century Italian dances now in the British Museum (Add. 29987). To the *estampie* principle is added, in some cases, that of the pairing of dances, the second being based on the material of the first (e.g. the *Lamento di Tristan* with *La Rotta*: *HAM*, i, no. 59a). The example we give is of a livelier character:

**Example 44**

London, Brit, Mus., Add. 29987, f. 63v.

Sparse though these examples are, they testify through their widely differing periods and places of origin to the universality of the principles which they illustrate.

# Bibliography

## Musical sources

The collection known as *Carmina Burana* (Munich, Staatsbibliothek, MS lat. 4660 with 4660a) may be studied in the facsimile edition by B. Bischoff (*PMMM*, ix) and in transcription by Hilka and Schumann. The Cambridge songs (Cambridge, University Library, Gg v. 35) are edited by Breul. For the Florence MS see Chapter 5, Bibliography.

The principal MSS of troubadour and trouvère song are edited in facsimile by Aubry, *Le Chansonnier d'Arsenal* (Paris, Bibliothèque de l'Arsenal, MS 5198) and *Le Roman de Fauvel* (see Bibliography, Chapter 6), Beck, *Le Chansonnier Cangé* (Paris, Bibl. Nat., f. fr. 846) and *Le Manuscrit du Roi* (ibid., f. fr. 844), Jeanroy, *Le Chansonnier d'Arras* (Arras, Bibliothèque Municipale, 139, *olim* 657), Meyer and Raynaud, *Le Chansonnier français de St Germain-des-Prés* (Paris, Bibl. Nat., f. fr. 20050) and Sesini, *Le Melodie trobadoriche* (Milan, Bibl. Amb., R.71. supl.). Other editions are those of Gennrich (*Lo Gai Saber, Rondeaux* and a complete collection of the troubadour melodies in *SMMA*, iii–iv). *C'est d'Aucassin et de Nicolete*, ed. Bourdillon; Bernart de Ventadorn songs, ed. Appel, *Die Singweisen*; Adam de la Halle in *CMM*, XLIV, and Gennrich, *Le Jeu*. The *lais* are collected in Jeanroy, *Lais et descorts*.

The songs of St Godric are printed by J. B. Trend in *ML*, ix (1928). The two most important German sources, those from Jena (Universitätsbibliothek) and Colmar (Munich, Staatsbibl., germ. 4997) are available in facsimile in *SMMA*, xi and xviii respectively. Older editions are those by Müller and Holz of the former, and by Runge of the latter. The songs of Neidhart are edited by Hatto and Taylor, by Gennrich in *SMMA*, ix and, with facsimiles, in *DTO*, lxxi (=xxxvii. 1); those of Frauenlob and his contemporaries, Reinmar von Zweter and Alexander 'der Meister', are in *DTO*, xli ( = xx. 2). For Oswald von Wolkenstein see *DTO*, xviii ( = ix. 1) Two recent collections of German song are those of Taylor and of Moser and Müller-Blattau. The *cantigas* are edited by Anglès and the *laudi spirituali* by Liuzzi. Finally there is Gennrich's anthology *Troubadours* and the numerous examples in *HAM*, i, *NOHM*, ii and Reese, *Music in the Middle Ages*.

## Literary sources

The most important are the treatise of Johannes de Grocheo, edited with German translation by Rohloff (an earlier edition is that of Wolf in *SIMG*, i, with corrections by Müller in *SIMG*, iv) and Dante's *De vulgari eloquentia* (many editions, especially that by P. Rajna for the Società dantesca). The anthology of troubadour verse by Hill and Bergin is extremely useful. The best edition of the *Chanson de Roland* is that by F. Whitehead (Oxford, 1942). A convenient selection of old French poetry with English translation is available in *The Penguin Book of French Verse*, i (London, 1961); *Aucassin and Nicolette* has appeared in the Penguin Classics (London, 1971).

## Studies

The literature is vast. The reader is referred to the standard works of Aubry, Beck, Chaytor, Dronke and Gennrich. The standard bibliographical works are Jeanroy, *Bibliographie sommaire*, Pillet and Carstens, *Bibliographie*, and Raynaud, *Bibliographie*, revised by Spanke. A good recent general account for the English reader is H. Van der Werf, *The Chansons of the Troubadours and Trouvères*. Appel's *Bernart von Ventadorn* is a standard biography. Taylor's collection of Minnesang already mentioned includes a substantial commentary.

# 4 The growth of polyphony, 900–1160

Polyphony is not a peculiarity of Western music. Primitive forms of polyphony have been and are known almost over the whole world. Polyphony is inseparable from most forms of practical music-making, except for the unaccompanied use of the human voice or a purely 'melodic' instrument. Primitive polyphony may be considered as belonging to one of the following categories: parallel movement at different pitches, heterophony, drones of various kinds and canonic or imitative procedures. Heterophony has been explained (p. 91) and the others are self-explanatory. Parallelism is a particular property of the organ, the drone of bagpipe, hurdy-gurdy, and also of the organ again at certain periods. It is possible that more sophisticated forms of polyphony were known before the Middle Ages: for example in classical Greece and Rome, when the organ already possessed a balanced keyboard like the white notes of a piano. The air was provided by assistants and the performer had both hands free to play. Such organs may sometimes have had ranks of pipes causing them to play in parallel fifths and octaves (Perrot, *The Organ*, p. 97). If to this the player added a polyphony of his own, the result would be a 'three-dimensional' polyphony which is a special peculiarity of the organ. However, this is pure speculation.

Improvised polyphony was practised in the Middle Ages, both in the Church and outside it. We know very little about it in the latter context, but as far as the Church is concerned we are helped by the fact that its musicians wished to codify their methods for the more seemly ordering, no doubt, of divine worship. So it comes about that the history of polyphony in the West begins with the examples contained in two treatises written towards the end of the ninth century which in Gerbert's edition are entitled *Musica Enchiriadis* and *Scholia Enchiriadis* respectively, the latter a commentary on the former in question-and-answer form. The context of the 'new' art is monastic; the technique is parallel movement in fourths, fifths and octaves; and its usual name is *organum*, apparently because the technique was suggested by the sound of the instrument, or, possibly, because the existing method was found to bear a resemblance to it. We first hear of the organ in churches in the tenth century, and here too the church in question is usually a monastery or a cathedral served by monks.

Since theorists are usually some distance behind actual practice it is reasonable to assume that this method was in use by about 850. Unfortunately the notation of the two treatises (the Daseian notation already mentioned: see p. 28) raises more questions than it answers, quite apart from the obvious fact that the text is frequently corrupt. Accidentals are the chief difficulty, since the authors' curious scale, perhaps derived from Byzantine concepts and consisting of four disjunct tetrachords of equivalent form (tone, semitone, tone) plus two extra notes, avoids diminished fifths but incorporates tritones and augmented octaves: *GABb♭c|defg|abc′d|e′f♯′g′a′|b′c♯″*). The *organum* is either simple (in two parts) or composite (three or four parts). Already we find in *organum* of the fourth a desire to modify the strictly parallel movement at cadences, as in the following example from the *Scholia Enchiriadis* (as the two upper parts are represented here only by a repetition of the signs used for the two lower parts, the difficulties caused by the tritones and augmented octaves of the full Daseian system do not apply: however, a flattening of *b* seems necessary in accordance with later versions of the *tonus peregrinus*, cf. Example 14. The printing in Gerbert, *Scriptores*, i, p. 190, illustrates the kind of accident to which his edition is prone: the sign for *c* in the upper octave should be identical with that in the lower, but it has been printed back to front):

**Example 45**

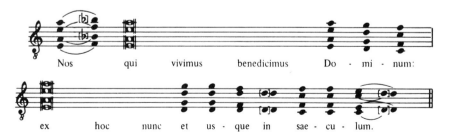

*Translation* We who live bless the Lord, from this time forth and for ever more.

Here the movement of the parts makes it clear which pair represents the original plainsong and which are added; in strictly parallel movement, of course, the point is purely academic. Normally the *vox organalis* was added below the plainsong or *vox principalis* at this very early stage, though there are complications in composite *organum*. A rather more sophisticated example of 'free' *organum* is provided by the *Musica Enchiriadis* in a pair of double versicles from a sequence:

**Example 46**

*Translation* King of heaven, Lord of the wave-sounding sea, of the shining sun and of the rough earth, your humble servants, adoring you with holy melodies, entreat you to free them of your command from their manifold ills.

Clearly we are now on the verge of written polyphonic composition; for the application of such methods in choir would result in chaos unless the music were carefully rehearsed in advance.

The earliest known practical source of polyphony is one of the two eleventh-century tropers from Winchester, the main contents of which were written before the Norman conquest. One of these (Oxford, Bod. Lib., Bodl. 775) has already been mentioned as an important document in the history of liturgical drama (p. 81). The other (Cambridge, Corpus Christi Coll., MS 473) contains 171 polyphonic parts to plainsong melodies (three of them duplicated) as additions to the manuscript, mostly in a separate section of their own (ff. 135r–190v; for a full discussion of the polyphony and a summary list of the contents of both manuscripts see Holschneider, *Die Organa von Winchester*).

The plainsong melodies themselves are mostly to be found written down in one or both of the two manuscripts. Altogether polyphony is provided for four antiphons (ff. 53v–54r), four troped and eight untroped Kyries (ff. 135r–138r), seven Gloria-tropes (ff. 138v–143r), nineteen Tracts (ff. 143r–152v), eight wordless sequences (though one has a partial text: see above, p. 63), of which one lacks neumes (ff. 153r–155r), four Easter Introit-tropes (ff. 162r–162v), fifty-three Alleluias interrupted by the Gloria in Greek, *Doxa en ipsistis theo* (ff. 163r–175r), fifty-nine responds, invitatories and processional antiphons (ff. 175v–189v) and seven additional items, including the three duplicates, on ff. 189v–190v and 197v–198v. All but the last seven pieces are thought to have been written down in the first quarter of the century. The notation is in virtually unheighted neumes, so that an absolutely faithful transcription is impossible. However, most of the *cantus firmi* can be reproduced in the normal manner by comparing them with decipherable sources, while the use of Notkerian letters (see above, p. 23) in the added part provides additional help. In the following example a transcription is attempted of the fourth of the eight sequences, based on the Alleluia 'Multifariae' already quoted (Example 27, p. 71).

**Example 47**

Oxford, Bod. Lib., Bodl. 775, f. 122v.
Cambridge, Corpus Christi College, MS 473, f. 153v.

MULTIFARIAE SEQUENTIA

*continued*

*continued*

Note: The version of the plainsong in Corpus Christi Coll. has not been used since it has been partially erased and does not materially differ from the Bodleian version insofar as it is extant.

\* MS reads:

† In Corpus Christi this phrase is written out twice with minor variants the second time.

The manuscript contains *organa* for soloists as well as for choir. In the responsorial chants the entire texts are set, without any stylistic distinction between the sections assigned in the liturgy to the cantors and choir respectively. When polyphony was sung by a choir, one side might sing the plainsong, the other side the *organum*, as is evident from a description of the dedication of Ramsey Abbey on 8 November 991 (Byrhtferth, *Vita Sancti Oswaldi* in *RBMAS*, LXXI, i, p. 464; quoted by Holschneider, op. cit., pp. 136–7, and in *NOHM*, ii, p. 279). The part-writing is now completely free with a preponderance of contrary motion, resulting from a genuine desire to write 'melliflua organorum modulamina' (f. 135r).

Indeed we are now worlds away from the majority of the examples from the *Musica* and *Scholia Enchiriadis*, in which each part tends to have its own range and in which, in the case of composite *organum*, the overall range is sometimes considerable. The type represented by Example 45, which may in any case be purely theoretical, has now disappeared for good except in a few backward-looking treatises. It is surprising that neither Guido of Arezzo (d. 1050) nor John of Afflighem (c. 1100) have anything of great interest to say concerning *organum*, though both include chapters on the subject. Both mention free *organum* with contrary motion, though Guido also concerns himself with obsolete parallelism. An anonymous treatise of about 1100, *Ad organum faciendum* (Milan, Bibl. Amb., MS 17), moves the plainsong fairly consistently to the lower voice: a Kyrie, 'Cunctipotens genitor Deus', has often been reprinted (e.g. *HAM*, i, no. 26a). But it is obvious that none of these sources represents any kind of stylistic advance over the Winchester Troper.

A number of small practical sources from the mid-eleventh to the early twelfth century have survived. The most important of these are from Chartres (Bibliothèque Municipale, 4, 109, 130, all now destroyed by fire) and Fleury (Rome, Biblioteca Vaticana, Reg. lat. 586 and 592). Of these the two from Fleury, and Chartres MS 4, are written in the same manner as the Winchester Troper, i.e. as a single part in neumatic notation. Chartres 130 is written in score in slightly diastematic neumes; the words are now under the lower part, which is the plainsong. This proves to be the normal subsequent arrangement. Chartres 109 uses a four-line staff in score.

Reg. lat. 586 contains a single page with *organa* to three Graduals. Only the solo portions are set, i.e. the intonation of the respond and the whole of the verse except for the last phrase. There is a facsimile in Holschneider, op. cit. (pl. 9) and an attempted transcription (pp. 172–7). Reg. lat. 592 includes a leaf (f. 78) containing various antiphons and responds, with *organa* to the respond-verses and to some of the respond-intonations; all but four of the twelve sections, however, are without neumes. (There is a facsimile of f. 78v in Bannister, *Monumenti*, ii, pl. 44). Chartres 4 contains three responds; Chartres 109 has six Alleluias and two processional antiphons, all for the Easter season; and Chartres 130 has six Alleluias for the Christmas and Easter seasons. Facsimiles of all three are in *PM*, I, xvii. Chartres 130 is the latest of the three (early twelfth century), and is the only one of the three to provide polyphony for soloists only. It also has the advantage of being in decipherable notation, although the manuscript was in a very damaged state even before it was destroyed. Its eight pieces were written on a single leaf (f. 75), but only the five pieces on the recto side were provided with notation. The last of these, the verse 'Dicant nunc Iudaei' to the Eastertide processional antiphon 'Christus resurgens', is only partially legible, but it survives virtually complete in an English source (Oxford, Bod. Lib., Rawl. C 892, ff. 67v–68), thus providing one of the very few remaining concordances for this primitive period of polyphony. The music has often been printed, most recently by Holschneider (op. cit., pp. 177–81, including the Bodleian concordance).

There is still a good deal of crossing of parts in this music, and the cadences are formed either above or below the plainsong according to the range and melodic direction of the latter. The movement is still entirely note-against-note, and indeed there is no indication of any real technical advance over the Winchester music of possibly a hundred years earlier.

We have labelled the period 'primitive', but it is a mistake to suppose that its polyphonic music is of purely academic interest. The sound of the perpetually intertwining male voices, whether solo or choral, can be very beautiful, and the transcriptions of Holschneider completely vindicate the attempt to restore the Winchester music and the other fragments. Nevertheless it is monotonous in the long run, unlike the plainsong which it embellishes. In a later era, the art of writing for equal voices in similar rhythm was to develop much further; but before that could come about there had to be a stylistic revolution in terms of both rhythm and texture.

## *Melismatic* organum

From about 1100, as far as can be determined, there arose a new style in which the two parts are clearly separated as to pitch (the lower being the *cantus firmus*), and in which the upper part moved at a rate of several notes to one in the lower part, the actual number varying considerably from one *cantus-firmus* note to the next. Note-against-note writing and crossing of parts were not wholly abandoned; but the former became less strict, and the latter a less constant feature. In the course of time various conventions arose governing the style of polyphony appropriate to various categories of chant, the picture being complicated somewhat by the appearance of the polyphonic conductus.

In a polyphonic conductus the lower part, or tenor, was normally (though by no means invariably) newly composed. Even when this was so, however, it still tended to have a decidedly melodic character of its own, and was written first, the upper parts being added afterwards. Such tenors, like monophonic conductus, could be either syllabic, melismatic, or a combination of the two. In the case of a syllabic tenor, the upper part could also be syllabic, though perhaps with an occasional group of two or three notes to the syllable. But an upper part against a syllabic tenor could equally well be highly melismatic, thus causing the notes of the tenor to move at a slow and irregular pace. If the tenor itself were melismatic, the upper part would often move in the same rhythm against it, though not always; while if the tenor were syllabic and melismatic in alternation the general tendency would be for the melismatic portions to be treated in note-against-note style and the syllabic portions in melismatic style in the upper voice.

This alternation between syllabic and melismatic style in the tenor is particularly characteristic of liturgical *organum*, which now began to concentrate exclusively on the solo-responsorial forms of the Office and Mass. (The fact that they were often troped in verse lends an added similarity to the conductus, though this feature was later abandoned.) The habit of treating the Gregorian melismas in roughly note-against-note style, and its syllabic portions melismatically, resulted in a considerable evening out of the syllables in the polyphonic setting as compared with their distribution in the original chant.

The sources of this repertory are four manuscripts associated with southern France and one with the ancient pilgrimage centre of Santiago (St James) at Compostela in north-western Spain (Galicia). Of the former, one (Paris, Bibl. Nat., lat. 1139) is from a set of nineteen tropers from Limoges, and like most of them from the abbey of St Martial there. It contains two* polyphonic items and dates from the early twelfth century; the notation is in Aquitanian neumes. The other three (Paris, Bibl. Nat., lat. 3719 and 3549 and London, Brit. Mus., Add. 36881) are later and are not so certainly connected with Limoges, but their notation is of the same regional type. Altogether about eighty pieces are preserved. The single manuscript now in the cathedral archives at Compostela is of a similar general style and date; but its music has some special characteristics which demand separate treatment.

An example of note-against-note writing in a purely syllabic conductus, 'Congaudet hodie', is given in *NOHM*, ii, p. 296 (Add. 36881, f. 12). The voices have approximately the same range and frequently cross. The melismatic treatment of a syllabic tenor is illustrated by 'Prima mundi seducti sobole', from the same source (f.

---

* The number is increased however by the recognition of 'hidden' polyphony in certain monophonic pieces, in which pairs of sections may be performed simultaneously. See Marshall (*JAMS* 1962), Treitler (*JAMS* 1964).

13v: *NOHM*, ii, p. 297). The voice-parts are now clearly differentiated in range. Another example, from lat. 1139, f. 41, is shown below: it is a trope to the versicle 'Benedicamus Domino', though not in the musical sense, since the tenor is an independent melody. Pieces of this kind stand in a similar relationship to 'Benedicamus Domino' as the later kind of sequence does to the Alleluia; the analogy being peculiarly striking owing to the similarity of their metrical schemes (8787 as opposed to 887887). We give the beginning of this fairly lengthy composition, with its full text, which is set in the same manner throughout:

**Example 48**

Paris, Bibl. Nat., f. lat. 1139, f. 41.

lu - bi - le - mus, ex - sul - te - mus, in - to - ne - mus can - ti - cum

Redemptori, Plasmatori, Salvatori omnium.
Hoc natali salutari, omnis nostra turmula
Deum laudet, sibi plaudat, per aeterna saecula,
Qui hodie de Mariae utero progrediens,
Homo verus, Rex atque Erus, in terris apparuit.
Tam beatum ergo natum, cum ingenti gaudio,
Conlaudantes, exsultantes, benedicamus Domino.

\* MS *a*

† MS a note between *e* and *d*

*Translation* Let us cry aloud for joy, let us rejoice, let us sing a hymn to the Redeemer, the Creator, the Saviour of all men. On this birthday of the Saviour, let our whole congregation praise God and be glad for ever and ever, since on this day, proceeding from the womb of Mary, he, true Man, King and Master, appeared on earth. Therefore with immense joy praising so blessed a child, let us rejoice and bless the Lord.

The next example shows fairly consistent note-against-note writing over a neumatic/melismatic tenor (Add. 36881, f. 2). The metre of the verse is now exactly that of the sequence; but it is no longer even textually a trope:

**Example 49**

London, Brit. Mus., Add. 36881, f. 2.

*Translation* Light has come down to the depths, a light illuminating the man coming into this world.

Finally we show both styles in juxtaposition in a troped version of the Christmas Gradual 'Viderunt omnes' (lat. 3549, ff. 151v–152). The trope-text amplifies the word 'viderunt', which was intoned by one or more cantors in a plainsong performance, so that the whole composition is intended for soloists. The chorus would pick up the

Gradual in plainsong at the word 'omnes'. The following printing of the text shows the original in italics and the trope in roman type:

Polyphony:  *Viderunt* Emmanuel, Patris unigenitum,
In ruinam Israel et salutem positum
Hominem in tempore, Verbum in principio,
Urbis quam fundaverat natum in palatio,
Plainsong:  *omnes fines terrae salutare Dei nostri* (etc.)

The following is a transcription of the first two lines of text. The complete piece is given in *HAM*, i, no. 27a, and in facsimile in Apel, *Notation*, p. 211. It will be noted that the original plainsong is transposed up a tone:

**Example 50**

Paris, Bibl. Nat., f. lat. 3549, f. 151v.

*continued*

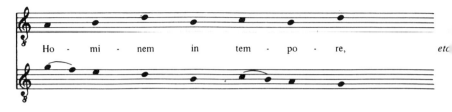

Ho - mi - nem in tem - po - re, *etc*

*Translation  All the ends of the earth have seen* Emmanuel, the only-begotten of the Father, created man in time, for the ruin of Israel and for [our] salvation, Word from the beginning, born in the palace of the city which he had founded, *the salvation of our God.*

As it happens the distinction between the treatment of the melismatic and syllabic portions of the tenor is abandoned in the continuation, in which note-against-note style is employed throughout.

The polyphonic repertory of Santiago de Compostela is contained in an appendix (ff. 185 seqq.) to the famous manuscript which also contains various monophonic Offices and Masses in honour of the patron saint of this important centre of pilgrimage. (It is also known as the Codex Calixtinus in view of the fact that Pope Calixtinus II (d. 1122) composed and selected some of the texts for the Offices; it cannot be taken as evidence of the date or provenance of the manuscript).

The polyphonic contents of the manuscript, which is usually dated 1137, include several conductus, some of them tropes for the 'Benedicamus', responds (including a Gradual and Alleluia), two troped Kyries and three settings of the 'Benedicamus Domino' untroped. As an example of note-against-note setting we quote part of the conductus 'Ad superni regis decus', in which the double-versicle structure is reminiscent of the sequence:

**Example 51**

Ad  su - per - ni  Re - gis  de  -  cus,  qui  con - ti -
Ce - le - bre - mus  lae - ti  tu  -  a,  Ia - co - be,

●) Liquescent first time only

*Translation* To the glory of the heavenly King, who is the author of all things, let us joyfully celebrate thy solemnities, O James.

The final melisma is the same in each of the first four double versicles, while the fifth and last appears as follows:

**Example 52**

*Translation* May he bless the Lord.

The melismatic style may be illustrated by the Gradual 'Misit Herodes' for the main Mass of the Saint's Day, possibly the most elaborate of all the pieces. Only the solo portions of the chant are set:

**Example 53**

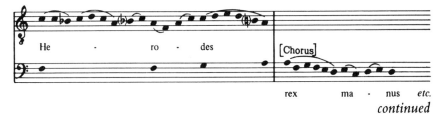

*continued*

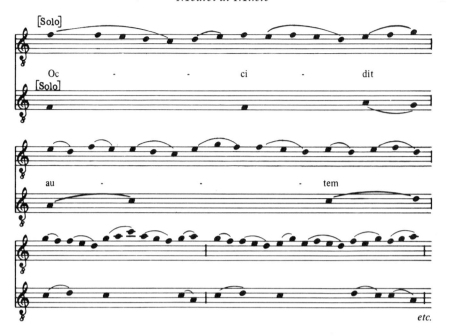

*Translation* Herod the King stretched forth his hands [to vex certain of the Church.] V. And he killed [James the brother of John].

The manuscript also contains a curiosity in the shape of a three-part conductus on two staves, 'Congaudeant catholici'. From the circumstance that the middle voice is written on the lower stave with the tenor, and that some (but not all) of its notes appear to have been added after the rest of the music, it has been conjectured that the middle voice was composed after the other two. But it is just as likely that it is the top voice which was composed last; or that the two upper parts were conceived independently and never intended to be combined. At all events, it makes an odd piece with all its three parts; an unsatisfactory attempt at best to reconcile melismatic and note-against-note writing. It has often been reproduced: two rhythmic versions are given in *NOHM*, ii, pp. 305–6, neither of them wholly satisfactory.

## Performance

The problem of rhythm is again the most difficult to solve in the music discussed in this chapter. Only the simplest of syllabic settings will yield to the kind of treatment previously suggested for some kinds of monophony, in which the natural rhythm of the words (but not necessarily their theoretical correspondence to classical metres) can sometimes help towards a solution. In polyphony melismas of any length, whether in the tenor or in the upper part *vis-à-vis* the tenor, preclude such treatment. For note-against-note treatment of tenor melismas we may sometimes predicate performance in notes of equal length; but this does not always yield satisfactory results in juxtaposition with other styles in the same piece. As for pieces and sections of pieces in which several notes are placed in the upper part to one in the tenor, the only possible solution seems to be a 'plainsong' treatment of the upper voice while the lower voice is fitted against it by means of purely pragmatic criteria.

Fortunately a solution, or at least a partial solution, to these problems was about to emerge in the 'modal' theory of rhythm and its attendant notation. A discussion of this theory and the music for which it was intended belongs properly to the next chapter.

# Bibliography

*Musical sources*

There is as yet no complete facsimile of the Cambridge Winchester Troper. There are plates in *EEH*, i, in Frere, *The Winchester Troper* and in Holschneider, *Die Organa von Winchester*, with attempted specimen transcriptions in the case of the last of these. The Chartres fragments are reproduced in *PM*, I, xvii, those from Fleury in Bannister, *Monumenti* (Rome, Bibl. Vat., reg. lat. 586 also in Holschneider, op. cit.).

The St Martial repertory is poorly dealt with, but apart from the references in the text there are facsimiles from two of the MSS (Paris, Bibl. Nat., lat. 1139 and London, Brit. Mus., Add. 36881) in Parrish, *Notation*, from which Examples 48–9 are drawn. Both Parrish and Apel (*Notation*) give single pages from the Compostela MS, which is transcribed in full in Wagner, *Die Gesänge der Jakobusliturgie*. A complete facsimile was published at Compostela in 1944.

*Theoretical sources*

These are of primary importance, as it is in them that written polyphony first appears. The *Musica Enchiriadis* and *Scholia Enchiriadis* are perhaps more properly known as *Enchirias de Musica* and *Scolica Enchiriadis* respectively, though the important Valenciennes MS of the early tenth century originally carried neither title. In the best MSS the former is ascribed to Hogerus or Otgerus, who can be identified as an abbot of St Amand near Valenciennes (the monastery where Hucbald was a monk); he died *c*. 940. The text must still be read from Gerbert, *Scriptores*, i, pp. 152–73 and 173–212; for the older literature see Reese, *Music in the Middle Ages*, p. 126. See also J. Smits van Waesberghe in *Revue grégorienne*, xxxi (1952), pp. 81–104, and *RISM*, B III (*The Theory of Music*), passim. A similar treatise from Paris was edited in Coussemaker, *Scriptores*, ii, pp. 74–8 and another from Cologne in Riemann, *Geschichte der Musiktheorie*, pp. 20–1 (another ed. by Handschin in *AcM*, xiv (1942), pp. 21–2). A third such treatise, the 'Bamberg dialogue', is described by E. M. Waeltner in *AMw*, xiv (1957), pp. 175–83. Guido's *Micrologus* is now in *CSM*, iv (also Gerbert, *Scriptores*, ii, pp. 2–24), and the *De Musica* of John of Afflighem (Johannes Affligemensis, formerly known as John Cotton) is in *CSM*, i (also Gerbert, *Scriptores*, ii, pp. 230–65). *Ad organum faciendum* and related tracts ed. Eggebrecht and Zaminer. Two treatises illustrating the transition from St Martial to Notre-Dame are those edited by Zaminer (first described by R. von Ficker in *KJb*, xxvii) and by A. Seay in *AnnM*, v (1957), pp. 7–42 (formerly ed. Lafage, *Essais*, pp. 355–63, and Handschin in *AcM*, xiv (1942), pp. 23–6). For a survey of recent work see A. Gallo in *AcM*, xliv (1972), pp. 85–6.

*Literature*

Apart from the standard histories and the descriptions in the books of Parrish and Apel (*Notation*), the best account of the earliest period, at least as far as practical sources are concerned, is to be found in Holschneider, *Die Organa von Winchester*. A useful list of sources is in L. B. Spiess, 'An Introduction to the pre-St Martial sources of Early Polyphony' in *Speculum*, xxii (1947). On the later period see especially *MGG*, article 'Saint-Martial'; Chailley, *L'École musicale de Saint Martial*; H. Spanke, 'Die Londoner St Martial-Conductushandschrift' and H. Anglès, 'La Musica del Ms. de Londres, Brit. Museum Add. 36881' in *Butlletí de la Biblioteca de Catalunya*, viii (1928–32), pp. 280–303, also published separately (Barcelona, 1935).

# 5 *The* ars antiqua, *1160–1316*

*Modal rhythm and modal notation*

Before the music of this period can be discussed it is necessary to devote some attention to its rhythmic basis, which is at the very root of its style. Indeed certain concepts and terms which date from this time were widely used until the sixteenth century and others have persisted until the present day. It is not easy to define 'modal rhythm', but it is quite certain that the definition must embrace every aspect of mensurality during the period under discussion. According to an anonymous Englishman who was evidently in Paris during the second half of the thirteenth century (referred to henceforth as Anonymus IV from his position in Coussemaker, *Scriptores*, i), 'modus vel maneries vel temporis consideratio est cognitio longitudinis et brevitatis meli sonique'.* For Franco of Cologne (*c.* 1260) 'modus est cognitio soni longis brevibusque temporibus mensurati'† (*CSM*, xviii, p. 26). Modal rhythm is characteristically (but not invariably) triple and embraced six basic modes ('modi generales') which fitted into an overall scheme. These may be demonstrated by setting each one of them down in its shortest possible form in modern notation, i.e. reduced to one sixteenth, the crotchet representing the original *longa* ( ♩ ) and the quaver the *brevis* ( ▪ ).

These represent the 'first *ordo* imperfect' of each mode in turn.

---

* '*modus* or *maneries* or *consideratio temporis* is the concept of length and shortness in a song or in a note [i.e. presumably of the rhythmic patterns in a piece of music, and of the relative lengths of single notes]'.
† '*modus* is the idea of pitch measured in long and short time-values'.

According to Walter Odington, who wrote around the year 1300, these patterns represent the following metrical feet: trochee ($-\cup$), iamb ($\cup-$), dactyl ($-\cup\cup$), anapaest ($\cup\cup-$), spondee ($--$) and tribrach ($\cup\cup\cup$) respectively. From this it can be seen that while the first, second and sixth modes transcribe these feet into their exact musical equivalents, the third, fourth and fifth have been modified in order that they may fit in with the rhythms represented by the former group. However, in the medieval terminology of the modes only two basic values were employed: *longa* and *brevis*. The value denoted by our ♩. in the third, fourth and fifth modes was termed *longa perfecta*, and that of ♩ in the third and fourth modes *brevis altera* (i.e. the second of a pair of breves). Thus the fourth and fifth modes genuinely corresponded, in the medieval view, to the dactyl and anapaest respectively. The unit of time corresponding to an ordinary breve or *brevis recta* was the *tempus* (cf. modern French *temps*, 'beat'); thus the *brevis altera* and the ordinary long (*longa recta* or *longa imperfecta*) were each worth two *tempora*.

Nevertheless it is only Walter Odington, possibly under the influence of St Augustine's *De Musica*, who actually relates the modes to their classical equivalents. Indeed, he goes much further than this, for the perfect forms of the first *ordo* in each mode (♩ ♪♩; ♪♩ ♪; ♩. ♪♩ ♩.;♪♩ ♩. ♪♩;♩ ♩ ♩.;♫♫ ♪) have quite different names: *amphimacrus, amphibracus, c[h]oriambus,* anapaest with *pyrrhicius, molossus proceleumaticus* respectively—and so on and so forth for subsequent extensions of the modal patterns. Odington is here clearly thinking of word-feet rather than verse-feet, and his system at least has the virtue as an illustration of the modes that, to use the examples given by St Augustine, the tonic accent or stress of such words as *párens* (iamb) or *Ératos* (anapaest) corresponds to that of the musical mode, whereas in verse the opposite stress-pattern (corresponding to the *ictus* falling on the long syllables) would prevail. It is true that it is possible, as St Augustine himself prefers, to adjust iambic or anapaestic verses so that they become respectively trochaic or dactylic with an up-beat (the so-called 'anacrustic scheme' of modern grammarians); but as this still leaves us without an equivalent of the second or fourth mode the analogy is far from complete. Since word-feet illustrate metre only in the abstract, it is clear that the use of metrical terms to clarify the modal system is of limited value.

So far the modes have been discussed in terms of triple metre only. Here of course it must be pointed out that, even in the form presented here, modes 3, 4 and 5 are more properly considered as binary rather than ternary (i.e. they correspond to a moderately fast § in modern notation); while the actual musical use of the other three modes implies a corresponding binary structure as often as not. Nevertheless in medieval terminology they all rank as being in triple time, corresponding to our § . Medieval theory also recognized a binary subdivision of modes 3 and 4 (i.e. ♩ ♫ and ♫ ♩ ) as representing the *mos lascivus* or jolly style (Robertus de Handlo, 1326, in Coussemaker, op cit., i, p. 402). Anonymous IV refers to various 'modi irregulares', of which the seventh is unmeasured, very dignified, and is called 'organum purum' (we shall return to this point later). Finally it should be mentioned here that even in their ternary aspect the modes were capable of all sorts of modifications which blurred the distinction between them.

'Modal notation' is a much more restricted concept than modal rhythm. It refers to a method whereby a rhythmic mode is indicated by the grouping of ligatures (a ligature is a series of notes written as one symbol). The following table shows the normal ligature-patterns for each of the six modes:

**See Table 4 overleaf**

This is an ingenious system, but it has numerous disadvantages, of which the most obvious are: (1) it can apply only to music in melismatic style, since separate syllables require separate note-forms; (2) repeated notes often cause confusion, since they cannot be combined in the same ligature; (3) any deviation from the strict modal pattern can lead to ambiguity.

The most important of these deviations, with their method of notation, are as follows.

1. *Fractio modi* or introduction of shorter time values. This is usually achieved by simply adding the necessary notes to the ligatures, e.g.

♩♩♪ (♩ ♪♩ ♪|♩ ♪♩ ) becoming ♩♪♪ (♩ ♪♩ ♪|♫♩ ) 

It may also be achieved by the *plica* ('fold'), a sign deriving from

## Table 4: Ligature-patterns in modal notation

| Mode | Pattern | Example* |
|---|---|---|
| 1 | 3 . 2 . 2 . . . . 2 | 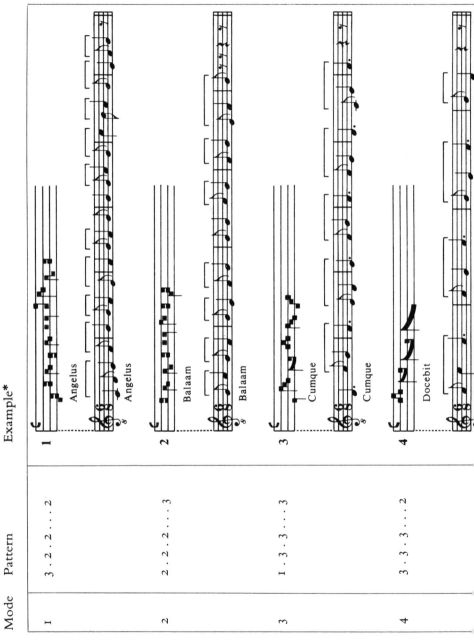 1   Angelus   Angelus |
| 2 | 2 . 2 . 2 . . . . 3 | 2   Balaam   Balaam |
| 3 | 1 . 3 . 3 . . . 3 | 3   Cumque   Cumque |
| 4 | 3 . 3 . 3 . . . . 2 | 4   Docebit |

\* The examples are taken from Johannes de Garlandia, *De mensurabili musica*. Neither the distinction between *longa* and *brevis* for repeated notes, nor the special form of the three-note ligature in mode 2 are apparent, however, in the regular sources of Notre-Dame music.

5

1.1.1.1...1
or 3 − 3 − 3
(This can be
confused with
the first *ordo* of
the first mode.
The first *ordo* of
the second mode
is written ▪▪
etc.)

6

4 · 3 · 3 · · · 3
or by means of
the *plica* (see
below):

the plainsong liquescent neumes:

♪ ┑ ┠ ( ♩ ♪♩ ♪| ♫♩ ♩ )

The final member of a plicated note or ligature, the pitch of which
depends on the context, was apparently performed 'by the partial
closing of the epiglottis combined with a subtle repercussion of the
throat' (Magister Lambertus, cited by Apel, *Notation*, pp. 226–7).

2. Extension of the mode, in which notes may be omitted:

♪ ╏ ┑ ( ♩ ♪♩ ♪| ♩. ♩ )

3. A figure called the *conjunctura*, of which the second and
subsequent notes are called *currentes*, is often used. It is derived from
the plainsong *climacus* and is always in descending motion, e.g. ❡•••• .
Here the rule is that the value of the last note is equal to the total value
of all the other notes in the symbol: ♫♫ ♩ . But the rule is not
always easy to apply, and *conjuncturae* are often used for ordinary
descending ligatures.

What has just been described is an outline of the perfected theory.
We are now in a position to consider its historical evolution and its
relevance to sources which are notated non-modally, of which the
most important are those which are syllabic. To begin with it must
be pointed out that the writings of the theorists, and indeed the
manuscripts which contain the music, are often of considerably later
date than the music itself—a fact which must be borne constantly in
mind.

Though the first mode has logical priority in the system and was
the first to be codified, there are grounds for believing that it was
preceded *de facto* by the fifth and possibly the third. We have already
pointed out the illogicality of applying the first and second modes to
monophonic music of the eleventh century on metrical grounds (see
p. 88). After about 1200, however, we may be justified in assuming
the influence of polyphony on monophonic song. This seems to
restrict us, before 1200, to the fifth mode for verse based on an
alternation between stressed and unstressed syllables, and to the third
mode for verse in which every third syllable is stressed. The latter is,
indeed, purely conjectural, and there are of course many other valid
ways of accomplishing the same stress-pattern in musical terms.

The fifth mode, on the other hand, is genuinely present whenever a succession of even note-values is in question. Such an ubiquitous rhythm, however, will scarcely qualify for systemization until it has to be fitted into some more complex scheme. Nothing could be more natural than that the first mode, and subsequently the second and the sixth, should have arisen out of the desire to rationalize the conduct of an upper part moving against this steady pulse in the tenor.* A growing tendency to replace the duple subdivision of the main beat ( ♫ ) by a triple one ( ♩ ♪ ) led ultimately to the construction of a completely ternary system: mode 2 followed by analogy with mode 1; mode 3 (and by analogy, mode 4) was created from the old 'dactylic' rhythm; mode 6 is merely mode 1 consistently 'broken' by the process of *fractio modi*. From the point of view of the notation, the decisive factor was the interpretation of the *ligatura binaria* ( ► or ▮ ) as 'short-long', wherever the stress: from this single development the notational system can be traced.

## The background to the sources

The centre of the new art was Paris, and the musical lead was now taken over by a great secular cathedral as opposed to the monasteries and monastic cathedrals which had previously been at the forefront of important musical developments. The earliest Parisian composer of whom we know the name is one Albertus, a cantor of Notre-Dame who appears in the cathedral records between 1147 and 1173; he is perhaps to be equated with Magister Albertus Parisiensis, the composer of a short and undistinguished conductus in the Compostela manuscript. He is however unknown to Anonymus IV, whose list of composers begins with Leoninus (or Leo) and Perotinus. What he has to say about these two is so important that a substantial passage from the treatise must be quoted:

Et nota quod magister Leoninus, secundum quod dicebatur, fuit optimus organista, qui fecit magnum librum organi de gradali et antifonario pro servitio divino multiplicando; et fuit in usu usque ad tempus Perotini magni, qui abbreviavit eundem et fecit clausulas sive

---

* Franco of Cologne grouped the fifth and first modes together as a single mode (CSM, xviii, pp. 27–8). In his terminology nos. 2–4 and 6 became nos. 2–5.

puncta plurima meliora, quoniam optimus discantor erat, et melior quam
Leoninus erat. . . .

Ipse vero magister Perotinus fecit quadrupla optima sicut 'Viderunt',
'Sederunt', cum habundantia colorum armonicae artis, similiter et tripla
plurima nobilissima sicut Alleluia 'Posui adiutorium', 'Nativitas' etc. Fecit
etiam triplices conductus ut 'Salvatoris hodie', et duplices conductus sicut
'Dum sigillum summi patris', ac etiam simplices conductus cum pluribus
aliis, sicut 'Beata viscera', etc.

'Master Leoninus was reputedly an excellent composer of *organum*; he
compiled a great book of *organum* from the Gradual and the Antiphonary
for the purpose of augmenting divine service. This was in use up to the time
of Perotinus the great, who shortened it, and composed many *clausulae* or
*puncta* which were better, since he was an excellent composer of *discantus*
and better than Leoninus. . . .

This master Perotinus composed excellent *quadrupla*, such as 'Viderunt'
and 'Sederunt', with an abundance of the refinements* of the art of music;
also many very noble *tripla*, such as the Alleluias 'Posui adiutorium',
'Nativitas', etc. He also composed conductus in three parts, such as
'Salvatoris hodie'; conductus in two parts such as 'Dum sigillum summi
patris'; and also monophonic conductus with various other types, e.g.
'Beata viscera', etc.)

We know nothing at all about Leoninus apart from what is stated
here. There is, however, some information which helps us to track
down Perotinus, though the evidence is purely circumstantial. In
1198 the bishop of Paris, Odo de Sully, issued an edict restricting the
ceremonial on the feast of the Circumcision, or *festum fatuorum* (see
above, p. 86), in which he allowed *organa* for two, three or four
voices for the respond and 'Benedicamus' of first Vespers, the third
and sixth responds of Matins, the Gradual and Alleluia of Mass, and
apparently the same items in second as in first Vespers. In the
following year, 1199, he issued a similar ordinance governing the
ceremonial on the feast of St Stephen, 26 December, when the priests
were accustomed to take charge of the services. In this it was laid
down that the singers of two-, three- or four-part *organum* were to be
paid six Parisian *denarii* for their pains. Now the interesting point is
that the four-part *organa* stated by Anonymus IV to be Perotinus are
actually pieces required for these very services: 'Viderunt' and

---

* *Color* was used as a synonym for *pulchritudo soni* (beauty of sound), which could be
interpreted in various ways, including ornamentation and repetition.

'Sederunt' are the Graduals for the Circumcision (also for Christmas Day) and St Stephen's Day respectively. Moreover, one four-part setting of each of these texts has survived in the sources. To ascribe these works to Perotinus and to date them around 1198 or 1199 is to make two fairly large assumptions; but the first of them seems to be a great probability and the second not unreasonable.

Perotinus has been identified with several persons named Petrus in the Paris archives, but none of them is a likely candidate for our composer. On the whole the evidence suggests that he was an unidentifiable *magister cantus* whose composing life fell into the period 1180–1205 (see Tischler in *Aspects*, p. 817).* This is not incompatible with the setting of the poem 'Beata viscera' by Philip the Chancellor (d. 1236).

Whereas at least a few works are attributed to Perotinus by name, the situation with regard to Leoninus is much vaguer. He is evidently a precursor of Perotinus, stylistically and chronologically; but our dating of his career will depend partly on our identification of Perotinus. On the whole it is difficult to be more precise than that he was active in the second half of the twelfth century. He is stated to have composed a 'magnus liber organi de gradali et antifonario pro servitio divino multiplicando'. It is not difficult to discern this compilation in the great liturgical cycle of two-part *organa* which appears in some form in all the main sources: it is a series of responds for Vespers and Matins, and Alleluias and Graduals for Mass, arranged in liturgical order. It is more of a problem to decide how closely the middle and late thirteenth-century sources of this repertoire resemble the original work of Leoninus himself; and which of the sources preserves it most faithfully. As far as the latter point is concerned, it is possible to recognize the version of Wolfcnbüttel, MS 677 (W¹: probably written at St Andrews in Scotland and published in facsimile by J. H. Baxter) as having the best claim, since it is the shortest version, and this manuscript is apparently the earliest of the principal sources. But is even this version pure Leoninus?

According to Anonymus IV Perotinus 'abbreviated the *Magnus Liber* and made many better *clausulae* or *puncta*'. Two of the three main sources of the whole repertoire, W¹ and Florence, Biblioteca

---

* Tischler rejects the interesting suggestion made by Husmann (in *JAMS*, xvi) that Perotinus was associated with St Germain l'Auxerrois rather than with Notre-Dame itself.

Medicea-Laurenziana, plut. 29.1 (F) do indeed contain a series (461 in F) of separate pieces in regular metre of which many could be regarded as substitutes for longer sections in the two-part *organa*. But it is not certain that Anonymus IV meant that the *Magnus Liber* was abbreviated through the process of substituting *clausulae* for sections in pure *organum*, or that it was improved by substituting better *clausulae* for the original ones. He merely says that Perotinus (1) abbreviated the *Magnus Liber* and (2) composed many and better *clausulae*. It has been pointed out that medieval scribes were not accustomed to writing out superannuated music in one section of a manuscript, and improvements to it in another, which suggests an independent function for the separate *clausulae*. It has also been stated that the actual practice of 'substitution' involves severe musical difficulties. Against this it may be mentioned that the 'original' *organa* and the 'substitute' *clausulae* are found in separate fascicles in our sources, and that these fascicles may originally have been separate books, either in the case of the manuscripts themselves, or at least in the prototypes from which they were copied. This is confirmed by Anonymus IV, who in another part of his treatise mentions a series of separate books containing different parts of the repertoire: (1) four-part *organa*; (2) three-part *organa*; (3) three-part conductus with *caudae*; (4) two-part conductus with *caudae*; (5) conductus without *caudae*; (6) two-part *organa*, and (7) many other volumes containing a variety of types. Among these last must be counted the *clausulae* and the motets.

There are thus two theories: (1) the two-part *organa* as we have them are the work of Leoninus, and the *clausulae* are substitute sections composed by Perotinus; and (2) the *organa* reach us in abbreviated form, and the *clausulae* are independent pieces with their own special liturgical function. However, it is misleading to suppose that the entire repertory of *clausulae* is uniform in function, style or technique, and the truth may lie somewhere between these extremes. We must now leave this intriguing problem on one side and examine the music as it appears in the sources (but see Bibliography, p. 158).

## Organum duplum

*Organum* in two parts is evidently the medium in which Leoninus mainly worked, and it is the medium adopted for by far the greater number of surviving Mass and Office responds, and for most settings of 'Benedicamus Domino'. As in the St Martial *organa*, melismatic chant is set in note-against-note style, now known as *discantus*, and syllabic chant is set melismatically. The principle is now applied far more thoroughly however (though by no means invariably); but *discantus* is strictly note-against-note only if the mode in each part is the same; more commonly mode 1 in the upper voice is heard against mode 5, or even a series of double longs, in the lower.

Franco divided *discantus* into three categories: 'discantus alius simpliciter prolatus, alius truncatus qui oketus dicitur, alius copulatus qui copula nuncupatur' (CSM, xviii, p. 26).* *Oketus*, or hocket, involved an alternation of rests and notes in two parts in such a way that the notes of one part sounded during the rests of another (ibid., pp. 77–9). *Copula* is a much debated term, but according to Franco it meant a quick passage, evidently cadential, resembling either mode 2 or mode 6 (according to our enumeration) but differing from either both in notation and in being performed more quickly (ibid., pp. 75–7).

The method of alternation between *discantus* and melismatic *organum* in settings of responsorial chant may be seen clearly at work in the verse 'Notum fecit' of the Gradual 'Viderunt' (M1; references are to the numbering in Ludwig's *Repertorium*):

* 'One kind of *discantus* is laid out in a straightforward manner, a second is discontinuous and is called *oketus*, while the third is run on and is called *copula*'.

## Example 54

W¹, f. 21.

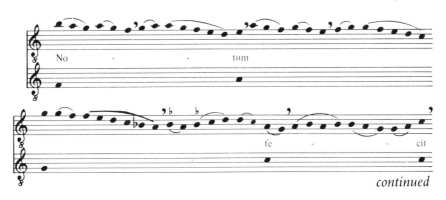

*continued*

*Translation* The Lord hath made known [his salvation].

The transcription of the sections in melismatic *organum*, here shown in 'non-committal' notation, is a matter of controversy. Some scholars, notably Waite, insist on a rigidly metrical transcription, and indeed there are many places where the grouping of ligatures suggests a modal pattern. But it is going too far to suggest that all Parisian *organum duplum* is in regular rhythm, and there can be little doubt that the melismatic sections as a whole correspond to the seventh of Anonymus IV's *modi irregulares*, which is unmeasured and is called *organum purum*. It is possible however that the passages suggestive of regular rhythm represent the hand of a reviser; and by the same token, a modal interpretation may be more suited to the manuscript versions as we have them, if not to the compositions in their original form. For as has been said, it would be rash to assume that any version of the *Magnus Liber* as we have it represents Leoninus' unaltered work. Even in W[1] the range of style is very wide; side by side with whole sections in melismatic *organum* we have such passages as the following in mode 2, from the verse 'Tamquam sponsus' to the respond 'Descendit de caelis' (02):

**Example 55**

W¹, f. 13v.

\* MS ♮ from here on

## *Organum triplum* and *quadruplum*

Of the dozen or so extant *organa tripla*, two are supposed to be by Perotinus, and the others are in the same style. The only two four-part *organa* ('Viderunt' and 'Sederunt') are likewise assumed to be his work; a third four-part piece, 'Mors', is a *clausula* (see below). Though the *organa* embody a distinction between *discantus* and melismatic *organum*, there is no rhythmical difference between them; all the upper parts are necessarily in regular rhythm throughout. In this music we see the first signs of a practice whereby a phrase is passed from one voice to another in imitative fashion, the ancestor of strict canon and in particular of a type in which all voices start simultaneously:

**Example 56**
(Gradual, *Exiit sermo*)

F, f. 18.

*continued*

143

* Exchange parts in repeat.

## *Clausulae* or *puncta*

These are evidently passages, or complete compositions, in *discantus* style: *punctum* or *punctus* is also the term for a section of an *estampie*. The controversy over their function, insofar as they survive independently in the sources, has been discussed above (p. 140). There are about 500 two-part and sixteen three-part *clausulae*, and one four-part *clausula* extant. They are usually settings of a single word—sometimes even a single syllable—taken from the melismas of Mass and Office responds or from the 'Benedicamus Domino'. Thus 'Mors' is from the Easter Alleluia 'Christus resurgens' (for a version of its music see *LU*, p. 827); 'In saeculum' is from the Easter Gradual 'Haec dies' (*LU*, p. 778; *GR*, p. 241); 'Domino' may be either from the same Gradual (verse 'Confitemi Domino') or from a setting of 'Benedicamus Domino'. Since the melodies of the latter are often drawn from Office responds their *clausulae* may bear instead a title drawn from the original text, e.g. 'Flos filius'—from the respond 'Stirps Iesse'—though this will indicate the complete melisma rather than merely the portion assigned to the word 'Domino'. The 'Benedicamus Domino'/'Flos filius' material is well presented in *HAM*, i, no. 28. The manuscripts usually group several settings of a particular melisma together, reiterating the text for each setting. Other settings consist of a double statement of the melisma, the words appearing once only. This is no argument against the substitution theory, however, for there are examples of this seemingly unliturgical practice even in the original discant sections of certain three-part *organa* (e.g. 'Haec dies': *HAM*, i, no, 31). It is possible, by carrying the substitution theory to absurd lengths, to create an entire Gradual, let us say, from separate *clausulae* (see *HAM*, i, no, 30). The 'independent composition' theory draws much of its strength from the facts that some *clausulae*, such as the three-part 'Flos filius' and the four-part 'Mors', can be assigned to no extant complete work; and that the *clausula* is the direct ancestor of the motet, which is undeniably an independent form.

*Conductus*

The polyphonic conductus, which may be in two, three or four parts, presents severe problems of transcription, in that the text is set syllabically, thus restricting the use of ligatures. Though the nature of the problem is often obscured in modern writings, its essence is usually a choice between fifth mode on the one hand and first or second mode on the other. It may be illustrated by two versions of the opening phrase of a well-known three-part conductus, 'Hac in anni ianua':

**See Example 57 overleaf**

A second-mode interpretation is offered by Janet Knapp in *CM*, vi, p.38. Apel (op. cit., p.222) transcribes the piece in duple metre. Though the choice here is particularly difficult, there are often factors which can affect the decision. Occasional groups of six or more notes on a single syllable render the fifth mode more appropriate in such cases than the first or second. On the other hand, many conductus are equipped with completely melismatic sections in modal notation

**Example 57**

(a)

Hac in an - ni ia - nu - a, hoc in ia - nu - a - ri - o

(b)

Hac in an - ni ia - nu - a,

hoc in ia - nu - a - ri - o

* From here top part third higher in MS F.

*Translation* At the beginning of the year, in this January

(called *caudae*, although they are by no means confined to the end of a piece) which are in first or second mode. This does not necessarily mean that the syllabic portions must be transcribed in the same mode: the important thing is that the style should remain constant.

When there are actual musical correspondences between the body of the conductus and its *caudae*, then the problem is solved.

The tenor of a conductus is usually newly composed, and is always independent of any Gregorian chant. There are however examples of simple, entirely syllabic conductus with tenors derived from secular song or from monophonic conductus. The texts are metrical and strophic, exactly as in the monophonic form. Though the purely syllabic type can have a simple charm, it is in the conductus with *caudae* that the genre reaches its highest level. There is all the lofty phraseology of *organum*, combined with a concession to pure euphony, in such passages as the following:

**Example 58**

(*Relegentur ab area*)                                    F, f. 202v.

*continued*

*etc.*

## Motet

The very earliest motets are simply two-part *clausulae* with words added syllabically to the upper part.* One manuscript (the St Victor MS) shows cues of motet-text in the margin of pages devoted to *clausulae* (see *NOHM*, ii, p. 349). Elsewhere the music was newly written out, but in view of the syllabic underlay the notation of the upper part or parts ceases to be modal. Nevertheless the rhythm can be inferred from the parent *clausula* if known; but where no such prototype is extant the rhythm can only be guessed at. The problem here is similar to that of the syllabic conductus.

There is a further connection between the motet and the conductus in that there are examples of three- and four-part motets with only one upper-voice text, of which the upper voices also survive separately without the tenor. In such cases the upper parts are written in score and the tenor (if it is present) is added separately.

---

* However, the St Martial MSS (12th cent.) already include settings of 'Benedicamus Domino' in which the upper part carries a troping text while the lower has the liturgical text set to the plainsong in long notes (see Handschin in *Kongressbericht Basel 1924*). The Notre-Dame repertory includes two three-part *organa* in which the two upper parts share a single troping text (Ludwig, *Repertorium*, pp. 100, 105). In none of these cases can a melismatic original be found. Such pieces, while they may not strictly qualify as 'motets', show that the technique of simultaneous troping was established very early, even without the prior existence of a purely melismatic version of the music. The Notre-Dame repertory also includes motets based on sections of existing three- and four-part *organa*, in both 'sustained-note' and 'discantus' style, mostly with a single text for the upper parts. These do not however necessarily predate the earliest works based on 'self-standing' *clausulae*. In all types of 'derived' motets the addition of parts to, or subtraction of parts from the model, is frequent.

(The reason for writing the tenor in this way is largely in order to save space: the melismatic tenor occupies much less room than the syllabic upper part or parts. When each upper part has a different text then these too are usually written out separately.) In the Florence manuscript there are two examples of a four-part work, each consisting of three parts in score followed by a tenor. Various selections from these four parts occur in other sources (see Ludwig, *Repertorium*, i, p. 99). In Wolfenbüttel, MS 1206 (W²), are seventeen three-part motets of which the two upper parts share a single text and are notated in score; some of these are also found elsewhere either as two-part *clausulae* (tenor and *duplum*) or as two-part conductus (*duplum* and *triplum*) or both (see Ludwig, op. cit., pp. 176–80). In the second case a two-part *clausula* appears to have given rise to a two-part conductus by way of a three-part motet. Occasionally one may see a three-part motet in which all three parts are identical to those of a three-part *clausula*, as in 'Flos filius' (*HAM*, i, no. 28i); but in this case a two-part motet, consisting of the tenor and *duplum* of the *clausula*, is also extant, and the relationship between all three compositions is difficult to establish.

A number of motets from the 'Notre-Dame' group of manuscripts are independent of any known *clausula*; but they do not differ essentially in style. Two-part motets initially had a Latin text in the *duplum* which alluded in some way to the text in the tenor: thus the text was a kind of trope. Just as the sequence in its melismatic form—a 'successive' trope—later acquired a syllabic text, so the *clausula*—a 'simultaneous' troping of plainsong—became a motet by the same process. Three-part motets at first shared the same text in the upper parts; later, a third part might have another Latin text or else a French one; and there are early examples of a single French text in a two-part work and of two French texts in three-part works. Normally a text in French would be profane in character, and it is not uncommon for a Marian text in Latin to be combined with a French text on the subject of profane love. Such a combination would seem to lead the motet right outside the liturgical (though not necessarily the clerical) sphere; and this is even truer of works in which the only sacred element is the tenor with its meagre text. But the whole question of the social function of the motet is one which has never been fully elucidated.

## The Bamberg manuscript (Ba)

The next stage in the history of the motet may be illustrated by this source, which dates from the late thirteenth century but contains a much earlier repertoire. It is a remarkably uniform document, with 100 motets, a conductus and seven textless pieces. The regular layout of two columns on each page, one for each upper voice, with the tenor across the bottom on a single stave, is interrupted only twice in the motets. Three works on ff. 31v–34 (Nos. 52–4) are written in three columns, the reason being that the tenor in these cases is a French song complete with text. No. 92 (f. 57v) ingeniously combines two tenors, which are written on two staves at the bottom of the page; this is the only four-part piece in the collection. Another kind of combination is shown in No. 81 (f. 52v), in which the song 'Robin m'aime, Robin m'a' from *Li Gieus de Robin et de Marion* appears with the tenor 'Portare':

**Example 59**

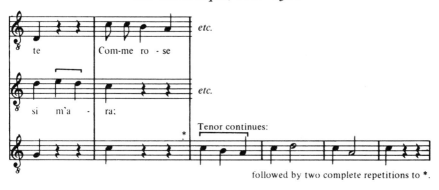

*followed by two complete repetitions to* \*.

*Translation  Triplum:* Greatly was I saddened by the departure of my love, the pretty one with the bright face, who is white, tinged with red like a rose. *Motetus:* Robin loves me, Robin has me, Robin has asked for me and he will have me;

Needless to say a certain amount of juggling with the tenor is necessary in order to preserve the French song in more or less its original state. The conductus, which is also found in a manuscript at Turin and in the Montpellier manuscript shortly to be described, has a short text in four stanzas beginning 'Deus in adiutorium.' In monophonic form it appears amongst the introductory material for First Vespers of the Circumcision in the Office of Pierre de Corbeil (p. 131). The textless pieces are written in score like the conductus although they have a plainchant tenor. They are generally taken to be for instruments, though only one bears a title suggestive of this: No. 105 is marked *In seculum viellatoris—In seculum* of the vielle-player—and even this is hardly conclusive. These seven pieces are perhaps best thought of as latter-day *clausulae,* sharing with them their problems of performance and function (No. 108 is in *HAM,* i, no. 32e). They do however employ hocket (see above, p. 141), a technique which might be thought to be of an instrumental nature, at least in origin.

The notation of this source is mensural, largely of a primitive type known as pre-Franconian. In this it corresponds to a section of the Montpellier manuscript now to be considered.

## *The Montpellier manuscript (Mo)*

This important source contains eight fascicles which between them cover practically a century of musical and notational development. The first fascicle contains the 'Deus in adiutorium' just mentioned; two of the Bamberg textless pieces with a fourth, texted, part added; a three-part 'Benedicamus Domino' and a textless piece of the Bamberg type ('Portare') which are unique to this source, and five three-part *organa* from the Notre-Dame repertory (though the last is found in this source only), but in mensural, not modal, notation. The second fascicle has seventeen motets in four parts; the third, eleven motets with a Latin *duplum* and French *triplum*, with four two-part motets; the fourth, twenty-two Latin motets in three parts; the fifth, one textless *In seculum* (actually the same as No. 2 of the manuscript and one of the Bamberg pieces) and 104 three-part motets; the sixth, 75 French motets in two parts; the seventh, 39 three-part motets and a few miscellaneous addenda; and the eighth, a conductus on the same text as No. 1 of the manuscript, and 42 three-part motets. Of these eight fascicles the first six are written in some form of pre-Franconian mensural notation, and are to be dated *c.* 1280; the seventh and eighth use Franconian notation with various modifications. The seventh fascicle was written at the very end of the thirteenth century and the eighth perhaps in the second decade of the fourteenth. All in all it is not too much to say that every important aspect of thirteenth-century music is represented in this enormous collection.

In mensural notation it is the actual shape of the notes and ligatures, and not merely the disposition of the latter, which indicates the rhythm. To begin with, the forms ¶ , ■ and ◆ were adopted to represent the long, breve and semibreve respectively. As for the ligatures, their interpretation depends on the concept of 'normal meaning for normal shape'. A 'normal' ligature was said to possess both propriety and perfection; deprived of one or both of these attributes its values changed. Thus a 'normal' two-note ligature ( ⊳ descending and ⌐ or ⌐ ascending,* meaning breve-long as in modal

---

* The second of the ascending forms gradually replaced the first as being easier to write. Steps towards a distinction in the shape of notes and ligatures are already found in the work of Johannes de Garlandia (*c.* 1250).

notation) could be modified as follows:

|  | Descending | Ascending |  |
|---|---|---|---|
| *sine proprietate, cum perfectione* | ↘ | ♩ , ♩ or ♩ | Long-long |
| *cum proprietate, sine perfectione* | ↘ | ♪ | breve-breve |
| *sine proprietate, sine perfectione* | ↘ | ♪ or ♪ | long-breve |

A final refinement was ↳ (↳), or ↳ (↳), *cum opposita proprietate*, meaning two semibreves. This also applied to the first two notes in ligatures of three or more notes; but in other ligatures of more than two notes all middle notes were breves. Since most music was in triple time there were elaborate rules governing the value of the long (perfect or imperfect) and the breve (*recta* or *altera*). This system is due in large part to Franco of Cologne, whose treatise *Ars cantus mensurabilis* may be dated *c.* 1260.

Once the motet had emerged from the womb of the Notre Dame liturgical repertory, it underwent little real stylistic development until the very end of the century. Differences of notation did not really affect the issue. The tenor continued to be laid out in *ordines* or phrases based on one of the six modes, or sometimes on two of them in alternation.* In the upper parts there was greater freedom, but one still senses a considerable dependence on the modes, more noticeable in some pieces (especially where the third mode is retained) than in others. A very few pieces—one in Montpellier, two in Bamberg—are in duple metre.

Towards the end of the century, however, Petrus de Cruce, who appears to have come from Amiens, did make real musical and notational innovations. He was the first composer, according to Jacobus of Liège (*c.* 1330), to write more than three semibreves to a breve. This he would do in the *triplum* of a three-part motet; and since the declamation remained syllabic, the style began to approach a fairly rapid *parlando*. Any group of semibreves occupying the space of a breve was marked off at each end by a point known as the *punctus divisionis*. Two of his compositions (the only ones extant), identified by citations in theoretical works, are found at the beginning of the seventh fascicle of the Montpellier manuscript. The idiom may be illustrated by the opening of the first motet (No. 253):

* A further device was to state the tenor twice or even three times in a different rhythmic pattern, a method later used by Petrus de Cruce, Philippe de Vitry and others.

**Example 60**

Mo, f. 270.

*Translation   Triplum:* If Love had any power I ought to have perceived it, who have served him\* all my life with loyal heart. *Motetus:* At the renewal of the fair weather one must, etc.

\* The participle *servie* indicates the usual medieval feminine gender for 'love'; yet although the composer undoubtedly set it thus it is almost certain that the poet originally wrote 'servi', appropriate to (masculine) personified Love, yielding a normal octosyllabic line.

Whatever the merits of this style, it was destined to herald a revolution of unparalleled thoroughness.

*Manuscripts of Turin and Las Huelgas; the Roman de Fauvel (Tu, Hu, Fa)*

These are all early fourteenth-century manuscripts which retain strong links with the previous century. The Turin manuscript has affinities with the Bamberg manuscript. A particular interest of the codex from Las Huelgas (a monastery near Burgos in northern Spain) is the use of conductus style for settings of the Ordinary of the Mass. The *Roman de Fauvel* is a satirical poem on the vices of *Flatterie, Avarice, Vilenie, Variété, Envie* and *Lacheté*. In one source (Paris, Bibl. Nat., fr. 146) this poem is provided with musical interpolations constituting an anthology of monophonic and polyphonic pieces ranging over more than a century up to 1316, when the music was copied.

The bulk of this music belongs firmly to the *ars antiqua*, except for the thirty-four motets. Indeed Apel has regarded even these as belonging to the preceding epoch on the grounds of their notation, and in particular the fact that the upward and downward tails on semibreves are a later addition to the manuscript. The former is the *semibrevis minima* or minim and a cornerstone of the *ars nova*. But the point is not its actual presence or otherwise in the source (whether or not as a later addition) but its inherent presence in the music itself. Since the *Roman de Fauvel* includes a number of motets cited by Philippe de Vitry in his *Ars nova* (whether they are actually by him is another matter); and since this treatise specifically deals with the interpretation of groups of two, three, four, five and six unmarked semibreves in terms of the minim as a basic unit, the conclusion is inescapable that in the polyphonic music of this source we have precisely the kind of situation with which Philippe de Vitry was attempting to deal.

# Bibliography

## Musical sources

Practically all the major sources are available in facsimile. $W^1$ is edited by Baxter (to be used with Hughes, *Index*); $W^2$, F and Ma (Madrid 20486) are in *PMMM*, ii, x–xi and i respectively; the St Victor MS (Paris, Bibl. Nat., lat. 15139) is edited by E. Thurston. The Bamberg MS is edited by Aubry (*Cent Motets*), the Montpellier by Rokseth (*Polyphonies*), the Las Huelgas by Anglès, the Turin by Auda and the *Roman de Fauvel* by Aubry. The first four of the second group include transcriptions, and the first three extensive commentaries. Among editions of Notre-Dame music may be signalled the transcriptions of two-part *organa* in Waite, *Rhythm*, of the three- and four-part *organa* by Husmann in *PAM*, ix, of 35 conductus by Knapp in *CM*, vi and of the works of Perotinus by Thurston. The motets of the important 'La Clayette' MS are now in *CMM*, LXVIII.

### Literary sources

The most important theorists are Anonymus IV (Ed. Reckow; Coussemaker, *Scriptores*, i, pp. 327–65), Johannes de Garlandia (*De mensurabili musica*, ed. Reimer; partly in Coussemaker, op. cit., i, pp. 175–82; the unauthentic version included in Hieronymus de Moravia's *Tractatus de musica*, ibid., i, pp. 97–117 and ed. Cserba, pp. 194–229) and Franco of Cologne (*Ars cantus mensurabilis*, in *CSM*, xviii; in the version included by Hieronymus de Moravia, ed. Coussemaker, op. cit., i, pp. 117–36 and also Cserba, pp. 230–59). Anonymus IV wrote after 1272, since he refers to the court of the last King Henry (Henry III died in that year); he was almost certainly an Englishman and possibly a monk at Bury St Edmunds. Johannes de Garlandia, perhaps Anonymus IV's 'Johannes dictus primarius', is dissociated by Reimer from the famous English scholar of that name; but the date of his treatise will be about 1250. Anonymus IV refers to a 'Franco primus', who was evidently a Parisian, as well as to Franco of Cologne, and in one source the *Ars cantus mensurabilis* is indeed attributed to Franco of Paris (ed. Gerbert, *Scriptores*, iii, pp. 1–16); but Franco of Cologne's authorship is nowadays regarded as certain. Magister Lambertus' treatise, attributed to 'a certain Aristotle' in the source, is in Coussemaker, *Scriptores*, i, pp. 251–81; his identity is established with the aid of another anonymous treatise, the 'Anonymus of St Emmeram', 1279 (ed. Sowa). The contributions of Petrus de Cruce are enshrined in the fourteenth-century compilations of Robert de Handlo and John Hanboys (Coussemaker, op. cit., i, pp. 383–403, 403–48), as well as in the work of Jacobus of Liège (see especially ibid., ii, pp. 401, 429). Walter Odington (ibid., i, pp. 182–250) has been newly edited in *CSM*, xiv; for St Augustine see bibliography to Chapter 1. Minor treatises edited separately include those of Alfredus or Amerus (ed. J. Kromolicki, 1909) and Dietricus (ed. H. Müller (1886)).

### Studies

Ludwig's *Repertorium*, supplemented by Gennrich, *Bibliographie* and Ludwig in *AMw*, v (1923), is basic. An important contribution was made by J. Handschin, 'Zur Geschichte von Notre-Dame' in *AcM*, iv (1932), pp.

5–17, 49–55, 104–5. The rhythmic interpretation of the two-part *organa* is the subject of Waite, *Rhythm* (which may be consulted for additional bibliography up to 1954), while more specific questions of rhythm are referred to by Sanders in *JAMS*, xv (1962), pp. 249–91. For the problems of conductus-rhythm see G. A. Anderson in *JAMS*, xxvi (1973), 288–304. An important criticism of Ludwig's substitution theory was made in Harrison, *Music in Medieval Britain*, pp. 122–6. His arguments have been countered by Waite, 'The Abbreviation of the *Magnus liber*' in *JAMS*, xiv (1961), pp. 147–58; subsequently two important articles by Husmann have appeared: 'The Enlargement of the *Magnus liber organi*...' in *JAMS*, xvi (1963), pp. 176–203, and 'The Origin and Destination of the *Magnus liber organi*' in *MQ*, xlix (1963), pp. 311–30; the most recent survey of the entire problem is Flotzinger, *Der Discantussatz*. (See also H. Tischler in *ML*, l (1969), pp. 273–9.) A further important contribution is A. Machabey, 'À Propos des Quadruples Perotiniens' in *MD*, xii (1958), pp. 3–25; the latest review of the identity of Perotinus is provided by H. Tischler, 'Perotinus Revisited', in *Aspects*, pp. 803–17. A substantial bibliography of the thirteenth century is incorporated in Rokseth's *Polyphonies*, iv, itself a masterly volume of commentary on the period; see further the studies of Reckow (*Die Copula*) and Apfel in the Bibliography.

# 6 French music in the fourteenth century

*The* Ars nova *and Philippe de Vitry*

France in the early fourteenth century was in a state of musical ferment. On the one hand were the progressives, led by Philippe de Vitry and Johannes de Muris; and on the other the conservative musicians, of whom the most profound was the author of the *Speculum Musicae*, Jacobus of Liège. One of his criticisms was that the new, smaller note-values introduced by the moderns were identical with the old values in actual effect by virtue of the slowing down of tempo—the old composers, such as Petrus de Cruce, he said, really had greater rhythmic variety. It is true that at that level the modern music was more uniform in style; but the protagonists of the *ars nova* had the tremendous advantage of retaining the old values, though at a greatly reduced speed, and consequently of being able to organize the metrical structure of their music on a much broader scale.

Philippe de Vitry, well-known as poet and ecclesiastic, is a vague figure to the musician. His surviving works amount to fifteen motets at the very outside, including some highly dubious cases and one work whose text only survives. Of the fourteen with music, only six are referred to as by Philippe either in a musical source or an external literary source—and not all these attributions are trustworthy. One of them supports the doctrine that a motet cited in the *Ars nova* may be taken to be by him. As for the treatise itself, which may be dated *c.* 1320, it survives only in a variety of corrupt or abbreviated forms, with a varying relationship to what he must originally have written—if indeed the work ever existed as a formal literary product. The earliest source (itself only from the late fourteenth century) is merely a summary, but valuable in that it deals with the *ars vetus* before the *ars nova*. The treatment of the *ars vetus* must inevitably have formed an integral part of Philippe de Vitry's teaching on rhythm; and indeed he certainly taught on other musical subjects as well. The summary also makes it clear that the treatment of the *ars nova* itself is deficient in the other sources: in particular they omit the detailed treatment of prolation.

The fundamental doctrine of the *ars nova* is the analogy between the three relationships of breve to long, semibreve to breve, and minim to semibreve. Franco of Cologne had already stated that the relationship of the semibreve to the breve was comparable to that between the breve and the long: and, since for him *modus* was always perfect, the *tempus* or beat was also inherently perfect and therefore contained three semibreves (*semibreves minores*). The second of a pair of semibreves was to be doubled in length on the analogy of the *brevis altera* (*semibrevis maior*). When Petrus de Cruce and his followers increased the permissible number of semibreves occupying the time of a *brevis recta* from three to nine this slowed down the speed of the music but did not result in a variety of different *tempora* or beats.

To Philippe de Vitry however, basing his theories on the equality of all minims, it became necessary to make such distinctions. For him, Franco's breve was a *minimum tempus perfectum*: a triply-subdivided beat of the smallest possible value. Its constituent semibreves were from his point of view *semibreves minimae* and could be divided only into semiminims, since they correspond in speed to the minims of the new *tempora* (see Table 5). There was a difference, however, between the old and the new art, apart from the possibility of semiminims, in that in the former the second of two unmarked semibreves would be doubled in length, while in the latter the opposite was the case: thus a new concept of 'natural rhythm' obtained. Some of the motets of the *Roman de Fauvel* can be interpreted on the assumption that they correspond to Philippe de Vitry's *tempus perfectum minimum*, in which case groups of two semibreves should be performed as ♩ ♪ .

The remaining two varieties of *tempus perfectum* allowed two and three minims respectively to each of the three semibreves. Evidently these were respectively twice and three times as slow as *minimum tempus perfectum*, at least in theory. *Tempus imperfectum* was a beat of only two semibreves, each divisible into two or three minims (*minimum* and *maius tempus imperfectum* respectively).

Whereas the word *tempus* referred to the beat itself, the word *prolatio* ('setting-forth')* was used to describe the arrangement within the beat, except in the case of *minimum tempus perfectum*. This resulted in the dual terminology shown in the Table; later the bracketed words were omitted from the descriptions, so that *prolatio* could be held to mean the number of minims in a semibreve and *tempus* the number of semibreves to a breve.

## See Table 5 overleaf

It has already been mentioned (at the end of Chapter 5) that the minim could be inherently present in music without being present in the notation. If his breve is reduced to a crotchet, Philippe de Vitry's values for groups of two, three, four, five and six unmarked semibreves in *tempus imperfectum* are ♫ , ♫♩ , ♩♫♩ , , ♫♫♩ and ♫♫♩♩ ; and similar rhythms obtained in *tempus perfectum*. The underlying assumption here, of course, is that the *prolatio* is *maior*, as indeed it usually is in the early fourteenth century. In theory only rhythms which conflicted with these required the marking of the minim by an upward tail (for a short time a downward tail, indicating a *semibrevis maior*, was also employed), but it was soon realized that it was simpler to mark all the notes which were to be interpreted as minims. The *Roman de Fauvel* belongs to the very early stage, in which no semibreves carry tails except for some additions in a later hand, mostly of downward tails. Moreover the *tempus* is very rarely marked, though we sometimes possess external information on this point from a theoretical source such as the *Ars nova* itself. Transcriptions of this music inevitably involve a certain amount of conjecture.

French music of the fourteenth century also knew the possible extension of the old *duplex longa* to three longs. It became known as the *maxima* and its relation to the long *maximodus* or *modus maximarum*. The possible permutations are given in Table 5(2); and they could in theory be combined with any of the four 'prolations', giving a total of sixteen possible mensurations and a variation of

---

* *Prolatio* is used by Franco to mean the performance of music as opposed to its written appearance.

**Table 5:** French *ars nova* notation

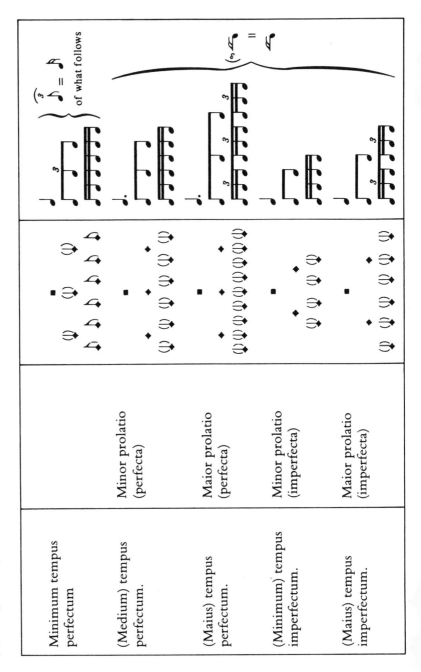

*(1) Tempus and prolatio*

| | | |
|---|---|---|
| Minimum tempus perfectum | Minor prolatio (perfecta) | |
| (Medium) tempus perfectum. | Maior prolatio (perfecta) | |
| (Maius) tempus perfectum. | Minor prolatio (imperfecta) | |
| (Minimum) tempus imperfectum. | Maior prolatio (imperfecta) | |
| (Maius) tempus imperfectum. | | |

*(2) Modus and maximodus*

from sixteen to eighty-one minims to the *maxima*. The combinations of *modus* and *tempus* were indicated by various signs, which are rarely found in the sources, however.

A feature of the *ars nova* was the employment of red notes. Their use, described in a complex manner in the sources, can be reduced to two fundamental points; the imperfecting of a note or group of notes which would otherwise have been perfect; and the raising of a note by an octave. (No instance of the latter use is known.)

## The motet

The following complete short work illustrates the simpler style of *ars nova* motet in the *Roman de Fauvel*. *Tempus* is assumed to be imperfect, and groups of more than two semibreves are interpreted according to the principles of Philippe de Vitry. The tenor is interesting. A rhythmic *ordo* in the old first mode is repeated eight times against a threefold melodic repetition. The technique of rhythmic repetition has become known in modern times as isorhythm, and it was to assume great importance in fourteenth- and fifteenth-century music:

**Example 61**

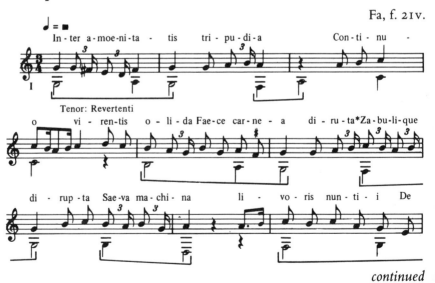

Fa, f. 21v.

*continued*

glo - ri - a    se    re - fo - vent    mu - tu - a    Per in - nu - me-

ra    mi - li - tis    in    au - la    re    gi - ae    cae -

- le - stis    ag - mi - na:    Sic    po - li    cli - ma - ta    se - re    na    Sa - cro    iu - bi-

- lo    re - ni - tent    ple - na.    Non i - ta    sub    a - e - ris

li - mi - te    vin - ci - tur;    Nam al - ter    al - te - ri - us    Ho - no -

re    te - ri - tur    li - ben - ti - us    Ex - tran - ne - o    quam    cu - i

sub - di - tur    Et non ad - ver - ti - tur    Quod di - vi - sum    reg - num    de - so - la - bi - tur.

\* MS durita

Trent MS 87, no. 177 (ff. 231v–232r), adds a middle part *O livor anxie*. The latter was also present in the now fragmentary *Chansonnier de Trémouilles*, dated 1376, to judge from the entry *O livor* in its list of 'Motez ordenez et escriz ci aprés'. The middle voice cannot be included in this transcription, as it is associated in Trent with a slightly different version of the top part, and may itself have suffered corruption. On the other hand Trent corrects a number of obvious errors in Fa. See the Critical Commentary to *PMFC*, i, and E. Droz and G. Thibault in *Revue de Musicologie*, vii (1926), pp. 1–8.

*Translation* Among the sweet-smelling joys of an ever-burgeoning paradise, having overthrown the impurities of the flesh and having broken the evil machinations of the devil [and] of Envy his messenger, they refresh themselves from each others' glory throughout the innumerable ranks of the heavenly host in the hall of the royal palace: thus the untroubled regions of heaven fully resound with the sacred chant of joy. Not so is [Envy] vanquished within the limit of the lower air; for each man is crushed by the honour of another more readily than he is subjected to any other external influence, and does not take heed that a kingdom divided shall be laid waste.

If the *modus* is imperfect the transcription will be in $\frac{2}{4}$ time. This may occur not only by itself, but also in connection with perfect *maximodus*, as in the well-known 'Firmissime/Adesto/Alleluia', which has been attributed to Philippe de Vitry. In another work which may also be his, 'Garrit Gallus/In nova fert animus/Neuma', the *modus* is alternately perfect and imperfect, the latter being indicated in the tenor by means of red notation:

**Example 62**

Fa, f. 44v.

etc.

⌐  ¬ = red notation

A French motet, 'Douce playsence/Garison selon nature/Neuma quinti toni', is attributed to Philippe de Vitry by the poet Gace de la Bigne, and it is cited twice in the *Ars nova*. Here both *modus* and *tempus* are varied: the following opening illustrates its rhythmic orbit:

**Example 63**

[rather slow]

*continued*

*Translation Triplum:* It is a sweet pleasure to love loyally, for otherwise a lover could not easily suffer that burning pain which is born of love. When those looks, by her subtle attraction, in looking . . . *Motetus:* [Every human creature] hopes that nature will cure him of his pain . . .

There are also a few four-part works by Philippe de Vitry. The end of 'O canendi/Rex quem metrorum/Contratenor/Rex regum' will illustrate the prevailing texture and also the technique of hocket as practised at the time (cf. p. 141):

**See Example 64 opposite**

The texts of fourteenth-century motets are as often satirical or polemical as religious in character; others are frankly profane. It is unlikely that the famous decree of Pope John XXII, which was issued at Avignon in 1324/5 and prohibited complex polyphony in the modern style, had much effect on the development of fourteenth-century church music as a whole. It probably curbed a growing

**Example 64**

tendency to revert to religious subjects in the motet, as exemplified by 'Firmissime/Adesto/Alleluia', as well as several other works by Philippe de Vitry and Machaut's 'Bone Pastor', which was written for the election of Guillaume de Trie as archbishop of Rheims in 1324. But the old books of Notre Dame, with their complex settings of respond, Gradual, Alleluia and 'Benedicamus Domino', which would certainly have provoked as much opposition as the modern style, had fallen out of use except possibly in remote areas like St Andrew's in Scotland, and the general tendency everywhere was to write severely functional settings of the liturgy, particularly the Ordinary of the Mass, in conductus or at the very most a simple motet style. Pope John's naive remarks about simple consonances could not be taken literally, but their spirit was widely accepted at first. Even so, Philippe de Vitry, who was after all to become bishop of Meaux in 1351, apparently found it possible to write a motet, 'Petre Clemens/Lugentium siccentur/Tenor', on the election of Pope Clement VI in 1342; while Machaut's *Messe de Nostre Dame* (discussed below) contains lengthy passages in hocket which would hardly have found favour in the time of John.

## Music for the Ordinary of the Mass

It is in the fourteenth century that one finds the earliest settings of the complete, or nearly complete, Ordinary of the Mass. These are not unified works of art in the later sense, and in three of them—the so-called Masses of Toulouse, Tournai and Barcelona—we cannot even be certain that they are the work of a single composer in each case*. In fact they are exactly comparable to the plainsong 'Masses' (which however are without Credo) of the modern plainsong books, an arrangement which was beginning to be favoured during the preceding century. A fourth such work is of course Machaut's Mass, which is not only immeasurably superior to the other three, but is indeed one of the enduring monuments of medieval musical art. But it is legitimate to inquire whether its pretensions to unity are any

---

*Yet another such work is the Sorbonne (or Besançon) Mass, in part at least by Johannes Lambuleti. See Chailley in *AnnM*, ii (1954). Modern research continues to uncover various more or less haphazard groupings of unrelated movements.

greater than those of its companions. As far as tonality is concerned it is divided into two equal halves, the Kyrie, Gloria and Credo being in D minor (the final note of the plainsong in the Kyrie (A) being treated as the fifth of the chord), and Sanctus, Agnus and Ite in F major. From the point of view of style, however, the Kyrie is linked to the last three movements, since it is like them in motet style on a plainsong, while the Gloria and Credo stand together by being freely composed in conductus style. Thus the effect of the sharp tonal division is modified by the stylistic link between the two halves. The idea that the work is intentionally unified by a single melodic figure is a myth, the motive in question being ubiquitous in fourteenth-century music. All this perhaps does not greatly matter in the context of a liturgical performance, in which the individual movements (except for the Kyrie and Gloria) are separated; but in view of the subsequent history of the polyphonic Mass as a strongly unified entity, the point deserves serious consideration.

The title of the work has been much discussed. The suggestion that it was written for the coronation of Charles V at the Cathedral of Notre-Dame at Rheims in 1365 (Machaut was a canon of Rheims) is wholly without foundation. Perhaps the simplest theory—that of F. Ll. Harrison—is the best: that the work is a votive Mass of the Blessed Virgin Mary. It calls not for large forces but preferably for four solo singers; instruments are unnecessary although an organ may have doubled the tenor part in the motet-like sections.

## Guillaume de Machaut

Machaut has been called a 'worldly ecclesiastic'; but the imputation depends on an equation of life with art. Like Philippe de Vitry he was a poet and a diplomat as well as an ecclesiastic and a composer. His works are preserved in a series of beautifully copied manuscripts in which his complete poems are followed by sections devoted to *lais*, motets, the Mass, the *Hoquetus David*, ballades, rondeaux and *virelais* (usually in that order). The music for the *Remède de Fortune* is preserved in the context of the poem itself (Schrade in his edition removes these seven works to the end of the sections to which from a formal point of view they belong). There are also numerous 'unofficial' copies of various works.

Most of the *lais* are purely monophonic. They raise to a great height a form which had already reached distinction. It would seem that a purely melodic and rhythmic expressiveness could hardly go further than in a work like 'Par trois raisons' (no. 5). The double-versicle structure is used throughout each work, mostly with new music for each double versicle; frequently, however, each half of the versicle has its own repetition with *ouvert* and *clos* endings (first- and second-time bars), resulting in a four-fold repetition altogether. In *Le lay de la fonteinne* each monophonic section is separated by a three-part *chace*; of the twelve sections, nos. 2, 4, 6, 8, 10 and 12 are *chaces*. The *chace* in France was a three-part round. Those of Machaut differ from their few predecessors only in their extraordinary ingenuity, which may be illustrated by the following extract from the second *chace* (section 4) from *Le lay de la fonteinne*:

**Example 65**

[fast]

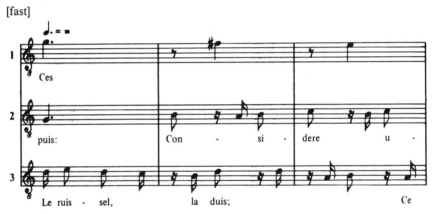

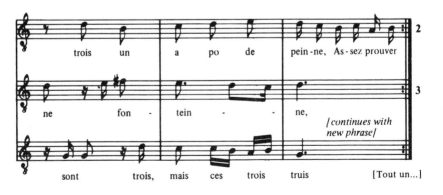

*Translation* That these three are one I can well prove without difficulty. Consider a spring, the stream, the conduit. These are three, but these three I find [to be all one . . . ]

The whole work amounts to 444 bars of quick $\frac{3}{8}$ in Schrade's transcription; but it would come to around 800 with all repetitions observed. *Le lay de confort*, which consists entirely of rounds, is even longer, with 616 bars (*c.* 1100 with repetitions). There are nineteen *lais* in all (including the one from the *Remède de Fortune*); they are followed in Schrade's edition by a *Complainte* and a *chanson roial* from the same poem. The polyphonic nature of nos. 18 and 19 has been recently demonstrated (see Bibliography).

The motets follow in the manuscripts. Many of them are entirely profane in subject-matter, apart from the liturgical tenor. The upper parts may be both French, both Latin, or the *motetus* Latin and the *triplum* French. If there is a fourth voice, it will be a contratenor sharing the range and rhythmic characteristics of the tenor. They are skilful compositions, but they do not show much advance on the style of Philippe de Vitry and the later *Roman de Fauvel* music. One feature, found in Philippe de Vitry but amplified by Machaut, is the *Introitus*, or prelude before the entry of the tenor (and contratenor). In Machaut, the tenor and contratenor may enter in the *Introitus*, prior to the commencement of the liturgical melody itself. Here is the *Introitus*, possibly instrumental, of the motet 'Christe qui lux/Veni Creator Spiritus/Tribulatio proxima est' (no. 21):

**Example 66**

*continued*

The *Messe de Nostre Dame* has already been discussed. It is followed in most manuscripts by the work known as *Double Hoquet* or *David Hoquetus*. The voices are entitled 'David Triplum', 'David Hoquetus' and 'David Tenor'. The tenor melody is the setting of the final word of the Alleluia 'Nativitas gloriosae virginis Mariae ex semine Abrahae orta de tribu Iuda clara ex stirpe David' (*GS*, pl. u). It is laid out in a complex fashion, eight rhythmic repetitions overlapping with three statements of the melody, followed by a fourth statement to a different rhyme which is heard four times. The work is clearly in the tradition of the appendix to the Bamberg manuscript (see above, p. 151).

The ballades (also called *ballades notées* to distinguish them from poems without music in this form) were amongst the most popular of Machaut's works. All but one are polyphonic: fifteen in two parts, eighteen in three parts and eight (including two from the *Remède de Fortune*) in four parts. The verse-form of the ballade is as follows: three stanzas with identical rhymes, the last line being a refrain common to each stanza. The *envoi* is not used. The musical setting invariably begins with a section which is repeated with *ouvert* and *clos* endings. What follows is usually free, but the very end may repeat the *clos* ending of the first section. No. 6, 'Doulz amis', has the form $AA_1BB_1$. There are two triple ballades, with one text to each voice-part (the three texts sharing the same rhythms and refrain-line): no. 17, 'Sans cuer/Amis/Dame' and no. 29, 'De triste cuer/Quant vrais amans/Certes'. The first of these is in canon: since each ballade has three stanzas the canon will of course be continuous until the end of the whole poem, when the three parts will stop at different times as in the *chace*. There is also one double ballade: the four-part 'Quant Theseus/Ne quier veoir' with tenor and contratenor (no. 34).

The rondeaux have much in common with the ballades. Of the twenty-two examples (one from the *Remède de Fortune*) one is without music and the others are in two, three or four parts. The poetic form is a single stanza in eight sections with an internal refrain, corresponding to the music as follows (italic letters indicate the refrain): *ABAAABAB*. In its most concise form each section corresponds to a single line of verse, as in the very short first rondeau:

**Example 67**

*continued*

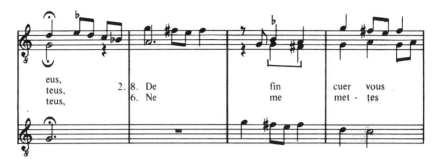

*Translation* Gentle gracious face, I have served you with a pure heart. Have pity on me, gentle gracious face; if I am a little timid, do not forget me. Gentle gracious face, I have served you with a pure heart.

The texture of the polyphony is interesting. The uppermost part, which does not appear in all the sources, has evidently been added to the melody and tenor on the analogy of the *triplum* in a motet. This also occurs in the ballades, and is of necessity an element in four-part textures; but far commoner in the three-part music is a single melodic part against a tenor and contratenor:

## See Example 68 opposite

This raises the whole question of Machaut's polyphonic technique in the ballades, rondeaux and polyphonic *virelais*, and the wider dissemination of these works compared with the *lais* and the monophonic *virelais*. (The *virelai*, or *chanson balladée*, had a bipartite musical structure and a three-stanza text in which the refrain links the

**Example 68**

*Translation* Your gentle looks

stanzas together: *ABBAABBAABBAA*. All but eight of Machaut's thirty-three *virelais* are monophonic, including the one from the *Remède de Fortune*).

Compared with his genius as a melodist, Machaut's ability as a polyphonic composer might appear at first sight to be very limited on the evidence of these works. But the motets show no insecurity of technique, and neither does the Mass; and it would be hard to show that the polyphonic rondeaux, ballades and *virelais* as a whole were earlier than these. The fact is that if Machaut writes what appears to be a perverse accompaniment to a charming melody, it is not because he could do no better. Apart from anything else, due allowance must be made for the probable timbre and pitch of the music. Nearly all these works are solo songs; and though they all demand an adult male voice (at least if the subject-matter is any guide), most of them will gain from an upward transposition of up to a fourth or so. There is evidence that male falsetto singing was well-known at the time; and the *instruments bas* or soft instruments—recorder, flute, vielle, psaltery, etc.—which would have accompanied such music were themselves small and high-pitched. A piece like the ballade (no. 20), 'Je sui aussi', seems to require a sustaining instrument for the tenor—rebec or portative organ, perhaps—and a plucked instrument for the contratenor: here it is transposed up a fourth and fairly liberally supplied with additional accidentals (shown of course above the staff):

**Example 69**

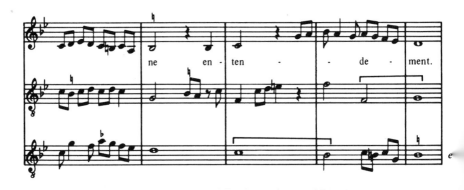

*Translation* I too am like one who is rapt, who has neither power, sense nor understanding.

When due allowance has been made for all this, however, and also for the possibility of mistranscription in the modern editions, it remains true that Machaut seems to be cultivating a deliberately 'modern' and somewhat dissonant style. That this was to the taste of his contemporaries is evident not only from the number of copies made outside Machaut's own 'edition', but also from the way in which these features of his style were taken up and developed still further by younger composers.

## Music of the later fourteenth century

Secular music after about 1360, when it was not merely a pale imitation of Machaut, cultivated a refinement, especially in the matter of rhythm, which was sometimes self-defeating. Syncopation had been part of the equipment taught by Philippe de Vitry (*CSM*, viii, p. 65, lines 59–63), but in this music the principle was carried to an extreme. A single note (semibreve or minim) would be added (or omitted) from the regular metre, and dropped (or replaced) at some later point in the music. Cross-rhythms were also extensively used. Composers of this period also experimented with extremes of chromaticism, though not in rhythmically complex pieces. On the other hand there was little attempt at variety of form or texture. Though a few pieces of this repertory are undeniably charming the overall effect is of preciosity. An extensive selection has been edited by Apel (*French Secular Music*) and he has dealt fully with its problems of notation in *The Notation of Polyphonic Music*. Not all the composers are French: one of the more interesting of them is an Italian, Matheo da Perugia. For it was at this period that French and Italian music began once again to tread similar paths after nearly a century of artistic independence.

After about 1400 a new simplicity began to be cultivated, particularly at the Burgundian court. Church music, which had fallen into obscurity, began once more to take its rightful place in musical art. Not all early fifteenth-century music belongs to the new manner: some of it is as complex as that of the preceding epoch. But it is more satisfactory to relate the various aspects of early fifteenth-century music to subsequent developments, and the multifarious strands of the transitional period will be gathered together at the beginning of Chapter 9.

# Bibliography

## Musical sources

The *Roman de Fauvel* was edited in facsimile by Aubry. The MS also includes 34 pieces (one polyphonic, the rest monophonic) by Jehannot de l'Escurel, first edited by Gennrich, *Rondeaux*, i, pp. 307–72, and more recently in *CMM*, XXX. The motets from this source, together with the remaining works of Philippe de Vitry, are in *PMFC*, i. The works of Machaut are in *PMFC*, ii–iii; there is also the edition of Ludwig. The Mass of Machaut is separately edited in *CMM*, II, in a pseudo-facsimile in *SMMA*, i, and by J. Chailley (Paris, 1948), A. Machabey (Liège, 1948) and H. Hübsch (Heidelberg, 1953). The Masses of Toulouse, Tournai and Barcelona are in *PMFC*, i; the Mass of Tournai is also in *CMM*, XIII. More sacred music of the period is in *CMM*, XXIX (music for the Mass) and *PMFC*, v (motets). Secular music is represented by Apel, *French Secular Music* and *CMM*, XXXVI and LIII. See also Bibliography for Chapter 9.

## Literary sources

The standard editions of Philippe de Vitry and Jacobus of Liège are those in *CSM*, viii and iii respectively; the sixth and seventh books of the latter are also in Coussemaker, *Scriptores*, ii, pp. 193–433, where they are misattributed to Johannes de Muris. The genuine works of Johannes, a protagonist of the *ars nova*, are printed ibid., iii, pp. 46–113 and in Gerbert Scriptores, iii, pp. 189–315; the important *Notitia artis musicae* of 1321, formerly known as *Ars novae musicae* and misdated 1319, is now available in *CSM*, xvii. *La Louange des Dames* (Machaut's lyric verse with a selection of 22 musical settings), and an anthology of ballades, rondeaux and virelais, have been edited by Wilkins.

## Studies

A large specialized bibliography up to *c.* 1958 is given in *NOHM*, iii, pp. 504–8. Note especially O. Gombosi, 'Machaut's *Messe Notre-Dame*' in *MQ*, xxxvi (1950), pp. 204–24, and Machabey, *Guillaume de Machaut*. A more recent introductory work is G. Reaney, *Machaut*. The difficulties of Machaut's notation are considered by R. Hoppin, 'Notational Licenses of Guillaume de Machaut' in *MD*, xiv (1960), pp. 13–27; the polyphonic nature of his last two *lais* is revealed by Hoppin, 'An unrecognized

Polyphonic Lai of Machaut' in *MD*, xii (1958), pp. 93–104, and M. Hasselman and T. Walker, 'More Hidden Polyphony in a Machaut Manuscript' in *MD*, xxiv (1970), pp. 7–16. An important recent general study is U. Günther, 'The 14th-Century Motet and its Development' in *MD*, xii (1958), pp. 29–58. For a commentary on Johannes de Muris see Michels, *Die Musiktraktate*.

# 7 Italian music in the fourteenth century

## Notation and sources

As in the case of French music, the notational system of Italian music is the clue to its rhythmic style. The fundamental treatise is the *Pomerium in arte musicae mensuratae* by Marchetus de Padua, written *c.* 1325. Compared with the *Ars nova*, however, this work suffers from two great disadvantages: it is written in a highly involved and scholastic style, which makes it very tiresome to read; and it is illuminated by hardly any contemporary sources. Nevertheless we learn from it that, as in France, the *tempus* could be perfect or imperfect, represented by three and two equal semibreves respectively. These were further subdivided as shown in Table 6 (a slightly simplified version of Marchetus' teaching). When fewer than the maximum number of untailed notes in any one *divisio* is found, the longer ones come last (*via naturae*) according to Franconian principles; and not in the new French manner except in (*senaria*) *gallica*, indicated by the letters G or .sg. Other rhythms are indicated by the use of the downward stem (*semibrevis maior*) and upward stem (*semibrevis minima*). But the minim never attained the status of a note with its own distinct value, so creating further divisions of the *tempus*, as it did in France. Nevertheless the minim was more freely used in the actual musical sources and in time the *quaternaria, senaria imperfecta* and *perfecta*, and *novenaria* came to occupy a similar position to Philippe de Vitry's 'four prolations'. As in France the tempo gradually slowed down and in fact there are few compositions extant in which the breve can be satisfactorily rendered by a crotchet or dotted crotchet: it is more likely to be transcribed as a value between the minim and the dotted semibreve according to circumstances.

**Table 6:** Italian *ars nova* notation

## (1) Tempus perfectum

| Divisio | | Abbreviation[1] |
|---|---|---|
| ternaria or perfecta | | .p. |
| senaria or senaria perfecta | | .s. or .sp. |
| novenaria | | .n. |
| duodenaria | | .d. |

## (2) Tempus imperfectum

| Divisio | | Abbreviation[1] |
|---|---|---|
| binaria or imperfecta | | .i. |
| quaternaria | | .q. |
| senaria gallica or senaria imperfecta[2] | | .sg. or .si. |
| octonaria | | .o. |

1. The abbreviations are those found in Rome, Bibl. Vat., MS Rossi 215.
2. The distinction between *senaria gallica* and *senaria imperfecta* lies in the values adopted when fewer than six unmarked semibreves are present. The former is the equivalent of Philippe de Vitry's *maius tempus imperfectum* (see p. 162); the latter uses the *via naturae*.

e.g.:

.sg. ♦♦♦♦ =

.si. ♦♦♦♦ =

One of the earliest documents of Italian notation, with a lower part notated in letters, is a fragment of keyboard music which may have been written down by an Englishman (London, Brit. Mus., Add. 28550, the so-called Robertsbridge Fragment). It has been dated *c.* 1325 and contains dances in an Italian style and transcriptions from motets, two of them from the *Roman de Fauvel*. The former use the *ternaria* and *quaternaria* divisions of the breve, which at this stage is still the beat. For the *Roman de Fauvel* motets, the *senaria gallica* division might have been appropriate: but in fact all the minims are specifically notated in a normal *senaria imperfecta* (facsimiles in *EEH*, i, pls. 42–5; transcriptions in *CEKM*, i, nos. 1–5). Another early source is the Codex Rossi (Rome, Bibl. Vat., Rossi 215), the notation of which corresponds in many respects to the teaching of Marchetus. It has been dated *c.* 1350 and includes amongst other things a *caccia*, 'Or quà conpagni', in the *senaria gallica* (its complete contents in *CMM*, VIII, ii). Later sources include the finely written Squarcialupi Codex, written for an organist of Florence Cathedral and a major source of the works of Francesco Landini: it has been edited in full by Johannes Wolf.

## *The* caccia

The *caccia* is the earliest of the distinctive Italian trecento forms to reach maturity, though it is not an easy one to define. As a poem, it is a vividly descriptive piece with dialogue, generally of a hunting or similar scene. The verse-form varies, but the stanza generally consists of a large number of short lines of differing length. As for the music, it is invariably a canon in two parts, nearly always over a free bass. The concluding ritornello was borrowed from the madrigal at a fairly early stage: there are also examples of canonic madrigals and a canonic *ballata*, distinguishable by their verse-form.

There is an early description of the *caccia* in an anonymous treatise on word-setting attached to Antonio da Tempo's *Summa artis vulgaris dictaminis* (1332). It indicates a canonic form of up to five parts in which all voices begin simultaneously (with a different phrase: i.e. the *rondellus*). There is nothing like this extant in Italian music, and the earliest surviving *cacce* are in the standard form. Of these 'Or quà conpagni', already mentioned, may serve as an illustration; it is without a ritornello, and there are two stanzas:

**Example 70**

Rossi MS, ff. 19v–20.

*continued*

*Translation* 'Now here, companions, here with great enjoyment, call the dogs here immediately!' 'Black-mouth, fetch, fetch!' 'White-skin, stay here, stay!' 'I think I see a chamois!' 'Where is it coming from?' 'From here, from here!' 'Which way is it going?'

However, the ritornello is found in some only slightly later works, such as the famous 'Tosto che l'alba del bel giorno appare' by Ghirardello da Firenze; and it may be absent from rather later *cacce*, such as 'Cacciando per gustar' by 'Magister Zacharias'.* Here the tenor, after its initial melisma, adds a lively commentary:

## See Example 71 opposite

*The madrigal*

Like the *caccia*, the madrigal appears in a stable form at an early date. It consists of two, three or four short stanzas (much shorter than in the *caccia*), followed by a ritornello of two lines. The ritornello does not imply a musical repeat of anything that has gone before (though in some cases the music of the ritornello itself is repeated to accommodate the text); the word is to be explained rather as a verbal 'turning-back' in the sense of an explanation or resolution of the allegory or conceit proposed at the beginning (cf. French *envoi*, Provençal *tornada*, which however require a partial musical

---

* Although described as a papal singer in the Squarcialupi Codex he cannot be identified with Nicholaus Zacharie, papal singer in 1420 and subsequently, the style of the latter's attested music being too dissimilar from that ascribed to Magister Zacharias. Through a number of somewhat tenuous links an identification with Antonio Zachara da Teramo is at least a possibility. In Example 71 Wolf's verbal text has been lightly emended.

**Example 71**

Squarcialupi MS, f. 176v.

*continued*

[na] *etc.*

*Translation* (I and II) Hunting through rough mountains and dangerous woods in order to taste that treasure, I found in a copse with small golden trees plenty of flowers, open and shut. Tasting and smelling the finest of them... *Tenor:* 'Any old rags, any old timber, any old glass, any old iron, any old broken copper?' 'Needles and spindles!' 'Haberdashery for sale, my lady!'

repetition of the last stanza). It is emphatically not a refrain. It is usually distinguished, musically, from the main part of the setting by a change of metre.

The madrigals and *cacce* of three early composers—Magister Piero, Giovanni da Firenze and Jacopo da Bologna—have been collected together in *PMFC*, vi. By far the majority of the works are madrigals (there is one *ballata* by Jacopo), and a very considerable majority of the madrigals are for two voices. Unlike the French chanson of the period and indeed the *caccia* in most cases, the madrigal is a form in which all parts are to be sung and are provided with words in the manuscripts, except in a few works in which *caccia* technique is adopted. The following example of a madrigal by Jacopo da Bologna illustrates the characteristics of the form:

**Example 72**

*continued*

189

*Translation* Phoebus entered with glowing rays into the house of the Ram, causing every field to put on grass and flowers, when I was fishing in a river of pure and clear water with that fair one who is more beautiful than Thetis, presenting the catch to her. She gave me thanks for it and I accepted them with a bow; I have never experienced a sweeter moment.

Note the tendency, typical of trecento music, for each bar in any one part to be occupied with notes of a single value (see bars 30–3 in this respect); or alternately with a rhythmic pattern which is enclosed

within a single bar and can be isolated as such (e.g. ♪ ♩ ♪ ;
♫ ♫♫ ). This 'bar-line' characteristic is strongly opposed to
French style and stems at least in part from the notational peculiarity
of Italian music in marking off each breve with a point (*punctus
divisionis*: the breve is represented here by ♩ and ♩. , and the two
sections are in *tempus imperfectum* (*divisio octonaria*) and *tempus
perfectum* (*divisio duodenaria*) respectively). Note finally the use of
hocket in the ritornello.

A few of Jacopo's madrigals are in three parts; but for a study of
this texture we may turn to the *ballata*.

*The ballata*

The Italian *ballata* is the formal equivalent of the French *virelai* (cf.
Machaut's alternative term *chanson balladée*). The great master of
this form is the blind Florentine organist Francesco Landini
(1325–97). Of his 154 compositions (*PMFC*, iv), 141 are in *ballata*
form (one being actually a *virelai* to French words); and of these, fifty
are for three voices. A good many of these have the text in the top
voice only, the other two parts being a tenor and contratenor. What
the modern listener will appreciate in Landini is the sheer beauty of
sound in his music, compared with (say) the asperity of Machaut.
This may, from the scholarly point of view, be an incorrect attitude:
but there is no reason why personal taste should not enter into the
appreciation of medieval music. Here is his *ballata* 'Nella mi vita':

**Example 73**

*continued*

[*D. C. al Fine*]

*Translation* I feel my heart fail within me, since I must part from you. With grief I set out since Fortune wills it, who forces it upon me. But wherever I may be, as long as I retain some strength, Lady, you cannot prevent me from being yours; since my soul can sooner die with my body than abandon you. I feel my heart fail within me, since I must part from you.

Landini's technical skill may be illustrated by the ritornello of his canonic madrigal 'De! dimmi tu,' where the canon is in three parts at the octave and fourth below:

**Example 74**

*Translation* Ah! What can I say of you compared with what I feel? Every estate of man seeks vanity.

His three-part madrigal 'Sì dolce non sonò' has an isorhythmic tenor (also in *HAM*, i, no. 54).

## Later Italian music; church music and keyboard music

Secular music in the later fourteenth century followed much the same path as in France, becoming somewhat artificial and stilted in its rhythmic complexity. The notation of Italian music had adopted some French features from about 1375, and eventually lost its own identity completely. Whereas French music underwent a rejuvenation soon after 1400 (so much so that it has been taken for the Renaissance itself), there was no such revival in Italy in the fifteenth century. Nevertheless, as we have seen, one of the more interesting composers setting French texts in the late fourteenth century was an Italian, Matheo da Perugia; and several Italian composers of the early fifteenth century compare favourably with the more backward-looking of their French counterparts.

Church music was not completely dormant in fourteenth-century Italy, though it forms a very small part of the whole corpus. A few scattered items occur in the volumes of *CMM*, VIII; liturgical music was either written in conductus style, or in discant style with the appropriate liturgical tenor; in either case it approached the idiom of the madrigal. The motet was also known: the few survivals include a fragment of one by Landini. Though the sum total of the extant repertoire appears small, it must be remembered that much of the anonymous church music associated with the papal chapel at Avignon is as likely to be by Italian as by French composers.

Apart from the existence of an early fourteenth-century English manuscript of keyboard music in Italian notation (see above, p. 184), Italy plays an important part in the history of keyboard music through the Faenza Codex (Faenza, Biblioteca Comunale, MS 117). This has been dated cautiously as late as *c.* 1420; but the style and character of the music is closely linked to that of the fourteenth century. Here the music is laid out on two staves in the modern fashion. There are a few liturgical pieces, consisting of organ verses designed for alternation with the liturgical plainsong: the Kyrie and Gloria of the Mass, and some other similar pieces. The rest of the contents consist of keyboard settings of vocal works, Italian and French, often highly ornamented. Some of the keyboard idioms adopted are startlingly modern:

**Example 75**

Faenza, Bibl. Com., MS 117, f. 57.

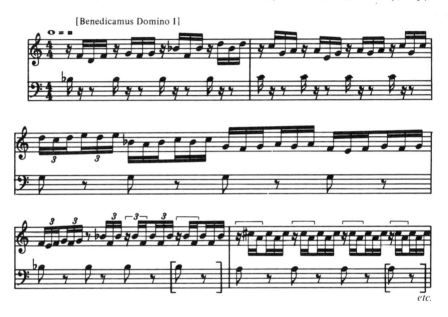

There is nothing like this in the extant keyboard music of any other nation before the sixteenth century.

# Bibliography

## Musical sources

The 'Robertsbridge Codex' is in *EEH*, i (facsimile) and *CEKM*, i (transcription). The *cacce* have been edited complete by Marrocco. The Squarcialupi Codex, which includes most of Landini's music, has been edited by Wolf; there is a complete edition of Landini by Ellinwood, and another in *PMFC*, iv. *PMFC* vi–ix contain more Italian secular music, while there are five volumes of trecento music in *CMM*, VIII. There is a facsimile of the Faenza Codex in *MSD*, x, and a complete transcription by Plamenac in *CMM*, LVII. Sacred music in *PMFC*, xii.

## Literary sources

The *Pomerium* of Marchetus is now in *CSM*, vi; the older edition was that of Gerbert, *Scriptores*, iii, pp. 121–88. The anonymous *Capitulum de vocibus applicatis verbis* attached to Antonio da Tempo's treatise has been edited by S. Debenedetti in *Studi Medievali*, ii (1906–7), pp. 59–82.

## Studies

A good bibliography is available in *NOHM*, iii, pp. 508–9: note especially Kurt von Fischer, *Studien*. In addition the study by L. Ellinwood, 'Francesco Landini and his Music' in *MQ*, xxii (1936), pp. 190–216, still has value. There is an excellent survey of the sacred repertory by von Fischer in *Proceedings of the Royal Musical Association*, c (1973–4). The three volumes entitled *L'Ars nova italiana del trecento* have many studies of value, including in vol. iii Plamenac's latest contribution to the Faenza literature. The two fundamental articles on that source, with transcriptions, are his 'Keyboard Music of the 14th Century in Codex Faenza 117' in *JAMS*, iv (1951), pp. 179–201 and 'new Light on the Codex Faenza' in *Kongressbericht Utrecht 1952* (Amsterdam, 1953), pp. 310–26. See also his 'A Note on the Rearrangement of Fa' in *JAMS*, xvii (1964), pp. 78–81, and Kugler, *Die Tastenmusik*.

# 8 English music from the Norman Conquest to the death of Dunstable

English music was last mentioned in Chapter 4 in connection with the early eleventh-century polyphony of the Winchester troper. It did not subsequently influence the course of the art in Europe until the early fifteenth century. The opportunity is therefore taken of extending the limits of this chapter beyond 1400 in order to throw light on the development of early fifteenth-century music in France and Burgundy. Of all the various peripheral repertories of the Middle Ages, that of England (or rather of Great Britain) is probably the most interesting to English-speaking readers, and possibly of the greatest intrinsic merit in absolute terms.

*Polyphony to c. 1300*

There is no evidence that a specifically English style of polyphony was in existence before about 1250 at the earliest. The oldest fragment after the Winchester collection, a two-part setting of the verse 'Ut tuo propitiatus' from the respond 'Sancte Dei pretiose' for the feast of St Stephen (facsimiles in *EEH*, i, pl. 1, *EBM*, iii, pl. 16 and Apel, *Notation*, p. 205; transcriptions in *HAM*, i, no. 26b and *NOHM*, ii, pp. 308–9), is in note-against-note style like the Winchester music and the fragments from Chartres and Fleury (see p. 120). The date is *c.* 1100 and the notation alphabetic. A rather later fragment, the verse 'Dicant nunc Judaei' from the Easter processional antiphon 'Christus resurgens' (*EBM*, iii, pl. lxiv), actually proves to be identical with one of the Chartres pieces (transcription in Holschneider, *Die Organa*, pp. 180–1). Also from the twelfth century is a group of pieces including two-part conductus and tropes of 'Benedicamus Domino,' and a three-part conductus, 'Verbum patris humanatur' (*EEH*, i, pls. 25–30). The analogy here is with the repertories of St Martial and Compostela rather than that of Notre Dame.

The important manuscript of Notre-Dame music now known as Wolfenbüttel 677 (W[1]) was almost certainly written, or at least put together, for the Augustinian priory of St Andrew's in Scotland. In the body of the manuscript occur two additions to the standard corpus of two-part responds: these are the Office responds 'Vir perfecte' and 'Vir iste' for the feast of St Andrew. They are however stylistically indistinguishable from their fellows and may have originally been composed for some continental foundation dedicated to St Andrew. Rather different are some troped settings of the Sanctus and Agnus, which have no counterpart in the French repertory, while it is primarily this manuscript which preserves a group of motets without their tenors, thus transforming them into conductus (see above, p. 148). The eleventh fascicle is entirely separate in style and content from the rest of the manuscript and contains Alleluias, sequences, Offertories, and troped settings of the Kyrie, Gloria, Sanctus and Agnus, all for the Lady-Mass or votive Mass of the Blessed Virgin Mary. The style here is predominantly discant, often actually note-against-note.

The date and provenance of this music, and its relation to the rest of the manuscript, have been much discussed; that it is 'insular' can hardly be doubted. The nearly note-against-note style of some pieces might suggest an archaic idiom; yet the almost constant use of discant style in the Alleluias suggests a refinement, rather than a tentative adumbration, of Notre-Dame technique. In all probability what we have is a collection modelled for the most part on Notre-Dame style but incorporating older elements, and composed between 1225 and 1275. A complete Alleluia, 'Post partum', has been quoted by Harrison (*Music in Medieval Britain*, p. 131, from W[1], f. 181). The first of the Kyries, 'Rex virginum amator', is in *HAM*, i, no. 37. Here is the beginning of the sequence 'Laudes Christo decantemus', incorporating the melody later used for 'Lauda Sion Salvatorem':

**Example 76**

Lau - des Chri - sto de - can - te - mus, Ma - tris ei - us qui gau - de - mus Spe - ci - a - li glo - ri - a.

*Translation* Let us, who rejoice in the particular glory of his mother, sing praises to Christ.

The next stage in the history of English music is represented by a manuscript containing the most famous of all English medieval compositions, 'Sumer is icumen in' (London, Brit. Mus., Harley 978; see *EEH*, i, pls. 12–22). The date of this composition has been a subject of controversy; but its date and that of the manuscript as a whole are not necessarily the same thing. In fact 'Sumer is icumen in' shows every sign of having been added on a blank page at a later period. If the manuscript as a whole was written around 1260, then 1280 is not an unreasonable date for the addition. Moreover, it has itself been altered, both in the notation and in the addition of a Latin text; but these alterations could have been made immediately afterwards by a different scribe. In its original form the piece was almost certainly intended to be sung in binary rhythm, for which there are continental parallels around the year 1280 (see above, p. 153):

**Example 77**    London, Brit. Mus., Harley 978, f. 11v.

*continued*

*Translation* Summer has come, loudly sing cuckoo. Now is the seed growing and the meadow flowering and the forest springing to life. Sing cuckoo. The ewe bleats after the lamb, the cow lows after the calf, the bullock leaps, the buck breaks wind. Merrily sing cuckoo. Cuckoo, cuckoo, well dost thou sing cuckoo, never cease now.

The reviser of the music may have been the person who added the Latin text; contrary to what a present-day musician might suppose, he would certainly have regarded 'triple' rhythm (actually our $\frac{6}{8}$) as more suitable than duple for a sacred text. He also made alterations to the melodic line:

**Example 78**

Ibid.

Per - spi - ce Chri - sti - co - la, quae di - gna - ti - o:

Per - spi - ce Chri - sti - co - la,

[Instrumental or vocalised]

(tune continues:)

Cae - li - cus a - gri - co - la pro vi - tis vi - ti - o, Fi - li -

- o Non par-cens ex - po - su - it mor - tis ex - i - ti - o;

Qui cap - ti - vos se - mi - vi - vos a sup-pli - ci - o Vi - tae

do - nat Et se - cum co - ro - nat in cae - li so - li - o.

*Translation* Observe, O follower of Christ, what an honour this is: the
heavenly husbandman, because of the blemish in the vine, not sparing his
Son, has exposed him to the pain of death; and He [the Son] restores the
half-alive captives from torment to life and crowns them with himself on
the throne of heaven.

The bounding $\frac{6}{8}$ rhythm is in fact utterly characteristic of the English church music being written during the last quarter of the century. But the technical skill involved in writing a four-part canon over a two-part *pes*, itself consisting of two melodic elements, which are interchanged between the voices, is far in advance of any other known music of the thirteenth century.

This manuscript also includes a dramatic dialogue, 'Samson dux fortissime'; a motet, 'Ave gloriosa/Duce creature/[Domino]', which also occurs in French sources; and three two-part textless pieces in modal notation, which may be regarded as instrumental dances (facsimiles in *EEH*, pls. 18–19). These last have aroused some interest and are available in modern transcriptions (one in Walker, *History of Music in England*, 3rd ed., p. 15; the other two in *HAM*, i, no. 41). Finally it includes an index to a lost collection of music once belonging to Reading Abbey, which contains liturgical polyphony, conductus and motets. The list includes the names of some composers: W. de Winton, R. de Burg[ate] (abbot of Reading, 1268–90), and W. de Wicumbe (William de Winchecumbe). This reminds us of that other thirteenth-century list of English composers (or rather singers), provided by Anonymus IV: an anonymous 'Anglicus' who taught in France, Johannes Filius Dei, Makeblite of Winchester and Blaksmit 'at the court of the last King Henry' (Henry III, who died in 1272).

A good deal of polyphony of the late thirteenth and early fourteenth century has survived, though in fragmentary form. Many pieces are incapable of completion. Most of the music belongs to a collection of fragments which are rather vaguely said to be from Worcester. That some of them ended up at Worcester is undeniable, since they were used as fly-leaves and paste-downs in the bindings of books in the library of Worcester Cathedral. Other fragments can be recognized as belonging to the same series of volumes of polyphony. But that the original manuscripts of which these fragments are all that remain were themselves part of the Cathedral library is another question; that the music was composed or even written down at or near Worcester is highly debatable. In the last resort the question is of minor importance: there are other fragments extant which supplement and complement our knowledge of the English musical vernacular of the time, and which must be considered alongside the Worcester pieces; and any attempt to define regional idioms is premature. A selection of the music deemed to be from Worcester was published in 1928 by Dom Anselm Hughes under the title of *Worcester Medieval Harmony*; a more complete transcription was published by L. Dittmer as *The Worcester Fragments* in 1957; and photographs of all the Worcester manuscripts have appeared in *PMMM*, v and vi. Other sources are discussed in Harrison, *Music in Medieval Britain*, pp. 136–47.

The survivals are sufficient to give us an idea of the liturgical, and in particular the monastic, repertory of the time (Worcester Cathedral was served by Benedictines, and other fragments are said to derive from monastic institutions). The motet was prominent, but it was virtually always Latin and always sacred; there is no English counterpart to the collections of Montpellier and Bamberg. Practically all liturgical compositions underwent troping: either successive or simultaneous (in the manner of the motet) or a combination of the two. There are a number of examples of conductus, many of them using the technique of *rondellus* or interchange (see above, p. 143), which was also applied to the motet.

This music has a style and character all of its own. The two parts of the St Andrew's music are now enriched by a third, and in the case of some motets by a fourth voice. The plainsong is in the lowest voice though there is a good deal of crossing. The voices are of similar range and the writing is rich and euphonious with an abundance of triads. English music did not always suffer a rhythmical slowing-down during the thirteenth century in the manner of continental music; a $\frac{6}{8}$ transcription is appropriate for much of the music, though it should not be sung too fast. In other words, English composers around 1300 were still often thinking in terms of the long and breve as the usual values, with an occasional pair of semibreves as rapid passing-notes. The combination of this rhythmically archaic style with an extraordinary contrapuntal fluency is what gives this music its special flavour. Our example is from a troped setting (now incomplete) of the Alleluia 'Gaude virgo':

**Example 79**

*Worcester Fragments*, no. 45.

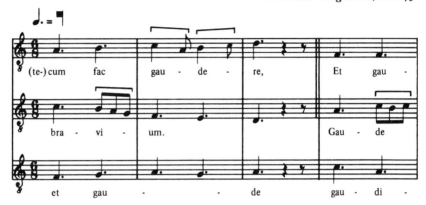

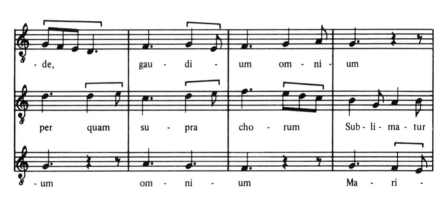

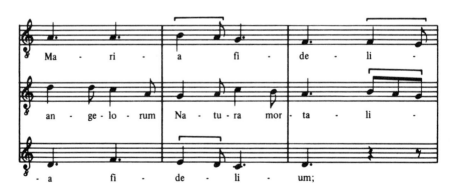

*Translation* And rejoice, O Mary, joy of all the faithful. Let the jubilant church rejoice with gladness though with decorum, assiduous, O Mary, in thy praises. (II) Rejoice, thou through whom the nature of mortals is elevated above the choir of angels. Rejoice because the illuminator of hearts has filled thee* [? with the spirit] and has rested upon thee. Rejoice, alone above all women, whose joy is complete in either robe. (III) And rejoice, O Mary, joy of all the faithful; let the Church rejoice assiduously in thy praises; and, O holy virgin...

* *Replere* can also mean to get a woman with child, which may be implied here, God (*illustrator cordium*) being regarded both as the Holy Spirit and as the child Jesus.

## The fourteenth and early fifteenth centuries

English music emerged painfully enough from the *ars antiqua*. One of two early or mid-fourteenth century motets on St Edmund (both printed in Bukofzer, *Studies*, pp. 29–33) uses the idiom of Petrus de Cruce; others show a tendency towards an Italian manner. There are various indications, mostly from fragmentary sources, of a somewhat desperate attempt to match the style of the contemporary French motet; but on the whole it was not until the end of the century that the idiom of the *ars nova* was completely assimilated and available as a medium for independent musical thinking. In the meantime, simpler types of polyphony retreated even further from the mainstream of musical development. This style, historically related to the Worcester music, was reserved for functional music in the liturgy, and has been termed 'English descant'. The expression, however, needs some qualification.

After the decline of *organum purum* in the thirteenth century the word *discantus* ('discant' or 'descant') properly refers to any kind of polyphony, since all polyphonic forms are the descendants of thirteenth-century discant style as exemplified by *clausula* and conductus. The expression 'English descant', when applied to music of the fourteenth and fifteenth centuries, is nowadays usually reserved for simpler three-part polyphony which is differentiated from motet style in that its parts are all in similar rhythm, and from chanson style in that they are differentiated in range. Such music is, however, by no means confined to British sources. A further limitation has sometimes been to reserve the term for music in which $\frac{6}{3}$ chords are predominant; but for this 'fauxbourdon style' (see below) would seem to be more appropriate. It is also pointless to be dogmatic about the particular voice in which a *cantus firmus* appears, since this does not in itself affect the style of the music, which may be without *cantus firmus* altogether. It is still not always fully understood that the early fifteenth-century treatises dealing with *discantus* and printed by Bukofzer (*Geschichte des englischen Diskants*) are referring to improvised polyphony by a single voice above or below a plainsong according to its range. The only exception to this was the technique known as 'faburden', in which a treble doubled the plainsong a fourth higher, while a third voice—the faburden itself—doubled it a third below, descending to a fifth below at cadences and some other points. This of course yields mostly sequences of $\frac{6}{3}$ chords. The technique appears to be derived from a very simple method of written composition which was current in the fourteenth century (see Harrison, *Music in Medieval Britain*, pp. 150–1, 345–6, and Example 82 below). The word itself must be derived from the French *fauxbourdon*, which meant 'false bass' and was evidently coined to describe a similar (and sometimes partially improvised) style. Later in the fifteenth century the plainsong in improvised faburden came to be regarded as being in the top, rather than the middle, voice (this is merely a theoretical distinction), and the faburden itself began to be used as a *cantus firmus* without the plainsong.

Such purely ritual polyphony as has survived from the fourteenth century appears so severely functional as to lead the casual observer to suppose that it is of no musical interest. Yet the best of it has real charm, as may be seen in the comparatively large number of such pieces in the Old Hall manuscript. This source (so called from its former location in the library of St Edmund's College, Old Hall, near Ware)* is also the earliest evidence for that revivification of English music which was to end with its dominating position in Europe between 1420 and 1460. The work of several hands, the manuscript appears at some stage to have become the property of the Chapel Royal and to have received additions from its repertory; but much of its history is uncertain, with the two editors of the new edition disagreeing over essential points, so that even now it is not possible to say with any certainty whether the composer Roy Henry was Henry

* It is now in the British Library, Add. MS 57950.

IV or Henry V. A large number of other composers are mentioned: some are otherwise unknown, and some are continental, such as the Italian composer identifiable from concordances as Zachara of Teramo (possibly the papal singer, Magister Zacharias, who composed the *caccia* quoted as Example 71); the most important single figure is undoubtedly Leonel Power. Dunstable and Forest are represented by late additions to the manuscript.

Both Italian and French elements are present in the style of the more complex pieces, the former being represented primarily by canonic procedures reminiscent of the *caccia*, and the latter by the use of isorhythm (often in all voices). Though English music had lagged behind that of the continent during the fourteenth century, it now began to catch up with a vengeance, so that in rhythmic complexity some English pieces of this period rival the most mannered and artificial products of the French and Italian schools. As an example of this we may cite a Gloria by Power, in which the flowing rhythm is apt to be held up by passages such as the following:

**Example 80**   London, Brit. Mus., Add. 57950, ff 17v–18

*Translation* We give thanks to thee for they great glory.

More frequently, however, the learning is worn lightly, as in some of the amazing canonic or isorhythmic compositions by Pycard, Byttering and others, such as Pycard's five-part, doubly-canonic Gloria:

**Example 81**

Ibid., ff 22v–23

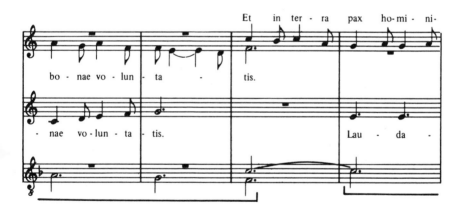

\* an alternative 'solus tenor' is here omitted

*continued*

*Translation* And on earth peace to men of good will. We praise thee, we bless thee, we worship thee, we glorify thee.

It is all too easy to concentrate exclusively on the more spectacular aspects of this collection, and to ignore the great range of styles represented in it. On the whole simpler styles are employed more frequently for the Marian antiphons which follow the settings of the Gloria in the manuscript (possibly for use as sequences at the Lady-Mass), and for settings of the Sanctus and Agnus, than for the Gloria or Credo. It should be mentioned that the manuscript was originally laid out in sections devoted to settings of the Gloria, Marian antiphons, Credo, Sanctus and Agnus, with a group of miscellaneous pieces to conclude. Later contents include both additions to the original scheme, and two groups of motets, on pages left blank by the original scribe. (The motets are discussed below, pp. 223–4.) The opening of a Sanctus by Lambe (or Lambertus?) exhibits the technique from which improvised faburden was to spring (see above, p. 209):

**Example 82**

Ibid., f 82

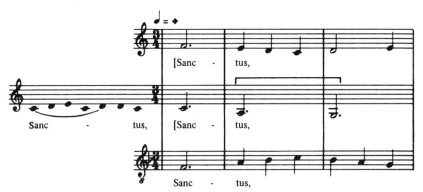

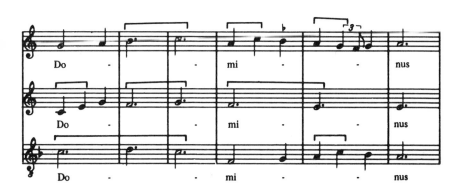

*continued*

*Translation* Holy, holy, holy, Lord God of hosts.

Another simple style was formed in imitation of the French chanson, with a melodious treble supported by a tenor and contratenor having the same range. The treble was either freely composed or a paraphrase of the plainsong; alternatively, the tenor could carry the chant. It may be added that in what might be called 'incipient faburden' style the chant could be present in any voice, or, alternatively, absent altogether. It was also possible for the chant to 'migrate' from one voice to another.

## From 1420 to 1460

The three basic polyphonic textures employed in the Old Hall manuscript—chanson, 'English descant' and motet—continued to dominate English music, and indeed European music generally, during the first half of the fifteenth century. The first two styles are employed in about equal measure in the polyphonic carol, a musical form almost unique to England which now arose after a long and largely unwritten monophonic prehistory, in which guise it was known throughout Europe.

The carol is characterized by a metrically distinct refrain which is sung at the beginning and end and between each stanza (the use of the term 'burden' for this type of refrain is anachronistic). The individual stanza may also have its own refrain, which may or may not in some cases be a substitute for the longer refrain between stanzas. Sometimes the long refrain is repeated to different music, usually a three-part variant of a two-part original. In that case the two-part version would probably be discarded after having been sung once. It is analogous to the first statement of the refrain-stanza of a processional hymn, which was sung by the cantors before being repeated by the choir. The analogy, however, must not be pressed too far. There are no grounds for regarding carols themselves as processional music; nor is it certain that their three-part sections were necessarily sung chorally: the term 'chorus' appears simply to denote 'refrain' and is not contrasted with the word 'unus' as in some continental sources (see below, p. 234).

In fact the actual function of the polyphonic carol in musical life is a difficult question. Their texts vary from those appropriate to specific liturgical occasions to the vaguely moralistic or completely secular. Their texts may be in English, Latin or both, or indeed in a mixture of English, French and Latin. The most famous of all the polyphonic carols, 'Deo gracias, Anglia', is a thanksgiving for the victory at Agincourt. The presence of the words 'Deo gracias' in the refrain, and similar evidence in a handful of other carols, has led to the suggestion that certain carols at least may have been intended as substitutes for the 'Benedicamus Domino', or its reply 'Deo gratias', on the analogy of certain conductus. It may be mentioned for what it is worth that carols and conductus are mentioned in the same breath in the fourteenth-century poem *Sir Gawain and the Green Knight*:

> and on fele wyse
> At the soper and after, mony athel songes,
> As coundutes of Krystmasse and caroles newe
> With al the manerly merthe that mon may of telle

The context here, however, suggests an informal milieu for both types; moreover the reference is certainly to the monophonic form of the carol if not of the conductus, and one hesitates to apply the evidence to the fifteenth-century polyphonic carol. No doubt, as earlier with conductus, *clausula* and motet, the form filled a variety of functions, sacred and secular, liturgical and non-liturgical.

The following short Latin carol shows the essentials of the form. Though the last line of each stanza partially repeats the full refrain, both musically and textually, the latter is probably to be performed between each stanza in order to preserve the contrast of texture between refrain and stanza. The three-part section exhibits chanson texture:

**Example 83**

London, Brit. Mus., Egerton 3307, f. 71v.

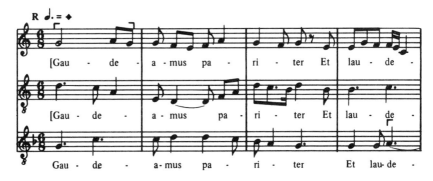

4 stanzas, of which the last two lines (from *) constitute an additional refrain. Performance: [R*a2*?]V[1]RV[2]RV[3]RV[4]R

† MB, iv, no. 72, has the reading *laudamus* in each stanza, though *laudemus*, as in the refrain, would seem to make better sense.

- mus Do - mi - num. No- vum mi- rum o - ri -

- mus Do - mi - num.]

- mus Do - mi - num. No- vum mi-rum o - ri -

- tur: De - us ho- mo na - sci - tur, Ut mor - ta - lis

- tur: De - us ho- mo na - sci - tur, Ut mor- ta - lis

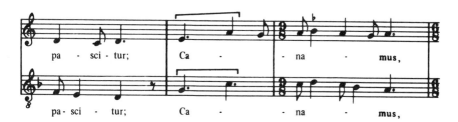

pa - sci - tur; Ca - na - **mus,**

pa - sci - tur; Ca - na - **mus,**

ca - na - mus a - la - cri - ter, Et

ca - na - mus a - la - cri - ter

lau - de - mus Do - mi - num.]

Et lau - de - mus† Do - mi - num.

*Translation* Let us rejoice together and praise the Lord. A new wonder has arisen: God is born man, he feeds as a mortal; let us sing, let us sing cheerfully and praise the Lord.

It is possible that the performance began with a two-part version of the refrain, obtained by omitting the middle part. This is explicit in the following carol, where however the two versions of the refrain have a different tenor. The three-part version is written at the end of the piece in the original, but is here transferred to its probable position:

**Example 84**

Ibid., f. 72.

7 stanzas, each ending 'Regali stirpe David'. Performance: $R^1R^2V^1R^2V^2R^2 \ldots V^7R^2$.

*continued*

* An allusion to Ps. xviii (A. V.xix), 5: 'tamquam sponsus procedens de thalamo suo'.

*Translation* A virgin brings forth a Son of the royal stem of David. He has come forth from the womb of Mary like a bridegroom from his chamber; from the royal stem of David.

The manuscript from which these carols are taken (London, Brit. Mus., Egerton 3307) also contains a set of polyphonic pieces for Holy Week and Easter, and a few other items. This collection illustrates the further development of severely functional liturgical music in the period after the compilation of the Old Hall manuscript. There are two Passions, the oldest known polyphonic settings. The Passion according to St Matthew is added as an afterthought in the manuscript, and is incomplete; the other one is a setting of St Luke, for the Wednesday in Holy Week. In both, the entire *synagoga* part is set polyphonically, whether the words are spoken by a crowd or by a single person. The last section of the St Luke version, setting the words of the centurion, sounds like the last breath of the *ars nova*:

**Example 85**                                                    Ibid., f 24v

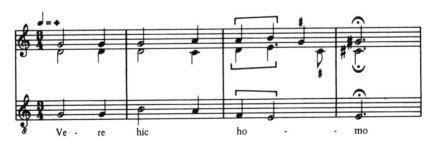

iu - stus e - rat.

*Translation* Truly this man was just.

Not all the music is as simple as that for the Passions or the ferial Mass: some of the Easter music in particular is highly melismatic. There is also a motet, 'Cantemus Domino', and an isorhythmic setting of a song also found in the *Carmina Burana*: 'O potores exquisiti'. The manuscript was almost certainly compiled for use at St George's, Windsor.

'O potores exquisiti' is not typical of English secular music of the period. Such polyphonic settings of English songs as have survived are mostly very primitive, if indeed it is not the notation itself which is hopelessly at fault. At all events, there is scarcely enough decipherable material to make generalizations. The main forms which remain to be considered are the votive antiphon, the motet, and the Mass.

The votive antiphon is not an easy form to define musically. It is properly distinguishable from the motet only at a time when the latter still preserved its medieval characteristics, such as the liturgical isorhythmic tenor and a separate text for each upper part. Even these features are not invariably present in some works to which no term other than 'motet' can properly be applied (e.g. the 'Cantemus Domino' just mentioned, the two upper voices of which have the same text); at the same time it is possible to have an antiphon in motet style (e.g. Leonel Power's 'Ave Regina caelorum', *EECM*, viii, no. 4). At a later stage an 'antiphon' may even have a liturgical tenor not associated with the main text (as in some items in the late fifteenth-century Eton Choirbook). The true definition of the votive antiphon is liturgical: the antiphon, with a versicle and response and a prayer, constituted a miniature Office of its own, dedicated to a particular saint (or to some aspect of the Divinity) and sung at a designated place, for example before a particular statue or altar. Since any text might serve for the antiphon itself, this is of no help in determining the proper label for a piece of music. Many continental works commonly designated as motets are no doubt antiphons, though it is impossible to be dogmatic in many cases. Thus, when specifically motet-like characteristics are absent (as they usually are after about 1450, though not invariably on the continent), the term 'motet' is best used only when it is quite certain that the piece in question is neither a functional setting of a ritual item (hymn, sequence, Magnificat, etc.), nor a votive antiphon.

We first met the votive antiphon in the context of the Old Hall manuscript, when however it was suggested that the items in question were included as substitutes for the sequence at Lady-Mass. (That, however, may not have been their original function.) The form grew much more popular in the period now under discussion, largely because of numerous new ecclesiastical foundations, in particular colleges, which specified the weekly or even daily singing of votive antiphons in their statutes. In this period the range of styles available was particularly wide, from simple 'insular' polyphony to the motet style itself. John Dunstable was a particularly notable contributor to the genre. His 'Crux fidelis', a votive antiphon of the Holy Cross, shows chanson texture with the plainsong in the tenor; our example is from the beginning of the second section:

**Example 86**

*continued*

\* MB, viii, has *d′c′* for *e′d′* in the middle part in this bar

*Translation* Assist us in guarding against [the arrows] of the enemy.

The finely-spun melodic line, hovering over the more static accompaniment, gives a rapturous quality to the music which is hardly ever attained by his contemporaries.

The earliest sign of the revival of the motet by English composers is in a work by a composer named in the text as Johannes Alanus: 'Sub Arturo/Fons citharizantium/In omnem terram'. The main source is a continental manuscript (Chantilly, Musée Condé, 1047), and the text of the *triplum* contains a list of English musicians, none of whom is known by any surviving compositions.* The composer may be the Aleyn of the Old Hall manuscript, which also contains a motet by the French composer Mayshuet amongst its original contents.

The Old Hall manuscript also contains two motets by English composers as part of its original layer, the first of which is Byttering's 'En Katerine solennia/Virginalis concio/Sponsus amat sponsam', in honour of St Catherine of Alexandria. This is the third work from the end of the manuscript, and is immediately followed by the Mayshuet motet, 'Arae post libamina', in which the latter part of the text of the top voice explains that it had been originally composed to a French text but had been re-set to Latin words to please the English: 'Practicus insignis Gallicus sub Gallicus hemus [verbis] hunc discantavit, sed post reformavit, Latini [*sic*] lingua Anglis sepius fit amena, reddendo Deo gracias'. This appears to imply that the work could replace the 'Deo Gratias' at the end of Mass. The last item of the manuscript is also a 'Deo gratias' substitute in motet style, but it is anonymous and the *duplum* and tenor are missing (it is possible that it too is by Mayshuet). These works between them demonstrate the predilection of the English towards Latin sacred texts, and point to the substitution of the 'Deo gratias' at the end of Mass as a possible function. It is not clear, however, whether this usage was restricted to works which are demonstrably tropes of the 'Deo gratias'.

The addenda to the Old Hall manuscript include motets by Damett, Cook and Sturgeon, all of whom were associated with the Chapel Royal, and as a final offering a group of three by Dunstable and Forest. Dunstable is represented (though anonymously) by his well-known 'Veni Sancte Spiritus' and Forest by 'Qualis est dilectus' and 'Ascendit Christus', the latter elsewhere ascribed to Dunstable. To the established framework of the motet Dunstable added his own brand of suave euphony. Of his eleven works in this category, all but two are in three sections, the outer ones in triple time and the middle ones in duple. Major prolation ($\frac{6}{8}$ or $\frac{9}{8}$) is avoided entirely. These sections always correspond to successive diminutions of the isorhythmic tenor, which is diminished in such ratios as 6:4:3 or

---

* Trowell (*AcM*, xxix (1957), pp. 65–75) has conjectured that the work was written for the celebration of the battle of Poitiers (1356) at Windsor Castle on St George's day, 1358. Ceremonial, as opposed to liturgically appropriate, motets remained rare in English music.

3:2:1. This results in a sense of building up towards a climax at the end, but not always, unfortunately, in the resolution of the climax, which is often more successfully achieved in less complex structures. A noteworthy feature is that the contratenor (when there is one) is now often provided with its own text; and the texts as a whole suggest that these works are of a purely devotional or para-liturgical nature, and were not written for specific occasions as were, for example, many of those of Dufay.

The most important development at this time, however, was the growth of the polyphonic *Ordinarium Missae*, unified by a single liturgical melody in the tenor. This tenor might be repeated isorhythmically within each movement, or from movement to movement, or else in a different rhythm in each movement. In the second case the melody might appear twice within each movement, but in different rhythms, the two statements being retained intact in each movement. Even in this second general category, moreover, the actual length of each movement may nevertheless differ as a result of variations in the number of rests in the tenor part.

On the whole the least important of these methods was the first. It is not found in any known complete Mass, but it is used in Dunstable's Gloria and Credo on 'Jesu Christe Fili Dei' (*MB*, viii, nos. 15–16). Here the tenor is repeated in halved note-values in both movements, which are of exactly the same length. Both style and technique suggest that this is an early, experimental work. The third method (with a different rhythmic layout of the *cantus firmus* for each movement) is adopted in a *Missa Rex saeculorum* which may be by either Dunstable or Power. Fragments of a troped Kyrie, 'Deus Creator omnium', have recently been found for this work (*MB*, viii, nos. 70, 19–22). Naturally each movement is slightly different in length.

The second general method of laying out the *cantus firmus*—with the same rhythm for each movement—was the most immediately productive. The technique may be seen in Dunstable's Mass *Da gaudiorum praemia*. Formerly only the Credo and Santus of this Mass were known (*MB*, viii, nos. 17–18). Now a fragmentary troped Kyrie (no. 69) and Gloria (no. 72) have turned up. The *cantus firmus* is divided into two sections, one triple and one duple. The surviving movements are not all of the same length, for in the Sanctus there are rests added at the beginning of the second section in the tenor to accommodate the word 'Benedictus' in the upper parts; while the Kyrie is still longer, with tenor rests at the beginning of both sections. Power's well-known *Missa Alma Redemptoris Mater* (which may once have had a troped Kyrie) is composed in a similar fashion.

A slightly later work, the anonymous *Missa Veterem hominem*, is interesting for several reasons. It is in four parts, the lower three of which are designated in the source (Trent 88) as Contra, Tenor, and Tenor Bassus. Thus, instead of four parts in 'motet' layout (*triplum, duplum,* tenor and contratenor) we have chanson texture underpinned by a tenor (or contratenor) bassus. As in the Masses just discussed, there is a troped Kyrie ('Deus Creator omnium'), but with the peculiarity that the first section is devoted to the first Kyrie only, and the second section to the Christe only; in spite of the scanty underlaying of the text, it is clear that the last three sections of the nine-fold Kyrie are not accommodated at all. This may be due, however, to the laxity of the continental scribe; for all the other extant English Kyrie tropes of the period set the full text, the nine invocations being spread in various ways over the conventional two sections into which the music falls. In the present work the *cantus firmus* is presented twice in each movement: in a triple-time version in the first section and in a duple-time version, rhythmically distinct from the former, in the second section. Finally, each movement is prefaced by an identical passage for the upper two voices only (not based on the *cantus firmus*), the so-called 'head-motive' or, better, introductory motto. Now it so happens that in all these respects this Mass resembles Dufay's *Missa Caput*: so closely, in fact, that its editor's suggestion that it may be by Dufay himself might be worth considering were it not for the fact that is is quoted by Thomas Morley in *A Plain and Easy Introduction to Practical Music* (1597) in a context which makes it clear that its composer was English. There are other reasons, which will be dealt with in the next chapter (see p. 243), for supposing that Dufay was influenced by the English in the *Missa Caput*, and even that it too may be by an English composer.

This list is far from exhausting the number of complete Masses known to have been written by English composers before 1460.* But

* See further *NOHM*, iii, pp. 208–13. Particularly interesting is the emergence of 'parody' technique (in which the given material is not a *cantus firmus* but a complete polyphonic piece) in works by Bedingham and Frye.

those cited may be considered to be representative. A surprising feature of recent research is the discovery of troped Kyries in English sources where these movements are omitted in continental sources (a further instance is the so-called *Missa sine nomine* regarded as a doubtful work of Dunstable in *MB*, viii). It was formerly thought that the Kyrie was normally omitted from English polyphonic Masses from the very beginning because of the popularity of troping in this country, which would have limited the usefulness of any one Mass. This was true enough after about 1460, except in the Lady-Mass in which the Kyrie was untroped. But before then the tropes appear to have been set as a matter of course, as indeed they were from time to time on the continent (for example in Arnold de Lantins' *Missa Verbum incarnatum*, which is named after its trope, and Dufay's *Caput*). The difficulty was that the English and the continental repertories of tropes differed; consequently the Kyries were omitted from continental copies of English works. Subsequently the problem of the tropes was resolved, in England by omitting the Kyrie altogether, and on the continent by omitting the words of the trope from the setting.

There are other ways of unifying a polyphonic Mass than by adopting the same *cantus firmus* in all movements: by unity of key, style, rhythmic layout, texture, and so on; and by repetition of actual material, especially in the introductory (and intermediate) mottos. Some of these were also employed by the English; most of them were already in use by continental composers before the device of the unifying *cantus firmus* reached them. But the latter, apparently invented by the English, was of decisive importance in musical history. That, and the English delight in euphony and fullness of sound, were adopted and transformed by Dufay and his successors in the last and most passionate phase of medieval music on the continent.

# Bibliography

## Musical sources

*EEH* and *EBM*, i, are valuable collections of facsimiles. The facsimile of W[1] is edited by Baxter (index by Hughes); 'Vir perfecte' and 'Vir iste' are included in Waite, *Rhythm*. The 'Worcester Fragments' are published as *MSD*, ii, with facsimiles in *PMMM*, v–vi; the edition of Dom A. Hughes also has some excellent facsimiles. The Old Hall MS is published as *CMM*, XLVI; the older edition by Ramsbotham, Collins and Hughes has some facsimiles and an interesting introduction to the third volume.

The carols are in *MB*, iv; the rest of Egerton 3307 is available in an edition by McPeek. Another anthology, *EECM*, viii, duplicates some of this music, while adding many other pieces, including some by Power, Dunstable, Plummer and Bennett. A good deal of music by Power, Bennett and other English composers is in the Trent codices (see Bibliography to Chapter 9); Dunstable is available complete in *MB*, viii, and Plummer nearly so in an edition by Trowell. The Mass *Alma Redemptoris Mater* by Power is in *DPL*, i:2; *Veterem hominem* is in *MPL*, I, ii:1, with an edition of 'Dufay's' *Caput*.

## Literary sources

A list of English medieval writers on music is beyond the scope of this book. Some of the most important treatises, such as those by Walter Odington and Robert de Handlo, and the anonymous *Quattuor principalia musicae* are printed in Coussemaker, *Scriptores* (the last under the name of Simon Tunstede); Odington is now available as *CSM*, xiv. The English treatises on discant were published by Bukofzer in his *Geschichte des englischen Diskants*, by Georgiades in his *Englische Diskanttraktate*, and by S. B. Meech in *Speculum*, x (1935), pp. 235–69. Carol-texts are published complete in Greene, *The Early English Carols* and *A Selection of English Carols* (the latter including those of the more recently discovered Egerton MS).

## Studies

Harrison, *Music in Medieval Britain*, is a first-rate general guide. Much useful information can be gleaned from Bukofzer, *Studies*, and Walker, *A History of Music in England*. The 'summer canon' is discussed by Bukofzer,

'Sumer is icumen in'; by B. Schofield in *MR*, ix (1948); and by Handschin in *MD*, iii (1949). There is an important contribution on the MS W[1] by Handschin in *MT*, lxxiii–lxxiv (1932–3), and on the Worcester music by L. Dittmer in *MD*, xi (1957), pp. 5–11; moreover, much of the article by Sanders in *JAMS*, xv (1962), especially pp. 264–78, is concerned with the Worcester repertory.

Faburden and *fauxbourdon* are discussed in works devoted to the subject by Besseler and Trumble (see main Bibliography), while there are important articles by Trumble in *Revue Belge de Musicologie*, xiv (1960), by Trowell in *MD*, xiii (1959), q.v. for summary of previous literature, and Harrison, ibid., xvi (1962). There are two recent articles of importance on the Old Hall MS: Andrew Hughes and M. Bent, 'The Old Hall Manuscript' in *MD*, xxi (1967), pp. 97–147, and M. Bent, 'Sources of the Old Hall Music' in *PRMA*, xciv (1967–8), pp. 19–35. On the origins of the cyclic Mass and the problems of the 'Dufay' *Missa Caput* see Bibliography to the next chapter.

# 9 The fifteenth century, especially in France and the Low Countries

## Music in the early fifteenth century

Broadly speaking, two opposing tendencies are to be seen in early fifteenth-century music: the continued cultivation of the artificial manner of the late fourteenth century, and the replacement of this by a new simplicity of style. In the case of church music, however, a rather different situation existed, in which the contrast was between the isorhythmic motet and a whole variety of functional liturgical styles. This opposition was not really resolved until the Mass replaced the motet as the main form of sacred music around 1450.

These different tendencies do not entirely correspond to different 'schools' of composers. The difficulty in classifying the latter arises from the distinction between the circumstances of a court with its private chapel, which tended to move about, and of a large fixed ecclesiastical institution such as a cathedral. To these must be added the Papal Chapel, the most important and most international musical institution of its day. Finally, many musicians were widely travelled on their own account. Nevertheless it is possible to distinguish between the Italians, the Burgundians (those employed by the Dukes of Burgundy), and a small group associated with Liège. One is left with an amorphous mass of Frenchmen, for many of whom biographical details are quite unknown. A few of these can be associated with the court and chapel of the antipopes at Avignon (until 1417, when the schism ended), to form a 'Mediterranean' school with the Italians. The remainder must be grouped together as a highly diffuse northern French school with no very special defining characteristics. The entire scope of the period can be found represented in the large retrospective collection in Oxford, Bod. Lib., Can. Misc. 213 (for modern editions see Bibliography).

*The fifteenth century, especially in France and the Low Countries*

The contrast of styles in secular music may be seen in a single composer of the French school, Baude Cordier, who came from Rheims and appears to have worked between 1390 and 1410. Even at his most complex, however, he retains a delicate sensibility:

**Example 87**

Oxford, Can. misc. 213, f. 108v.

*continued*

3. Prier convient le bel Ymeneüs
   Que l'amender vueille de bien en mieulx.

\* MS sons                                    Performance: ABAAB
† MS faut                                                    1 2 3 4 5

*Translation* Through the lack of the noble god Bacchus, comrades are very often reduced to shame; for Napeas, who governs lovers, causes them against his will to be rejected. On must pray fair Hymen to improve matters.

The simple chanson style is better represented by a contemporary, Richard de Loqueville (d. 1418), who was in the service of Duke Robert of Bar and taught at Cambrai Cathedral from 1413:

**Example 88**

*continued*

Puis - que je suy a - mou - reux De

vous, gra - ci - eu - se gen - te, 2.5. Ja

n'est do - lour que je sen - te, Tant suy li -

- ment joy -eux.

3. Si vodray estre songneux
De vous servir a m'entente

Performance: ABAAB
1 2 3 4 5

*Translation* Since I am in love with you, gracious lady, I shall never feel sorrow, I am so joyfully happy. I will be careful to serve you with all my intent.

Among their French contemporaries were three—Johannes Cesaris, Johannes Carmen and Johannes Tapissier—who were said in a poem by Martin le Franc, *Le Champion des Dames* (*c.* 1440), to have 'astonished all Paris' before the music of Dufay and Dunstable became known there. Tapissier, whose real name was apparently Jean de Noyers (*CMM*, XI, i, p. 1), was at the Burgundian court in 1408 and seems also to have been associated with Avignon; the other two have northern French associations. Cesaris, like Cordier, wrote mainly *chansons* in a rhythmically complex style. Carmen and Tapissier are known only for their sacred music. Their motets, like one by Cesaris, are in a rapid parlando style as regards the upper parts, far removed from the serenity of Dunstable. Parlando is also used in a Credo by Tapissier, a Gloria by Cordier, and a Gloria by a pupil of Tapissier. Tapissier's Sanctus, having a shorter text, is melismatic: all employ chanson texture and are freely composed. Similar works are extant by Bosquet (Jo. de Bosco, a singer at Avignon in 1394) and [Jo. de] Cameraco (a papal singer in 1418, doubtless from Cambrai), and others.

A slightly different attitude is to be found in settings of Mass movements by Loqueville, Guillaume Le Grant (a papal singer from 1419 to 1421), Estienne Grossin (in Paris, 1418–21) and R[eginaldus?] Liebert (*Magister puerorum* at Cambrai from 1424?). The first two of these wrote settings in which two-part sections, marked 'unus,' alternate with three-part sections marked 'chorus'. Such works are the earliest indications we have of polyphony sung chorally after the period of primitive *organum*. Neither of these two composers uses plainchant. Le Grant employed a highly chromatic idiom which was not destined to survive:

**See Example 89 opposite**

Loqueville's settings of movements from the Ordinary of the Mass are very close to early Dufay (see below, p. 243). Grossin wrote a *Missa Trompetta* (Kyrie, Gloria, Credo and fragmentary Sanctus extant), the lowest part of which is labelled 'Trompetta' in some sections. It is fairly certain that the slide-trumpet is actually intended here, since the sections in which it appears are marked 'duo', though they are in three parts: evidently the heading refers to the two upper, vocal, parts. Liebert wrote a complete Lady-Mass for the season from

**Example 89**

Ibid., f. 104r–105v.

Cum San - cto Spi - ri - tu

in glo - ri - a De - i Pa - tris.

A - - men.

Contratenor
Tenor

A men.

*Translation* With the Holy Spirit in the glory of God the Father. Amen.

the Purification (2 February) to Easter, with Introit ('Salve Sancta Parens'), Kyrie (IX), Gloria, Gradual ('Benedicta et venerabilis es'), Alleluia (with verse 'Ora pro nobis'), Sequence ('Ave mundi gaudium'), Tract for use after Septuagesima (only the verse 'Dei Genitrix' of the Tract 'Gaude Maria' is set), Credo, Offertory ('Ave Maria'), Sanctus (IV), Agnus (unidentified) and Communion ('Beata viscera'). Except in the Gloria and Credo, where it is absent altogether, the plainsong is paraphrased in the top part. Both chanson and *fauxbourdon* texture are used. The whole scheme is remarkably similar to that of Dufay in his *Missa Sancti Jacobi*.

The Italians need not be considered in detail here. Their forms and techniques were largely a continuation of those of the trecento. There was, however, an increase in the production of sacred music, papal disapproval having by now completely evaporated.

The Liège group included Johannes Ciconia (b. *c.* 1340), who is found in Padua from *c.* 1400, and in Liège again from *c.* 1413; he is not heard of after *c.* 1424. The Italian influence in his music was far-reaching. Arnold and Hugo de Lantins, who may have been brothers, also visited Italy (though separately). Arnold has left us the Mass with Kyrie 'Verbum Incarnatum' (Ed. Van den Borren, *Polyphonia Sacra*, nos. 1–5). The texture is that of the chanson and the idiom Italianate. Arnold's chansons are simple in style; those of Hugo, who also set Italian texts, tend towards rhythmic complexity.

The Burgundians are the most significant of these various schools, in that they represented all that was most forward-looking in the music of the day. Italian influence is minimal. They rejected rhythmic complexity and cultivated a directly appealing melodic style. Their church music is functional and of small importance. The early Burgundians included Pierre Fontaine, Nicolas Grenon and (probably for a short time only) Tapissier. A slightly later generation included Binchois and Dufay himself, the latter apparently for a short time at an uncertain date, the former from *c.* 1430 to his death in *c.* 1460. Their favoured medium was the three-part rondeau, ballade and *virelai*, the latter in a single-stanza form known as the *bergerette*.

Because of his range we may take Binchois as representative of the group. His chansons amount to sixty works in Wolfgang Rehm's edition. Binchois is often thought of as a rather shallow composer of whom the light-hearted rondeau in the manner of 'De plus en plus' is typical. The rondeau is certainly his favoured form, but it is often deeply felt. He was more successful with the *rondeau quatrain* (having a four-line refrain) than with the *rondeau cinquain* (in which the refrain is divided into three plus two lines), owing to the difficulty of providing a suitable phrase for the third line. This may be seen by comparing the first piece in Rehm's edition ('Adieu, adieu'), which is nevertheless a most expressive work, with the rather less ambitious 'Mon seul et souverain desir'. The latter is worth quoting in full for another reason. Both sources of the music (the Oxford manuscript and one from the Escorial) agree in giving a key-signature of *e'* flat and *a* flat for the tenor and contratenor, against the *b'* flat and *e'* flat of the upper part. (In both sources the actual clefs are missing, but can be deduced. Alternatively the piece could be presented a fourth lower or a tone higher by regarding the flat-signs merely as indications of the position of *fa* in the three hexachords—see Carl Dahlhaus in *Die Musikforschung*, xvii (1964), pp. 398–9—but this would imply an unconventional placing of the C-clefs.) Clearly the *b* is also to be flattened in the lower parts. This curious key-signature in the tenor and contratenor is misread by Marix and assumed to be mistaken by

Rehm; nor are its implications realized in *CW*, xxii, no. 9. Here is a new transcription, based on the Escorial manuscript, which is in other ways more consistent and helpful than the one from Oxford:

**Example 90**     El Escorial, Bibl. mon., MS V. III. 24, f. 20v.
Oxford, Bod. Lib., Can, misc. 213, f. 71v.

*continued*

3. Hellas mon bien, tout mon plaisir,
   Ne me mettez en non chaloir;

5. Car je voel a vous obéir,
   Et si n'ay nul aultre vouloir,

6.† Ne je ne puis riens sans vous voir
   Altre ne me peut resjoïr.

* Escorial *que je*                      Performance  ABAAABAB
† Escorial omits *Ne*                                 1 2 3 4 5 6 7 8

*Translation*  My sole and sovereign desire, my comfort and my true hope, I shall wear nothing but black until I may see you again. Alas my dear one, all my pleasure, do not show me indifference. For I wish to obey you, and indeed I have no other wish; nor can I do anything without seeing you; no one else can make me rejoice.

There is also a good deal of church music by Binchois, much of it severely functional in style. He used *fauxbourdon* technique extensively, sometimes leaving one of the two upper parts to be improvised. Most of this is printed in Marix's collection. Van den Borren (*Polyphonia Sacra*) adds a curious Gloria-Credo pair in which the alternate sections are marked to be sung at double speed, a technique used by some other early fifteenth-century composers. It seems likely that these directions are not to be taken literally, but that the sign indicating the diminution is to be read as a *poco più mosso*.*

## Dufay

Guillaume Dufay cultivated most of the early fifteenth-century styles and techniques, before his music underwent that profound change of manner which influenced all subsequent composers and which is his chief title to fame. Many details of his biography are uncertain, but he was in Italy (with short absences) from 1420 to 1433, and from 1435–7, sometimes as a singer at the papal court. In 1434–5 he was at the court of Savoy, and again at some time between 1438 and 1454, during which period he was apparently also singer and chaplain to the Duke of Burgundy. From 1454 his life was spent mainly at Cambrai (where he had received a canonry in 1436), and he died there in 1474.

There is very little external evidence for the chronology of Dufay's music. It is reasonable to suppose that the eight pieces with Italian texts belong to the Italian period—one of them, 'Quel fronte signorille', actually bears the inscription 'Rom[a]e composuit' in the Oxford manuscript. The most famous of these, the setting of the first strophe of Petrarch's 'Vergine bella', is remarkable for its sensitive reaction to the text, sometimes at the expense of the overall meaning of a passage. For instance, in dealing with 'the extreme wretchedness of human affairs', the 'wretchedness' and the 'affairs' are given strongly contrasted treatment:

## See Example 91 overleaf

French texts, on the other hand, might date from any period of his life, and in fact the earliest dateable piece, the ballade 'Resvellies vous', was written to celebrate the marriage of Carlo Malatesta in 1423. It is quite clear from a study of the development of his style (mainly in matters of rhythm) that Dufay continued to compose chansons until late in life. Normally he kept to the old texture with

---

* So Glareanus, Dodecachordon, III, viii. However, the signs actually used by Binchois are described in two contemporary treatises (Anon. XI and XII in Coussemaker, *Scriptores*, iii) as being the equivalent of $\frac{3}{2}$ ($\phi$, in the context of triple time), $\frac{4}{3}$ ($\bigcirc$) and $\frac{5}{3}$ ($\flat$) respectively).

**Example 91**

Oxford, Bod. Lib., Can. misc. 213, f. 133v.*

* the Oxford version of the text is not followed

overlapping tenor and contratenor parts; but in one rondeau, 'Ne je ne dors ne je ne veille', those parts have a different range. With its duple rhythm and chromatic experiments, the latter is strongly reminiscent of the Mass and motet 'Ave regina caelorum', and we may deduce that this is a late work:

**Example 92**

Florence, Bibl. naz., Magl. XIX. 176, f. 29v.

*continued*

Car con - traint suis de de - si - rer

Que mort con - tre moy se res - veil - - le.

3. Desir ne veult que je sommeille;
   L'oeil ouvert, ennuy me conseille
   Que je transisse de pleurer;

5. Je n'ay pas la coulleur vermeille;
   C'est par vous, dont je m'esmerveille
   Comment vous povez endurer

6. Que pour vous craindre et honnourer
   Je souffre doulleur nonpareille.

Performance ABAAABAB
             1 2 3 4 5 6 7 8

*Translation* I neither sleep nor wake; so suspicious am I, sighing is the least of it; for I am constrained to wish that Death should rise up against me. Desire prevents me from sleeping; while my eyes are open, Misery counsels me to die of weeping. I have not a rosy hue; that is your doing, at which I wonder how you can bear me to suffer unparalleled grief through fearing and honouring you.

The *Lamentatio Sanctae Matris Ecclesiae Constantinopolitanae* was performed in 1454 at the Feast of the Pheasant at Lille, a gathering intended to launch the crusade (which was never undertaken) to recover Constantinople from the Turks. It has a French text, 'O très piteulx de tout espoir fontaine', with a Latin tenor, 'Omnes amici eius spreverunt eam', set to a paraphrased psalm-tone without isorhythm. The work might be called a chanson-motet, a category later to be cultivated by Josquin and others in a small number of important pieces.

Dufay's dateable isorhythmic motets were written between 1420 and 1438, and on the whole the year 1440 is a safe *terminus post quem non* for compositions in this style. They are utterly different from those of Dunstable, being characterized by rhythmic urgency and immense contrapuntal ingenuity. Most of the non-isorhythmic works printed as motets are better classified as votive antiphons: this category includes two settings of 'Alma redemptoris mater' and three of 'Ave regina caelorum', the last of these apparently dating from 1464. There are also a number of functional liturgical works: hymns, Magnificats, and the like.

Dufay wrote a large number of separate movements for the Mass, but they cannot be considered here. The earliest complete Mass, apparently dating from *c.* 1425, is hardly an advance on the style of Loqueville. The *Missa Sancti Jacobi* is a complete setting of the Ordinary and Proper for St James on the lines of Liebert's Marian Mass, though some sections are in four parts. In the Communion the middle part has to be supplied to complete the 'faux bourdon', a technique employed also in some of the hymns, and of course as we have seen in the works of other composers, such as Binchois. It is not at all certain that this particular instance of the technique is the earliest. A *Missa Sancti Antonii* (anonymous except for a detached Kyrie) has been identified from Dufay's Will and from quotations by the theorist Tinctoris as his *Missa Sancti Antonii Viennensis*. This shows an advance, in the direction of a simpler rhythmic style, over the two previous Masses; it may date from the 1430s.

The authenticity of the *Missa Caput* has recently been questioned. The manuscript evidence for the ascription to Dufay is not strong, and its style is nearer to that of contemporary English composers than to any known work of Dufay himself. Parts of the Kyrie and Agnus have been found in English sources, and the text of the former seems to prove that it was originally composed to a nine-fold troped Kyrie rather than to the mutilated version found in the Trent codices. The fact and method of this mutilation, together with the actual choice of trope ('Deus Creator omnium') closely ally it to the anonymous English *Missa Veterem hominem* already discussed (p. 226); and there are numerous stylistic and technical resemblances besides. Then again there is the choice of an English version of the *cantus firmus*, which is identified as the final melisma (sung to the word 'caput') of the Maundy Thursday antiphon 'Venit ad Petrum'. All this might seem to add up to a very convincing case; but Dufay's authorship is not completely disproved as yet. The work was certainly believed to be by him in the later fifteenth century, and it provided a model for Masses based on the same *cantus firmus* by Ockeghem and Obrecht. It is curious that the Kyrie alone was copied at Cambrai in 1463. Possibly this was a lost shorter version of the Kyrie, newly composed on the untroped text. At all events it is a movement of this kind which begins the works of the two later composers, otherwise so faithful to their model. The style of the work as a whole suggests a date of *c.* 1440; if it is by Dufay it is certainly very English in character, based perhaps on *Veterem hominem* as a model.

If this was a case of transferring the English device of a unified *cantus firmus* to his own work, Dufay then proceeded to another innovation: the choice of a secular melody as *cantus firmus*. In the *Missa Se la face ay pale*, it is taken from the tenor of his own ballade of that title. Quite apart from its secular nature, the choice of a polyphonic model raises the question as to what extent the other voices are present in the music. Already in this Mass a triadic figure in the *cantus firmus* gives rise to similar figures in the other voices just as it does in the ballade:

**See Example 93 opposite**

Since the *cantus firmus* already has its own rhythm, it is not subjected to an arbitrary rhythmic shape as a plainsong melody would have been; but it does undergo various modifications in proportion, by doubling or halving the values, and by changing the metre. This is also done in the *Missa L'Homme armé*, where the original melody, though measured, is monophonic. These works represent a climax of polyphonic ingenuity in terms of the new four-part texture (with a

**Example 93**

bass part below the tenor and contratenor) as opposed to the older four-part 'motet' texture. They may be assigned to the 1450s.

The two late masses, *Ecce ancilla Domini* (copied at Cambrai in 1463) and *Ave regina caelorum* (partly based on the antiphon copied in 1464) return to plainchant tenors, and a simpler method of treatment. There is, however, a difference between these works and the *Missa Caput*, in that the loose-limbed structure of the latter has been replaced by a tauter and more economical style, no doubt learnt from the experiments of the two previous Masses. For instance, the long introductory duos of the *Missa Caput* have become short trios throughout the *Missa Ave Regina caelorum*. This work, based on the same plainsong as Dufay's third setting of that antiphon, foreshadows so-called parody technique in one short passage in the second Agnus, where the setting of the personal prayer for mercy which Dufay has added to the Marian text is transferred to the Mass:

**Example 94**

*The later fifteenth century*

The remainder of this history must be concerned with tendencies and trends, even though three towering figures would have deserved individual attention. Since the main scene of action lies in France and the Low Countries, we are justified in seeing in the music of this

period a counterpart to the other arts of the 'declining Middle Ages';
nevertheless, the main impression is not of a decline at all but of
vigorous growth which was to result finally in the breaking of the
shackles of medievalism.

In many ways it is the history of the chanson which is the
touchstone for development in the other forms. In terms of rhythmic
style the chanson, after changing from a predominant major
prolation ($\frac{6}{8}$ or $\frac{9}{8}$) early in the century to *tempus perfectum* ($\frac{3}{4}$), was
now more often in *tempus imperfectum* ($\frac{2}{4}$). At the same time the
traditional texture (upper part against tenor and contratenor in the
same range) was changed to one in which all three parts had different
ranges, the tenor being in the middle. Finally there was a tendency
towards greater length, and an inclination towards the rondeau in
preference to the ballade or *virelai*—but a rondeau equipped only
with the text of a refrain. Indeed, this last point is of some significance
in the disappearance of the *formes fixes*.* Many *chansons*, while
technically rondeaux, are in fact not susceptible of the rondeau's
characteristic scheme of repetition.

Though the *formes fixes* had been abandoned from time to time
before the mid-century, such chansons had been in the nature of
special cases; and they showed astonishing resilience up to 1500 and
even beyond, as is shown by the use of texts with the rhyme-scheme
of a rondeau refrain, and even the occasional use of ballade and
*virelai*, in the late chansons of Josquin. Dufay clung to the *formes fixes*
even when he had accepted other changes and had imbued the
chanson with the fascination of his late style (see Example 92). But
the new style may be judged more accurately from the work of
younger composers: Ockeghem, Busnois or Hayne van Ghizeghem.
It is seen to perfection in Ockeghem's 'D'un aultre amer':

## See Example 95 overleaf

In later years a fourth voice was added to the texture, often as a *si
placet* to an existing chanson. This voice was a *contratenor
altus*—above the tenor—as opposed to the existing *contratenor bassus*.
Hence the modern terminology for the voice-parts. Much the same

---

* *Formes fixes*: a term denoting a number of musico-poetic forms in which text and music
stand in a fixed relationship to one another; especially rondeau, ballade, *virelai*.

**Example 95**

Dijon, Bibl. Mun. 517, f. 42v–43.

*continued*

chan - - ge    Car mon hon - neur

en - ap - pe - tis - se - - roit.

3.   Je l'aime tant que jamais ne seroit
      Possible a moi de consentir l'eschange.

5.   La mort, par Dieu, avant me defferoit
      Qu'en mon vivant j'acoinctasse ung estrange.

6.   Ne cuide nul qu'a cela je me range;
      Ma leauté trop fort se mefferoit.

Performance ABAAABAB
1 2 3 4 5 6 7 8

*Translation* Would my heart stoop to love another? It must never be thought that I would estrange my love, nor that I would change my purpose for anything, for my honour would be the less for it. I love so much that it would never be possible for me to consent to the exchange. Death, God's my witness, would destroy me before I should love a stranger during my life. Let no one think that I would agree to that; my loyalty would suffer too much.*

* In older French as spoken, this poem could be placed equally well in the mouth of a man or of a woman. The former is more probable: the scribe may have intended the spellings 'un autre' ('another') and 'ung estrange' as common gender.

thing had been established in the Masses of Dufay (following the example of *Veterem hominem*); but here the inner voices are of the same range and the transformation is not quite complete. The importance of the discovery was not immediately felt: in the early sixteenth century there was a move led by Josquin towards the composing of chansons in five and six parts; but ultimately a four-voiced texture, indicated by the soprano, alto, tenor and bass clefs, became at least equal in importance to the standard five-part texture of the sixteenth century, not only in the chanson but in all forms of vocal music.

At the opposite pole from the chanson lies the Mass, which now became the recognized vehicle for musical thought *per se*. Here Johannes Ockeghem (*c.* 1420–95) is the unquestioned leader. His early work in this field is modelled, externally, on Dufay. After two early three-part works came the *Missa Caput*, in which Ockeghem went so far as to retain Dufay's own rhythmic version of the chant. But it is transposed down an octave and lies at the bottom of the four-part texture. Though the melody is in G (Mixolydian), Ockeghem chooses to end each movement on D (Dorian); and the constant harping on the note B in the melody leads to a curious harmonic style in which chords of B minor and D minor may occur in close proximity:

**Example 96**

Bukofzer has written so finely on Ockeghem's style in general and on this work in particular (*Studies*, pp. 278–91) that it is difficult to add anything to his comments. In his concern for the purely sonorous aspect of the art Ockeghem was a true romantic. He most nearly achieved the ideal in the *Missa Mi-mi* which is without a *cantus firmus*: but he also came close to it in the five-part work based on his 'Fors seulement', in the *Missa Prolationum* and in the beautiful, though restrained, Requiem.

Obrecht in his Masses reveals the more mechanical aspect of late medieval style. His *cantus firmi* tend to be markedly distinct in rhythm from the other voices; their layout gives the impression of having been pre-arranged without regard to the style of the music as a whole. He is much addicted to sequence, and to parallel movement in tenths. Curiously enough, all but two or three of Josquin's Masses are very much akin to those of Obrecht. The style of Josquin's *Missa Pange lingua*, which seems to have been composed after 1514, and in which the *cantus firmus* disappears in favour of a paraphrased treatment of the chant in all voices equally, is not at all typical of his Masses as a whole.

The musical distinction between antiphon and motet almost disappeared after 1450. It is true that one occasionally comes across large-scale pieces with a *cantus firmus* which is not that of the main text, up to about 1500. This is particularly true of Obrecht, who will even provide more than one text for the remaining voices. The 'motets' of Josquin are more often antiphons, hymns or sequences (though a sequence may be given a chanson tenor as *cantus firmus*). Otherwise they may be psalm-settings, anticipating a development which did not take place in England until the 1550s. Another important development may actually be seen in the work of an Englishman, Walter Frye, who lived on the continent. His 'Ave regina caelorum' is not a setting of the familiar text, but of another one which existed both as an antiphon and, with a repetition of the second half of the opening lines, as a respond. Frye chose the responsorial form of the text, and both it and the music have the form ABCB. This became the standard form for the sixteenth-century 'motet', whether the text were taken from a liturgical respond or not. Frye's piece became extremely popular in the later fifteenth century, and its tenor, which is not based on plainsong, was used as a *cantus firmus*, for example by Obrecht in his Mass of that name and in a sacred work composed independently of the Mass and using Frye's text.

In England itself, musical style became gradually isolated from that of the continent. The main form of the later fifteenth century—the large-scale votive antiphon—employed an increasingly florid style and an increasing number of voice-parts. The florid style was a perfect counterpart to the Perpendicular style in architecture, and like it remained in force until the Reformation. In the early sixteenth century there was a revival of Mass composition, and in the Masses of Taverner (d. 1545) the whole English heritage is summed up. Renaissance culture in early sixteenth-century England was a prerogative of the Italianate court of Henry VIII and extended to its music as to its other arts.

On the continent Johannes Tinctoris (*c.* 1435–1511) deplored the fact that the English no longer led the musical world. Yet even in France and the Low Countries, the use of *formes fixes*, the reliance on *cantus firmus* for large-scale forms, and the cultivation of a harmonic style which was 'non-functional' (except at cadences) and in which contrapuntal movement was the determining factor, combine to give the impression of an essentially medieval art. Even dance music—the courtly *basse dance*—was based on a *cantus firmus*, each long note corresponding to a single 'step' or *mesure*. Over these notes a second player improvised a florid counterpoint. There could be no better symbol of medieval culture.

In Germany, the spirit of the Middle Ages lived on until the end of the century at least. Typical of the art of the day are the contents of the three major song-books of the later fifteenth century, those of Lochamer, Schedel and Glogau.* Embedded in a quantity of foreign music are simple three-part songs with the tune in the middle voice, dances of various kinds, and monophonic mensural songs which may in some cases have originally belonged to complete polyphonic pieces. Included with the first of these books is the *Fundamentum organisandi* by the blind organist Conrad Paumann, dated 1452. This is simply a series of examples illustrating the various ways in which the common intervallic progressions of a *cantus firmus* could be dealt with in a two-part instrumental style; but added to it are a number of sensitive keyboard settings of monophonic melodies, sacred as well as secular. The largest of all fifteenth-century collections of keyboard music, the so-called *Buxheimer Orgelbuch* of *c.* 1470, includes several versions of Paumann's *Fundamentum*, as well as a large collection of transcriptions of vocal works by foreign and German composers, settings of *basse dance* melodies, of sacred and secular monophonic songs, and of plain-chant for use in the liturgy, as well as freely composed *praeambula*, etc. Most of this goes no further than the Netherlands style of the middle of the fifteenth century; but the medieval bonds were loosened later

* The first two are named after their early owners, the last after its place of origin.

in the century by a number of composers including Paul Hofhaimer (1459–1537), whose German part-songs are amongst the earliest examples of the four-part *Tenorlied* (with the tune in the Tenor), and who achieved a new flexibility even in his liturgical organ music. The *Tenorlied* was cultivated at an early stage also by Heinrich Isaac (*c.* 1450–1517), a native of Brabant who served under Lorenzo de' Medici before becoming attached to the imperial court under Maximilian. He cultivated secular song in Italian, French and Latin as well as in German, and wrote a considerable number of instrumental pieces. But his greatest contribution was in sacred music: he composed numerous Masses and motets in addition to the famous *Choralis Constantinus*, a cycle of liturgical works for the Mass completed by his pupil Senfl and eventually published in Nuremberg, 1550–5. Isaac, like Obrecht, is an ambivalent figure: the rhythmic complexity and schematic layout of some of his music binds him to the past, while in other works, such as the glorious six-part Mass *Virgo prudentissima* or the motet 'Angeli archangeli', he achieves a degree of harmonic stability unusual everi in Josquin.

In Spain, as in Germany, and with even better reason, the influence of Netherlands art was strong throughout the fifteenth century. The representative collection of secular music is the *Cancionero de Palacio*. The favoured form is the *villancico*, similar in structure to the *virelai* or *ballata*, and the best-known composer the playwright and courtier Juan d'Encina (1468 or 1469–1529 or 1530). The style of these songs, though they are homophonic and often written in four parts, is closer to that of the *lauda* and *canto carnascialesco* than to the *frottola* (see below). Though Spain enjoyed a buoyant musical life in the fifteenth century, with sacred music being composed by such figures as Cornago, Anchieta and Peñalosa, and even producing a brilliant and internationally known theorist in the controversial figure of Bartolomé Ramos de Pareja, its essential dependence on the Netherlands school is convincingly shown by a number of Spanish sources of Netherlands and Netherlands-inspired music, including an important Barcelona MS containing Masses by Isaac, and an equally important MS at Segovia preserving a number of hitherto unknown works by Obrecht.

The movement for change came from Italy, which had been musically dormant since the first quarter of the century. The *frottola*, born in Mantua around 1475, employed regular phrase-lengths and triadic harmonies. One method of performance was as an accompanied solo song; but the published collections of the early sixteenth century show them primarily as part songs for four voices. The *frottola* was a *forme fixe* in the sense that a number of possible verse-forms were reflected by the musical structure, but it did not have the fixity of the rondeau, ballade or *virelai*. (However, a single musical setting could serve for any sonnet.) The *frottola* was paralleled by the *lauda* and *canto carnascialesco* (sacred song and carnival song), which employed a similarly homophonic and melodically undistinguished style.

It was probably the *frottola* which provided the impulse for the substitution of the *basse dance* (or *bassadanza*) by a harmonically conceived form in the early sixteenth century. The *cantus firmus*, of irregular length, became a metrically regular bass above which harmonies could be improvised by several players simultaneously. The evidence for such improvisation is indirect, but the disappearance of the *cantus firmi* and the appearance of the standard basses are matters of historical fact. It was a decisive moment in musical history: a sixteenth-century pavan is not essentially different in its basic harmonic criteria from a nineteenth-century waltz.

The change did not occur so cleanly in the higher forms of art. A Mass by Palestrina is about as close to the dance idioms of his day as a symphony by Brahms is to those of his. The use of a *cantus firmus* persisted in sacred music; but it was no longer a fundamental procedure. There is a sense of harmonic progression in Palestrina (and in Gombert and Clemens non Papa) which is totally absent from Ockeghem. It is present to a limited extent in Obrecht (who visited Italy and died there in 1505), in that he favoured triadic harmonies and clear-cut cadences; and even more in Josquin, who linked Ockeghem's fluidity to Obrecht's harmonic sense. It is perhaps Josquin above all who was able to reconcile the demands of the highest forms of art with those of a new era. His creation of the paraphrase Mass (see above, p. 252) freed composers from the tyranny of the *cantus firmus* and enabled them to fashion an independent structure from given material. The development of the so-called 'parody' Mass by Josquin and Obrecht enabled composers to take an existing polyphonic model and rework it in its totality. In sacred music apart from the Mass, and in secular music, there was a new attention to the overall spirit of the words: this, and not their outward form, should be the composer's guide.

All this was the achievement of many men over many years; but above all it was the achievement of Josquin in the last years of the fifteenth century and in the first two decades of the sixteenth. In his lament on the death of Ockeghem, which occurred in 1495, Josquin abandons his Latin *cantus firmus* in the second half (though it is no great constraint in the first) and calls on his contemporaries to weep for their master in simple but affecting phrases:

**Example 97**

Medici Codex, ff 126v–127

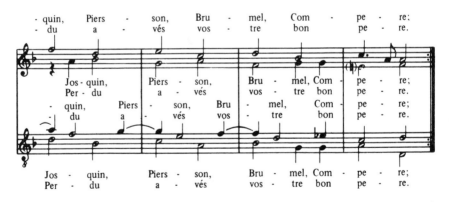

*continued*

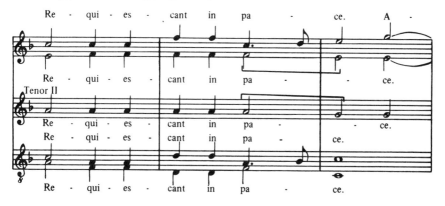

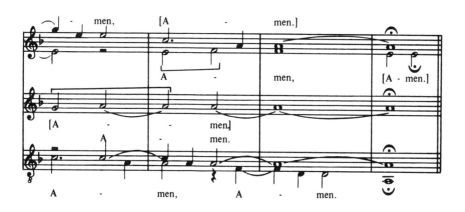

This work, until recently known only from inaccurate prints by Petrucci and Susato, is quoted here from *The Medici Codex of 1518*, ed. E. Lowinsky (*MRM*, iii-iv), no. 46.

*Translation* Clothe yourselves in garments of mourning: Josquin, Brumel, Piersson [i.e. Pierre de la Rue], Compère; and weep great tears from your eyes: you have lost your good father. May he rest in peace. Amen.

It is a Requiem for the Middle Ages.

# *Bibliography*

## *Musical sources*

*CMM*, XI, contains to date four vols. of early fifteenth-century music. The repertory of the Oxford manuscript is largely available in a series of older editions by Stainer (*Dufay*), Marix (*Les Musiciens*) and Van den Borren (*Polyphonia Sacra* and *Pièces polyphoniques profanes*). The complete works of Ciconia have been edited by Clercx-Lejeune; those of Dufay are in *CMM*, I. The *Caput* Masses of Dufay, Ockeghem and Obrecht are now available in an excellent single-volume edition as *CM*, v. The chansons of Binchois are edited by Rehm, the Masses of Ockeghem by Plamenac; and there are complete editions of the works of Obrecht and Josquin by Wolf and Smijers respectively. Smijers' *Van Ockeghem tot Sweelinck* is a useful anthology, while a great deal of fifteenth-century music is available in the series *CW*.

A substantial selection from the Trent codices, with a complete inventory of their contents, has been published in *DTO*, xiv–xv, xxii, xxxviii, liii, lxxvi and cxx, though in some of the earlier volumes the transcriptions are so close to the original notation as to be virtually impossible to read. There is now a complete (though not very clear) facsimile of all seven MSS (*Codex Tridentinus 87[–93]*), and one of the Codex Escorial by Rehm. The series *CMM* now includes the works of Brumel, Compère, Agricola and many others, as well as a substantial number of collections devoted to the fifteenth century; another important edition is *MPL*, which in the first volume of its first series includes the *L'Homme armé* Masses of Dufay, Busnois, Caron, Faugues, Regis, Ockeghem, de Orto, Basiron, Tinctoris and Vacqueras. Amongst the older editions which still have value are those of the Copenhagen and Dijon *chansonniers* by Jeppesen, and by Droz, Thibault and Rokseth; the latter is also available in facsimile in *PMMM*, xii. See also the editions by Hewitt of Petrucci's large retrospective publications *Harmonice Musices Odhecaton A* (Venice, 1501), and *Canti B* (1502); of *frottole* in *PAM*, viii (books I and IV ed. Schwarz) and in *IM*, I, i (books I–III ed. Cesari and Monterosso); of *laudi* by Jeppesen; of the Medici Codex by Lowinsky; and of the chanson MSS of Marguerite of Austria by Picken. The Brussels MS of *basse-dance* melodies was edited in facsimile and transcription by Closson and there is a complete edition of all known such melodies in vol. vi of The *Wellesley Edition*. The *Arte della danza* by Guglielmo Ebreo (or 'da Pesaro') was ed. in 1873 by Zambrini. For the *Lochamer Liederbuch* and Paumann's *Fundamentum organisandi* see the editions of Ameln (facs.) and Arnold. The

*Buxheimer Orgelbuch* is edited by Wallner in facsimile (DM, II, i) and transcription (*EDM*, xxxvii–xxxix). For music by Hofhaimer and his school, see Moser. Isaac: *Choralis Constantinus* ed. Beczeny and Rabl (vol I: *DTO*, x ( = v. I)), Webern (vol. 2: *DTO*, xxxii ( = xvi. I) and Cuyler (vol. 3); masses ed. Lerner (*CMM*, LXV), Cuyler, Fano and Staehelin; secular music ed. Wolf (*DTO*, xxviii ( = xiv. I)). The Spanish *Cancionero de Palacio* is in *MME*, v, x, xiv. The largest of the later fifteenth-century English sources, the Eton Choirbook, is in *MB*, x–xii. *Glogauer Liederbuch* in *EDM*, iv, viii.

## Literary sources

The most important theorists of the period are Ugolinus of Orvieto (*CSM*, vii, 3 vols.), Johannes Tinctoris (Coussemaker, *Scriptores*, iv, pp. 1–200) and Franchino Gafori. Tinctoris' Dictionary, the *Terminorum Musicae Diffinitorium*, has been edited separately by Machabey with French translation, and by Parrish with English translation.

## Studies

Apart from the invaluable general guides of Reese (*Music in the Renaissance*), *NOHM*, iii and Apel (*Notation*), there are monographs on Ciconia by Clercx-Lejeune, on Dufay by Van den Borren, on Obrecht by Gombosi and on Josquin by H. Osthoff. More specialized topics are dealt with by C. Hamm on the chronology of Dufay's works; by Sparks, *Cantus Firmus*, and by Bukofzer in his *Studies*. This last contains important accounts of the *Basse Dance*, the origins of choral polyphony and, most significantly, of the *Caput* Masses. Those who wish to pursue further the case of Dufay's *Missa Caput* and related topics should consult the recent articles: M. and I. Bent, 'Dufay, Dunstable, Plummer—a New Source' in *JAMS*, xxii (1969), pp. 394–424; A. Planchart, 'Guillaume Dufay's Masses: Notes and Revisions' in *MQ*, lviii (1972), pp. 1–23; and G. Chew, 'The Early Cyclic Mass as an Expression of Royal and Papal Supremacy' in *ML*, liii (1972), pp. 254–69. The standard work on the Burgundian school is Marix, *Histoire*; on Busnois see especially C. Brooks in *JAMS*, vi (1953), pp. 111–35. An important book on the emergence of Italian music in the later fifteenth and early sixteenth centuries is Torrefranca's *Il Segreto del quattrocento*, while a recent work of great value is Jeppesen's *La Frottola*. The emergent humanism of Germany is well described in Moser's *Paul Hofhaimer*; more recently L. Cuyler's *The Emperor Maximilian I and Music* has appeared. For the Segovia MS see Anglés in *AcM*, viii (1936), pp. 6–17. On English music of the later fifteenth century see especially Harrison, *Music in Medieval Britain*.

# *Bibliography*

The following is intended to serve the dual purpose of a general bibliography of medieval music, and of a list of works referred to in abbreviated form. The first list gives all symbols used in the book (in the main text and in the chapter bibliographies) in alphabetical order of the symbol itself. In a few cases cross-references are made to names of editors in the second list. The latter gives all works which are normally referred to by author's or editor's name and short title, or by short title only, as well as a few additional works of a general nature. Individual articles from journals, etc., are omitted, as are some highly specialized non-musical works, sufficient identification of which is provided in the text or chapter bibliographies. A star indicates a facsimile edition or a substantial collection of facsimiles with or without transcriptions; the symbol 'Ed.' is used for an edition even when a considerable amount of commentary is included in the publication.

*Symbols for journals, collected editions, etc.*

AcM     *Acta Musicologica* (1928–).
AH     *Analecta Hymnica medii aevi*, Ed. G. M. Dreves, C. Blume and H. M. Bannister, 55 vols. (Leipzig, 1886–1922).
AM     *Antiphonale Monasticum pro diurnis horis* (Paris, Tournai, Rome, 1934).
AMM     *Antiphonale Missarum juxta ritum Sanctae Ecclesiae Mediolanensis* (Rome, 1935).
AMw     *Archiv für Musikwissenschaft* (1918–27, 1952–).
AnnM     *Annales Musicologiques*, 6 vols. (Paris, 1953–63).
AR     *Antiphonale Sacrosanctae Romanae Ecclesiae* (Tournai, 1949).
AS     *Antiphonale Sarisburiense*, Ed. W. H. Frere, 6 vols. (London: The Plainsong and Mediaeval Music Society, 1901–25, repr. Farnborough, 1966).★

CEKM    *Corpus of Early Keyboard Music*, Ed. W. Apel (American
        Institute of Musicology, 1963–). See Apel.

CM      *Collegium Musicum*, Ed. M. Velimirović, Series 1, 6 vols.
        (Yale, 1955–65). See Knapp, Planchart.

CMM     *Corpus Mensurabilis Musicae*, Ed. A. Carapetyan (Rome:
        American Institute of Musicology, 1947–).

CSEL    *Corpus Scriptorum Ecclesiasticorum Latinorum* (Vienna, 1866–).

CSM     *Corpus Scriptorum de Musica* (Rome: American Institute of
        Musicology, 1950–).

CW      *Das Chorwerk*, Ed. F. Blume and K. Gudewill (2nd ed.,
        Wolfenbüttel, 1950–).

DM      *Documenta musicologica* (Kassel, etc., 1955–).★

DPL     *Documenta Polyphoniae Liturgicae Sanctae Ecclesiae Romanae*,
        Ed. L. Feininger (Rome: Societas Universalis Sanctae
        Ceciliae, 1947–).

DTO     *Denkmäler der Tonkunst in Österreich*, 123 vols. (Vienna etc.,
        1894–1971). See Adler, Bezecny, Rietsch, Schatz, Schmieder,
        Webern, Wolf.

EBM     *Early Bodleian Music*, Ed. J. Stainer and E. W. B. Nicholson, 3
        vols. (London, 1901–13, repr. Farnborough, 1967).★

EDM     *Das Erbe deutscher Musik* (Hannover, etc., 1935–). See Wallner.

EECM    *Early English Church Music*, Ed. F. Ll. Harrison (London,
        1963–). See Hughes.

EEH     *Early English Harmony*, vol. i (facsimiles), Ed. H. E.
        Wooldridge (London: The Plainsong and Mediaeval Music
        Society, 1897).★

EG      *Études Grégoriennes* (1954–).

GR      *Graduale sacrosanctae Romanae Ecclesiae* (Paris, Tournai, Rome,
        New York, 1961).

GS      *Graduale Sarisburiense*, Ed. W. H. Frere, 2 vols. (London: The
        Plainsong and Mediaeval Music Society, 1894, repr. in 1
        vol., Farnborough, 1966).★

GSJ     *Galpin Society Journal* (1948–).

HAM     *Historical Anthology of Music*, Ed. A. T. Davison and W. Apel,
        2 vols. (vol. i, 2nd ed., Cambridge, Mass., 1954).

IM      *Instituta et Monumenta* (Cremona, 1954–). See Cesari, Tintori.

JAMS    *Journal of the American Musicological Society* (1948–).

KJb     *Kirchenmusikalisches Jahrbuch* (1886–).

LU      *The Liber Usualis* (Tournai, 1957).

LVM     *Liber Vesperalis juxta ritum Sanctae Ecclesiae Mediolanensis*
        (Rome, 1939).

MB      *Musica Britannica* (London, 1951–). See Bukofzer, Harrison,
        J. Stevens.

MD        *Musica Disciplina* (1946–).
MGG       *Die Musik in Geschichte und Gegenwart*, Ed. F. Blume (Kassel, 1949–).
MHS       *Monumenta Hispaniae Sacra*, Series Liturgica (Barcelona, 1946–).
ML        *Music and Letters* (1920–).
MMB       *Monumenta Musicae Byzantinae* (Copenhagen, 1935–).*
MME       *Monumentos de la Música Española* (Barcelona, 1941–). See Anglés.
MMg       *Monatshefte für Musikgeschichte*, Ed. R. Eitner, 37 vols. (1869–1905).
MMMA      *Monumenta Monodica Medii Aevi*, Ed. Bruno Stäblein (Kassel and Basel, 1956–).
MMN       *Monumenta Musica Neerlandica* (Amsterdam, 1959–).
MMS       *Monumenta Musicae Sacrae* (Macon and Rouen, 1952–).*
MPL       *Monumenta Polyphoniae Liturgicae Sanctae Ecclesiae Romanae*, Ed. L. Feininger (Rome: Societas Universalis Sanctae Ceciliae, 1947–).
MQ        *The Musical Quarterly* (1915–).
MRM       *Monuments of Renaissance Music* (Chicago and London, 1964–). See Hewitt, Lowinsky.
MSD       *Musicological Studies and Documents* (Rome: American Institute of Musicology, 1951–). See Carapetyan, Dittmer.
MT        *The Musical Times* (1844–).
NOHM      *The New Oxford History of Music*, Ed. J. A. Westrup and others (vols. i–iii, London, 1954–60).
PAM       *Publikationen älterer Musik*, Ed. T. Kroyer and H. Schultz, 11 vols. (Leipzig, 1926–40, repr. Hildesheim and Wiesbaden, 1967). See Husmann, Ludwig, Plamenac, Schwarz, Wagner.
PG        *Patrologiae cursus completus, series Graeca*, Ed. J. Migne, 166 vols. (Paris, 1857–66).
PL        *Patrologiae cursus completus, series Latina*, Ed. J. Migne, 221 vols. (Paris, 1844–55).
PM        *Paléographie musicale: les principaux manuscrits de chant grégorien, ambrosien, mozarabe, gallican, publiés en fac-similés par les Bénédictins de Solesmes* (Solesmes, 1889–).*
PMFC      *Polyphonic Music of the Fourteenth Century*, Ed. L. Schrade and others, 12 vols. (Monaco, 1956–76).
PMMM      *Publications of Medieval Musical Manuscripts*, Ed. L. Dittmer (New York: Institute of Mediaeval Music, Ltd., 1957–).*
RBMAS     *Rerum Britannicarum Medii Aevi Scriptores* ['Rolls Series'] (London, 1858–).
SIMG      *Sammelbände der Internationalen Musik-Gesellschaft*, 15 vols. (Leipzig, 1899–1914).

## Bibliography

SMMA    *Summa Musica Medii Aevi*, Ed. F. Gennrich, 18 vols.
       (Darmstadt, later Langen bei Frankfurt a.M., 1957–67).*
       See Ludwig.
ZMw     *Zeitschrift für Musikwissenschaft*, 16 vols. (Leipzig, 1918–34).


### Books and individual editions

Adler, G., *Handbuch der Musikgeschichte*, 2 vols. (2nd ed., Berlin, 1930,
     repr. Tutzing, 1961).
Adler, G. and others, Eds., *Sechs* [later *Sieben*] *Trienter Codices*, 8 vols.
     (Vienna, 1900–70). *DTO*, xiv–xv ( = vii, 1–2), xxii ( = xi, 1), xxxviii
     ( = xix, 1), liii ( = xxvii, 1), lxi ( = xxxi), lxxvi ( = xl), cxx.
Ambros, A. W., *Geschichte der Musik*, 5 vols. (3rd ed., Leipzig,
     1887–1911).
Ameln, K., Ed., *Locheimer Liederbuch und Fundamentum Organisandi*
     *des Conrad Paumann* (Berlin, 1925, repr. Kassel, 1972).*
Andrieu, M., Ed., *Les* Ordines Romani *du haut moyen-âge*, 4 vols.
     (Louvain, 1931–56).
Anglés, H., Ed., *El Codex musical de las Huelgas*, 3 vols. (Barcelona,
     1931).*
     Ed., *La Música de las Cantigas de Santa Maria del Rey Alfonso el Sabio*,
     3 vols. (Barcelona, 1942–64).*
     Ed., *La Música en la Corte de los Reyes Católicos*, ii–iv: *Polifonía*
     *profana: Cancionero musical de Palacio*, 4 vols. (Barcelona, 1947–65).
     *MME*, v, x, xiv. 1–2.
Apel, W., *Gregorian Chant* (London, 1958).
     *The Notation of Polyphonic Music 900–1600* (5th ed., Cambridge,
     Mass., 1953).*
     Ed., *French Secular Music of the Late Fourteenth Century* (Cambridge,
     Mass., 1950).
     Ed., *Keyboard Music of the Fourteenth and Fifteenth Centuries* (American
     Institute of Musicology, 1963). *CEKM*, i.
Apfel, E., *Anlage und Struktur der Motetten im Codex Montpellier*
     (Heidelberg, 1970).
Appel, C., *Bernart von Ventadorn* (Halle, 1915).
     Ed., *Die Singweisen Bernarts von Ventadorn* (Halle, 1934).
Arnold, F. W., and Bellermann, H., Eds.,: *Das Locheimer Liederbuch*
     *nebst der Ars Organisandi von Conrad Paumann* (Leipzig, 1926,
     repr. Wiesbaden, 1969).
*L'Ars nova italiana del trecento*, 3 vols. (Certaldo, 1959–69).
*Aspects of Medieval and Renaissance Music: a birthday offering to Gustave*
     *Reese*, Ed. J. la Rue (New York and London, 1967).

Aubry, P., *Trouvères et troubadours* (Paris, 1909).

Ed., *Cent motets du XIII^e siecle*, 3 vols. (Paris, 1908, repr. New York, 1964).★

Ed., *le Chansonnier de L'Arsenal (Paris, 1909)*.★

Ed., *Le Roman de Fauvel* (Paris, 1907).★

Auda, A., Ed., *Les 'Motets Wallons' du manuscrit de Turin: Vari 42*, 2 vols. (Brussels, 1953).★

Bannister, H. M., *Monumenti Vaticani di Paleografia Musicale Latina*, 2 vols. (Leipzig, 1913, repr. Farnborough, 1969).★

Baumstark, A., *Liturgie comparée* (Amay à Chèvretogne, 1939).

*Nocturna Laus* (Münster Westf., 1957).

Baxter, J. H., Ed., *An Old St. Andrews Music Book* (London, 1931).★

Beck, J., *Die Melodien der Troubadours* (Strasbourg, 1908).

*La Musique des troubadours* (Paris, 1910).

Ed., *Le Chansonnier Cangé*, 2 vols. (Paris and Philadelphia, 1927).★

Beck, J. and Beck, L., Eds., *Le Manuscrit du Roi*, 2 vols. (London and Philadelphia, 1938).★

Besseler, H., *Bourdon und Fauxbourdon* (Leipzig, 1950, repr. 1974).

*Die Musik des Mittelalters und der Renaissance* (Potsdam, 1937).

*Handbuch der Musikwissenschaft*, i.

Bezecny, E., and Rabl, W., Eds., *Heinrich Isaac: Choralis Constantinus, Erster Theil* (Vienna, 1898). *DTO*, v. 1 ( = x).

Bourdillon, F. W., Ed., *Aucassin et Nicolete* (Manchester, 1930).

Ed., *Cest daucasī & de nicolete* (Oxford, 1896).★

Breul, K., Ed., *The Cambridge Songs* (Cambridge, 1915).★

Brightman, F. E., Ed., *Liturgies Eastern and Western*, i (Oxford, 1896, repr. 1965, 1967).

Bukofzer, M. F., *Geschichte der englischen Diskants und des Fauxbourdons nach den theoretischen Quellen* (Strasbourg, 1936).

*Studies in Medieval and Renaissance Music* (New York, 1950 and London, 1951).

*'Sumer is icumen in': a Revision* (Berkeley, 1944).

Ed., *The Works of John Dunstable* (2nd ed., London, 1970). *MB*, viii.

Burney, C., *A General History of Music*, 4 vols. (London, 1776–89). Ed. F. Mercer, 2 vols. (New York, 1935, repr. 1957).

Carapetyan, A., Ed., *An Early Fifteenth-Century Italian Source of Keyboard Music: the Codex Faenza, Biblioteca Comunale, 117* (American Institute of Musicology, 1961).★ *MSD*, x.

Cesari, G., and Monterosso, Eds., *Le Frottole nell'edizione principe di Ottaviano Petrucci* [Books I–III] (Cremona, 1954). *IM*, I, i.

Chailley, J., *Histoire musicale du moyen âge* (Paris, 1950).

*La musique médiévale* (Paris, 1951).

# Bibliography

Chaytor, H. J., *The Troubadours* (Cambridge, 1912).
*The Troubadours and England* (Cambridge, 1923).
Clercx-Lejeune, S., *Johannes Ciconia*, 2 vols. (Brussels, 1960). Complete
  works in vol. ii.
Closson, E., Ed., *Le Manuscrit dit de Basses Danses de la Bibliothèque
  de Bourgogne* (Brussels, 1912).★
*Codex Tridentinus 87 [–93]*, 7 vols. (Rome, 1969–70).★
Colgrave, B. and Mynors, R. A. B., Eds., *Bede's Ecclesiastical History of
  the English People*, [text and translation] (Oxford, 1969).
Corbin, S., *L'Église à la conquête de sa musique* (Paris, 1960).
de Coussemaker, C. E. H., *Histoire de l'harmonie au moyen-âge* (Paris,
  1852, repr. Hildesheim, 1966).
  Ed., *Scriptorum de musica medii aevi nova series*, 4 vols. (Paris, 1874–6,
  repr. Milan, 1931).
Cserba, S., Ed., *Hieronymus de Moravia O.P., Tractatus de Musica*
  (Regensburg, 1935). *Freiburger Studien zur Musikwissenschaft*, ii.
Cuyler, Louise: *The Emperor Maximilian I and Music* (London, 1973).
  Ed., *Heinrich Isaac's Choralis Constantinus, Book III* (Ann Arbor, 1950).
  Ed., *Heinrich Isaac: Five Polyphonic Masses* (Ann Arbor, 1956).
Davis, R. H. C., *A History of Medieval Europe from Constantine to
  St Louis* (London, 1957).
Denis, N. M.-, and Boulet, R.: *Euchariste ou la Messe dans ses variétés,
  son histoire et ses origines* (Paris, 1953).
Dittmer, L., Ed., *The Worcester Fragments* (American Institute of
  Musicology, 1957). *MSD*, ii.
Dolan, D., *Le drame liturgique de Pâques en Normandie et en Angleterre au
  moyen âge* (Paris, 1975).
Dronke, P., *The Medieval Lyric* (London, 1968).
Droz, E., Thibault, G. and Rokseth, Y., Eds., *Trois chansonniers français
  du XV^e siècle* (Paris, 1927). Only this first volume (*Chansonnier de
  Dijon*), was published. Facsimile ed. in *PMMM*, xii.
Duchesne, L., *Origines du culte chrétien* (5th ed., Paris, 1925. English trans.,
  *Christian Worship*, 5th ed., London, 1931).
Düring, I., *Ptolemaios und Porphyrios über die Musik* (Göteborg, 1934).
  Ed., *Die Harmonielehre des Klaudios Ptolemaios* (Göteborg, 1930).
  Ed., *Porphyrios Kommentar zur Harmonielehre des Ptolemaios* (Göteborg,
  1932).
Eggebrecht, H. and Zaminer, F., Eds., *Ad organum faciendum:
  Lehrschriften der Mehrstimmigkeit in nachguidonischer Zeit* (Mainz,
  1970).
Ellinwood, L., Ed., *The Works of Francesco Landini* (Cambridge, Mass.,
  1939).
*Essays presented to Egon Wellesz*, Ed. J. A. Westrup (Oxford, 1966).

Evans, P., *The Early Trope Repertory of St. Martial de Limoges* (Princeton, 1970). *Princeton Studies in Music*, ii.

Fano, F., Ed., *Heinrich Isaac: Messe* (Milan, [1962]). *Archivium musices metropolitanum mediolanense*, x.

Feltoe, C. L., Ed., *The Leonian Sacramentary* (Cambridge, 1896).

Ferretti, P., *Esthétique grégorienne* (Paris, 1938).

Fischer, K. von, *Studien zur italienischen Musik des Trecento und frühen Quattrocento* (Berne, 1956).

Fleischer, O., *Neumenstudien*, 3 vols. (Leipzig, 1895–1904).

Flotzinger, R., *Der Discantussatz im Magnus liber und seiner Nachfolge* (Vienna, 1969).

Frere, W. H., Ed., *The Winchester Troper* (London, 1894).

Friedlein, G., Ed., *Anicii Manlii Torquati Severini Boetii De Institutione Arithmetica libri duo; De Institutione Musica libri quinque; accedit Geometria quae fertur Boetii* (Leipzig, 1867, repr. Frankfurt a.M., 1966).

Froger, J., *Les Chants de la messe aux VIIIe et IXe siècles* (Tournai, 1950).

Galpin, F. W., *Old English Instruments of Music* (3rd ed., London, 1932; 4th edn., New York, 1965).

Gastouée, A., *Les Origines du chant romain: l'Antiphonaire grégorien* (Paris, 1907).

Gautier, L., *Histoire de la poésie liturgique au moyen âge. I: Les Tropes* (Paris, 1886, repr. Ridgewood, N.J., 1966).

Gennrich, F., *Die altfranzösische Rotrouenge* (Halle, 1925).

*Bibliographie der ältesten französischen und lateinischen Motetten* (Darmstadt, 1957, = *SMMA*, ii).

*Der musikalische Vortrag der altfranzösischen Chansons de geste* (Halle, 1923).

*Grundriss einer Formenlehre des mittelalterlichen Liedes* (Halle, 1932).

*Rondeaux, Virelais und Balladen*, 2 vols. (Dresden, 1921 and Göttingen, 1927).

Ed., *Adam de la Halle: Le Jeu de Robin et de Marion; Li Rondel Adam* (Langen bei Frankfurt a.M., 1962).

Ed., *Lo Gai Saber: 50 ausgewählte Troubadourlieder* (Darmstadt, 1959).

Ed., *Troubadours, Trouvères, Minne- und Meistersinger* (Cologne and London, 1960). *Das Musikwerk*, ii.

Georgiades, T., *Englische Diskanttraktate aus der ersten Hälfte des XV. Jahrhunderts* (Munich, 1937).

Gerbert, M., *De cantu et musica sacra*, 2 vols. (St Blaise, 1774).

Ed., *Scriptores ecclesiastici de musica sacra potissimum*, 3 vols. (St Blaise, 1784, repr. Milan, 1931 and Hildesheim, 1963).

Gérold, T., *Histoire de la musique des origines à la fin du XIVe siècle* (Paris, 1936).

*La Musique au moyen âge* (Paris, 1932).

*Les Pères de l'Église et la musique* (Strasbourg, 1931).

Gevaert, F.-A., *La Mélopée antique dans le chant de l'église latine* (Ghent, 1895).

Göllner, T., *Formen früher Mehrstimmigkeit in deutschen Handschriften des späten Mittelalters* (Tutzing, 1961). *Münchner Veröffentlichungen zur Musikgeschichte*, vi.

Gombosi, O., *Jacob Obrecht: eine stilkritische Studie* (Leipzig, 1925).

Greene, R. L., Ed., *The Early English Carols* (Oxford, 1935 repr. 1977).

Ed., *A Selection of English Carols* (Oxford, 1962).

Hamm, C., *A Chronology of the Works of Guillaume Dufay, Based on a Study of Mensural Practice* (Princeton, 1964). *Princeton Studies in Music*, i.

Hanssens, J. M., *Aux origines de la prière liturgique: Nature et genèse de l'office de Matines* (Rome, 1952).

Ed., *Amalarii Episcopi Opera Liturgica Omnia*, 3 vols. (Rome, 1948–50).

Harrison, F. Ll., *Music in Medieval Britain* (2nd ed., London, 1963).

Ed., *The Eton Choirbook*, 3 vols. (London, 1956–61). *MB*, x–xii.

Hatto, A. D. and Taylor, R. J., Eds., *The Songs of Neidhart von Reuental* (Manchester, 1958).

Hawkins, J., *A General History of Music*, 5 vols. (London, 1776; new ed. 1946).

Hesbert, R.-J., Ed., *Antiphonale Missarum Sextuplex* (Brussels, 1935).

Hewitt, H., Ed., *Harmonice Musices Odhecaton A* (Cambridge, Mass., 1946).

Ed., *Ottaviano Petrucci: Canti B numero cinquanta* (Chicago, 1967). *MRM*, ii.

Hilka, A., Schumann, O., and Bischoff, B., Eds., *Carmina Burana*, 4 vols. (Heidelberg, 1930–70. A reprint of the earlier vols., and a completion, are in progress). Facsimile, Ed. Bischoff, in *PMMM*, ix.

Hill, R. T., and Bergin, T. G., Eds., *Anthology of the Provençal Troubadours* (New Haven, 1941; 2nd edn. in 2 vols., 1973). *Yale Romanic Studies*, xvii.

Holschneider, A., *Die Organa von Winchester. Studien zum ältesten Repertoire polyphoner Musik* (Hildesheim, 1968).

Holz, G., Saran, F. and E. Bernouilli, Eds., *Die Jenaer Liederhandschrift*, 2 vols. (Leipzig, 1901, repr. Hildesheim, 1966).

Hughes, A., *Medieval Music: the Sixth Liberal Art* (Toronto and Buffalo, 1974).

Ed., *Fifteenth-Century Liturgical Music, I* (London, 1968). *EECM*, viii.

Hughes, Dom A., *Index to the facsimile edition of MS. Wolfenbuettel 677* (Edinburgh and London, 1939).

*Medieval Polyphony in the Bodleian Library* (Oxford, 1951).

Ed., *Anglo-French Sequelae* (Burnham and London, 1934, repr. Farnborough, 1966).

Ed., *Worcester Mediaeval Harmony* (London: Plainsong and Mediaeval Music Society, 1928).

Huglo, M., *Les Tonaires. Inventaire, analyse, comparaison* (Paris, 1971).

Huglo, M. and others, *Fonti e Paleografia del canto ambrosiano* (Milan, 1956).

Huizinga, J., *The Waning of the Middle Ages* (London, 1924; Penguin reprint, ibid., 1955).

Husmann, H., Ed., *Die drei- und vierstimmigen Notre-Dame-Organa* (Leipzig, 1940, repr. Hildesheim and Wiesbaden, 1967). *PAM*, xi.

Idelsohn, A. Z., *Jewish Music in its Historical Development* (New York, 1929, repr. 1967).

Ed., *Thesaurus of Hebrew Oriental Melodies*, 10 vols. (Leipzig, New York and Jerusalem, 1914–32).

Jackman, J. L., Ed., *Fifteenth Century Basse Dances* (Wellesley College, 1964). *The Wellesley Edition*, vi.

Jacobsthal, G., *Die chromatische Alteration in liturgischen Gesang der abendländischen Kirche* (Berlin, 1897).

von Jan, C., Ed., *Musici Scriptores Graeci* (Leipzig, 1895, repr. Hildesheim, 1962).

Jeanroy, A., *Bibliographie sommaire des chansonniers français du moyen âge* (Paris, 1918).

Ed., *Le Chansonnier d'Arras* (Paris, 1925).*

Jeanroy, A., Brandin, L., and Aubry, P., Eds., *Lais et descorts français du XIIIe siècle* (Paris, 1901).

Jeppesen, K., Ed., *Der Kopenhagener Chansonnier* (Copenhagen and Leipzig, 1927).

Jeppesen, K., *La Frottola*, 3 vols. (Copenhagen, 1968–70).

Ed., *Die mehrstimmige italienische Laude um 1500* (Copenhagen and Leipzig, 1935).

Jungmann, J. A., *Missarum Sollemnia*, 2 vols. (5th ed., Vienna, 1962. English trans., *The Mass of the Roman Rite*, 2nd ed., New York, 1954).

Kinsky, G., *Geschichte der Musik in Bildern* (Leipzig, 1929).

Knapp, J., Ed., *Thirty-five Conductus for Two and Three Voices* (Yale, 1965). *CM*, vi.

Kugler, M., *Die Tastenmusik im Codex Faenza* (Tutzing, 1972). *Münchner Veröffentlichungen zur Musikgeschichte*, xxi.

de Lafage, A., *Essais de diphthérographie musicale*, i (Paris, 1864, repr. Amsterdam, 1964).

# Bibliography

Lindsay, W. M., Ed., *Isidori Hispalensis Episcopi Etymologiarum sive originum libri XX*, 2 vols. (Oxford, 1911).

Lipphardt, W., Ed., *Der karolingische Tonar von Metz* (Münster in Westf., 1965). *Liturgiewissenschaftliche Quellen und Forschungen*, xliii.

Liuzzi, F., Ed., *La Lauda e i primordi della melodia italiana*, 2 vols. (Rome, 1935).*

Loriquet, H., Pothier, J., and Collette, A., Eds., *Le Graduel de l'Église cathédrale de Rouen* [Paris, lat. 904], 2 vols. (Rouen, 1907).*

Lowinsky, E., Ed., *The Medici Codex of 1518* (Chicago, 1968). *MRM*, iii–v.

Ludwig, F., *Repertorium Organorum recentioris et motetorum vetustissimi stili*, vol. i, pt. 1 (Halle, 1910, repr. Hildesheim, 1964). The originally unpublished vol. i, pt. 2, and the incomplete vol. ii have been printed by Gennrich in *SMMA*, vii–viii (the former also incorporating 'Die Quellen der Motetten ältesten Stils' from *AMw*, v (1923), pp. 185–222, 273–315) and vol. ii also by Dittmer (*Musicological Studies*, xvii).

Ed., *Guillaume de Machaut: Musikalische Werke*, 4 vols. (Leipzig, 1926–9, repr. Wiesbaden, 1954). The first 3 vols. = *PAM*, i.1, iii.1 and iv.2.

McCann, J., Ed., *The Rule of Saint Benedict in Latin and English* (London, 1952).

Machabey, A., *Guillaume de Machaut*, 2 vols. (Paris, 1955).

Ed., *Johannis Tinctoris Terminorum Musicae Diffinitorium*, with French translation (Paris, 1951).

McPeek, G. S., Ed., *The British Museum Manuscript Egerton 3307* (London, 1963).

Macran, H. S., Ed., *The Harmonics of Aristoxenus* (Oxford, 1902).

Marix, J., *Histoire de la musique et des musiciens de la cour de Bourgogne sous le règne de Philippe le Bon* (Strasbourg, 1939).

Ed., *Les Musiciens à la cour de Bourgogne au XV^e siècle* (Paris, 1937).

Marrocco, T. W., Ed., *Fourteenth-Century Italian Cacce* (2nd ed., Cambridge, Mass., 1961).

Meibom, M., Ed., *Antiquae musicae auctores septem*, 2 vols. (Amsterdam, 1652).

Meyer, P. and Raynaud, G., Eds., *Le Chansonnier français de Saint-Germain-des-Prés* (Paris, 1892).*

Michels, U., *Die Musiktraktate des Johannes de Muris* (Wiesbaden, 1970). *Beihefte zum AMw*, viii.

Misset, E. and Aubry, P., Eds., *Les Proses d'Adam de Saint Victor* (Paris, 1900).

Moser, H. and Müller-Blattau, J., Eds., *Deutsche Lieder des Mittelalters* (Stuttgart, 1968).

269

Moser, H. J., *Paul Hofhaimer: ein Lied- und Orgelmeister des deutschen Humanismus* (Stuttgart 1929; repr. Hildesheim, 1965, with additions drawn from subsequent articles and the transcriptions cited below).

Ed., *91 gesammelte Tonsätze Paul Hofhaimers und seines Kreises* (Stuttgart, 1929; repr. Hildesheim, 1965, in Moser, *Paul Hofhaimer*).

Müller, K., Ed., *Die Jenaer Liederhandschrift* (Jena, 1896).★

Munrow, D., *Musical Instruments of the Middle Ages and Renaissance* (London, 1976).

Mynors, R. A. B., Ed., *Cassiodori Senatoris Institutiones* (Oxford, 1937, repr. 1961).

Norberg, D., *Introduction à l'étude de la versification latine médiévale* (Stockholm 1958).

Osthoff, H., *Josquin Desprez*, 2 vols. (Tutzing, 1962).

Ott, C., Ed., *Offertoriale sive versus Offertoriorum* (Tournai, 1935).

Parrish, C., *The Notation of Medieval Music* (New York, 1957 and London, 1958).★

Ed., *Dictionary of Musical Terms by Johannes Tinctoris* (New York, 1963). With English translation.

Perrot, J., *L'Orgue de ses origines hellénistiques à la fin du XIIIᵉ siècle* (Paris, 1965. English trans., *The Organ*, London, 1971).

Picken, M., Ed., *The Chanson Albums of Marguerite of Austria* (Berkeley and Los Angeles, 1965).

Pillet, A., and Carstens, H., *Bibliographie der Troubadours* (Halle, 1933).

Pirro, A., *Histoire de la musique de la fin du XIVᵉ siècle à la fin du XVIᵉ* (Paris, 1940).

*Plainsong Hymn Melodies and Sequences* (London: The Plainsong and Mediaeval Music Society, 1896).

Plamenac, D., Ed., *Johannes Ockeghem: Collected Works*. 2 vols., containing the Masses, have appeared (vol. i, = *PAM*, i.2, Leipzig, 1927, repr. New York, 1959; vol. ii, New York, 1947).

Planchart, A. E., Ed., *Three Caput Masses* (Yale, 1964). *CM*, v.

Quasten, J., *Musik und Gesang in der Kulten den heidnischen Antike und christlichen Frühzeit* (Münster Westf., 1930).

*Patrology*, 3 vols. (Utrecht, 1962–3).

Raby, F. J. E., *A History of Christian-Latin Poetry from the Beginnings to the Close of the Middle Ages* (2nd ed., Oxford, 1953).

*A History of Latin Secular Poetry in the Middle Ages*, 2 vols. (Oxford, 1934).

Ed., *The Oxford Book of Medieval Latin Verse* (Oxford, 1959).

Ramsbotham, A., Collins, H. B., and Hughes, Dom A., Eds., *The Old Hall Manuscript*, 3 vols. (London: The Plainsong and Medieval Music Society, 1933–8).

*G. Raynauds Bibliographie* s.v. Spanke, H., Ed.

# Bibliography

Reckow, F., Ed., *Der Musiktraktat des Anonymus 4*, 2 vols. (Wiesbaden, 1967). *Beihefte zum AMw*, iv–v.

Ed., *Die copula* (Mainz and Wiesbaden, 1972).

Reaney, G., *Machaut* (London, 1971).

Reese, G., *Music in the Middle Ages* (New York, 1940).

*Music in the Renaissance* (rev. ed., New York, 1959).

Rehm, W., Ed., *Die Chansons von Gilles Binchois* (Mainz, 1957). *Musikalische Deukmäler*, ii.

Ed., *Codex Escorial . . . Ms.V.III.24* (Kassel etc., 1958).* *DM*, II, ii.

Reimer, E., Ed., *Johannes de Garlandia: De mensurabili musica. Kritische Edition mit Kommentar und Interpretation der Notationslehre*, 2 vols. (Wiesbaden, 1972). *Beihefte zum AMw*, x–xi.

Riemann, H., *Geschichte der Musiktheorie im IX–XIX Jahrhundert* (2nd ed., Leipzig, 1921).

Rietsch, H., Ed., *Gesänge von Frauenlob, Reinmar von Zweter und Alexander* (Vienna, 1913).* *DTO*, xli (=xx, 2)

Roberts, A. and Donaldson, J., Eds., *The Ante-Nicene Fathers. Translations of the Writings of the Fathers down to A.D. 325*, 10 vols. (New York, 1917–25).

Rohloff, E., Ed., *Der Musiktraktat des Johannes de Grocheo* (Leipzig, 1943).

Rokseth, Y., *La Musique d'orgue au XV$^e$ siècle et au debut du XVI$^e$* (Paris, 1930).

Ed., *Polyphonies du XIII$^e$ siècle*, 4 vols. (Paris, 1935–9).

Runge, P., Ed., *Die Sangweisen der Colmarer Handschrift und die Liederhandschrift Donaueschingen* (Leipzig, 1896).

Schatz, J., and Koller, O., Eds., *Oswald von Wolkenstein: Geistliche und weltliche Lieder* (Vienna, 1902). *DTO*, xviii ( = ix. 1).

Schwarz, R., Ed., *Ottaviano Petrucci: Frottole, Buch I und IV* (Leipzig, 1935, repr. Hildesheim and Wiesbaden, 1967). *PAM*, viii.

Schering, A., Ed., *Geschichte der Musik in Beispielen* (Leipzig, 1931).

Schmieder, W. and Wiessner, E., Eds., *Lieder von Neidhart [von Reuental]* (Vienna, 1930). *DTO*, lxxi ( = xxxvii.1).*

Seay, A., *Music in the Medieval World* (Englewood Cliffs, N.J., 1965).

Sesini, U., Ed., *Le Melodie trobadoriche nel canzoniere provenzale della Biblioteca Ambrosiana R.71 Sup.* (Turin, 1942).*

Smijers, A., Ed., *Van Ockeghem tot Sweelinck*, 6 vols. (Amsterdam, 1939–52).

Smijers, A. and others, Eds., *Josquin des Prés, Werken*, 54 fascicles (Amsterdam, 1921–68. Reprinted with Supplement in 12 vols., 1969).

Smoldon, W. L., Ed., *Officium Pastorum* (London, 1967).

Ed., *Peregrinus* (London, 1965).

Ed., *Planctus Mariae* (London, 1965).

Ed., *The Play of Daniel* (London, 1960).

Ed., *The Play of Herod* (New York, 1965).★

Ed., *Sponsus (The Bridegroom)* (London, 1972).

Ed., *Visitatio Sepulchri* (London, 1964).

Sowa, H., Ed., *Ein anonymer glossierter Mensuraltraktat 1279* (Kassel, 1930). *Königsberger Studien zur Musikwissenschaft*, ix.

Spanke, H., Ed., *G. Raynauds Bibliographie des altfranzösischen Liedes*, rev. ed. (Leiden, 1955).

Sparks, E. H., *Cantus Firmus in Mass and Motet, 1420–1520* (Berkeley and Los Angeles, 1963).

*Speculum*. A journal of mediaeval studies (1926–).

Staehelin, M., Ed., *Heinrich Isaac: Messen*, 2 vols. (Mainz, 1970–73). *Musikalische Denkmäler*, vii–viii.

Staerk, A., *Les Manuscrits latins du $V^e$ au $XIII^e$ siècle conservés à la bibliothèque impériale de Saint-Pétersbourg*, 2 vols. (St. Petersburg, 1910).★

Stainer, J., Ed., *Dufay and his Contemporaries* (London, 1898).

Sternfeld, F. W., Ed., *A History of Western Music*, i (London, 1973).

Stevens, J., Ed., *Medieval Carols* (2nd ed., London, 1958). *MB*, iv.

Strunk, O., Ed., *Source Readings in Music History* (New York, 1950).

Suñol, G., *Introduction à la paléographie musicale grégorienne* (Paris, 1935).★

Symons, Dom T., Ed., *Regularis Concordia Anglicae Nationis Monachorum Sanctimonialiumque*, text and translation (London, 1953).

Taylor, R. J., Ed., *The Art of the Minnesinger*, 2 vols. (Cardiff, 1968).

Thibaut, J.-B., *L'Ancienne liturgie gallicane* (Paris, 1929).

*Monuments de la notation ekphonétique et neumatique de l'église latine* (St. Petersburg, 1912).★

Thurston, E., Ed., *The Music in the St. Victor Manuscript* (Toronto, 1959).★

Ed., *The Works of Perotin* (New York, 1970).

Tintori, G., Ed., *Sacre rappresentazioni nel manoscritto 201 della Bibliothèque Municipale di Orléans* (Cremona, 1958).★ *IM*, I, ii.

Torrefranca, F., *Il Segreto del quattrocento* (Milan, 1939).

Trowell, B., Ed., *Four Motets by John Plummer* (Plainsong and Mediaeval Music Society, 1968).

Trumble, E., *Fauxbourdon: an Historical Survey* (New York: Institute of Medieval Music, 1959).

Van den Borren, C., *Guillaume Dufay, son importance dans l'évolution de la musique au $XV^e$ siècle* (Brussels, 1925).

Ed., *Pièces polyphoniques profanes de provenance liégeoise (XV^e siècle)* Brussels, 1950).

# Bibliography

Ed., *Polyphonia Sacra* (London: The Plainsong and Mediaeval Music Society, 1932, repr. 1962).

Van der Werf, H., *The Chansons of the Troubadours and Trouvères* (Utrecht, 1972).

Van Dijk, S. J. P., and Walker, J. H., *The Origins of the Modern Roman Liturgy* (London, 1960).

Vecchi, G., Ed., *Uffici drammatici padovani* (Florence, 1954).*

Villetard, H., Ed., *Office de Pierre de Corbeil* (Paris, 1907).

Ed., *Office de Saint Savinien et de Saint Potentien* (Paris, 1956).

Vollaerts, J. W. A., *Rhythmic Proportions in Early Medieval Ecclesiastical Chant* (Leiden, 1958).

Wace, H. and Schaff, P., Eds., *A Select Library of the Nicene Fathers of the Christian Church*, 28 vols. (Oxford and New York, 1886–1900). English translations.

Wagner, P., *Einführung in die Gregorianischen Melodien*, 3 vols. (final ed., Leipzig, 1911–21, repr. Hildesheim, 1962; English trans. of vol. i, *Introduction to the Gregorian Melodies*, London, 1907).

*Geschichte der Messe* (Leipzig, 1913).

Ed., *Die Gesänge der Jakobusliturgie zu Santiago de Compostela* (Freiburg, Switz., 1931).

Ed., *Das Graduale der St. Thomaskirche zu Leipzig als Zeuge deutscher Choralüberlieferung*, 2 vols. (Leipzig, 1930–2, repr. Hildesheim and Wiesbaden, 1967).* *PAM*, v, vii.

Waite, W., *The Rhythm of twelfth-century Polyphony, its theory and practice* (New Haven and London, 1954).

Walker, E., *A History of Music in England* (3rd ed. by J. A. Westrup, Oxford, 1952).

Wallner, B. A., Ed., *Das Buxheimer Orgelbuch* (Kassel, 1955).* *DM*, II, i.

Ed., *Das Buxheimer Orgelbuch*, 3 vols. (Kassel, 1958–9). *EDM*, xxxvii–xxxix.

Webern, A. von, Ed., *Heinrich Isaac: Choralis Constantinus, Zweiter Theil* (Vienna and Leipzig, 1909). *DTO*, xvi. 1 ( = xxxii).

Wellesz, E., *Eastern Elements in Western Chant* (London, 1947, repr. Copenhagen, 1967).

*A History of Byzantine Music and Hymnography* (2nd ed., Oxford, 1961).

Werner, E., *The Sacred Bridge* (London and New York, 1959).

Wilkins, N., Ed., *La Louange des Dames* [the collected lyric poems of Guillaume de Machaut, with 22 musical settings] (Edinburgh, 1972).

Ed., *One Hundred Ballades, Rondeaux and Virelais from the Late Middle Ages* (Cambridge, 1969). Texts, with fifteen musical settings.

Wilson, H. A., Ed., *The Gelasian Sacramentary* (Oxford, 1894).
Ed., *The Gregorian Sacramentary* (London, 1915).
Wolf, J., *Geschichte der Mensuralnotation von 1250–1460 nach den theoretischen und praktischen Quellen*, 3 vols. (Leipzig, 1904, repr. in 1 vol., Hildesheim, 1963).
*Handbuch der Notationskunde*, 2 vols. (Leipzig, 1913–19, repr. Hildesheim, 1963).
*Musikalische Schrifttafeln* (Bückeburg and Leipzig, 1923).
Ed., *Heinrich Isaac: Weltliche Werke* (Vienna and Leipzig, 1907). *DTO*, xiv. 1 ( = xxviii).
Ed., *Jakob Obrecht: Werken*, 30 fascicles (Amsterdam and Leipzig, 1912–21. Repr. in 7 vols., Farnborough, 1968).
Ed., *Der Squarcialupi-Codex Pal. 87 der Biblioteca Laurenziana in Florenz* (Lippstadt, 1955).
Young, K., *The Drama of the Medieval Church*, 2 vols. (Oxford, 1933, repr. 1951, 1962).
Zambrini, F., Ed., *Trattato dell'arte del ballo di Guglielmo Ebreo* (Bologna, 1873). *Scelta di curiosità letterarie*, cxxxi.
Zaminer, F., Ed., *Der Vatikanische Organum-Traktat Ottob. lat. 3025* (Tutzing, 1959). *Münchner Veröffentlichungen zur Musikgeschichte*, ii.
Zöbeley, H. R., *Die Musik des Buxheimer Orgelbuch: Spielvorgang, Niederschrift, Herkunft, Faktur* (Tutzing, 1964). *Münchner Veröffentlichungen zur Musikgeschichte*, x.

# Indexes

Matter is indexed under four headings: Persons, Places, Works, Subjects. The symbol *n* after a page-number indicates that the reference occurs *only* in a note on that page; the symbols *e* and *t* indicate that the reference *includes* material in the form of a musical example (*ee* = examples) or in a table respectively.

# 1 *Persons*

Modern scholars are not indexed. The usual form of ancient and medieval names is followed, but where modern usage is variable forenames are preferred to surnames and authenticated Latin forms to hypothetical vernacular ones.

# 2 *Places*

The list includes a few places referred to as the provenance of manuscripts.
These are listed according to their present location in Index 4 under
Manuscripts.

# *3 Works*

# 4 *Subjects*

Manuscripts are listed under that heading according to their present location. A few are also listed in Index 2 according to their provenance if known. The present index includes some cross-references to manuscripts according to their general type or commonly accepted name.